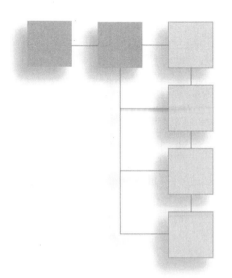

CREATING ADVENTURE GAMES FOR TEENS

JASON DARBY

Course Technology PTR
A part of Cengage Learning

COURSE TECHNOLOGY
CENGAGE Learning·

Australia • Brazil • Japan • Korea • Mexico • Singapore • Spain • United Kingdom • United States

COURSE TECHNOLOGY
CENGAGE Learning·

Creating Adventure Games for Teens
Jason Darby

Publisher and General Manager, Course Technology PTR:
Stacy L. Hiquet

Associate Director of Marketing:
Sarah Panella

Manager of Editorial Services:
Heather Talbot

Senior Marketing Manager:
Mark Hughes

Senior Acquisitions Editor: Emi Smith

Project Editor: Jenny Davidson

Technical Reviewer: Joshua Smith

Copy Editor: Laura Gabler/
Caroline Roop

Interior Layout Tech: MPS Limited

Cover Designer: Luke Fletcher

Indexer: Valerie Haynes Perry

Proofreader: Megan Belanger

For product information and technology assistance, contact us at
Cengage Learning Customer & Sales Support, 1-800-354-9706

For permission to use material from this text or product, submit all requests online at **www.cengage.com/permissions**
Further permissions questions can be emailed to
permissionrequest@cengage.com

Library of Congress Control Number: 2012942781

ISBN-13: 978-1-133-72802-3

ISBN-10: 1-133-72802-2

Course Technology, a part of Cengage Learning
20 Channel Center Street
Boston, MA 02210
USA

Cengage Learning is a leading provider of customized learning solutions with office locations around the globe, including Singapore, the United Kingdom, Australia, Mexico, Brazil, and Japan. Locate your local office at: **international.cengage.com/region**

Cengage Learning products are represented in Canada by Nelson Education, Ltd.

For your lifelong learning solutions, visit **courseptr.com**

Visit our corporate website at **cengage.com**

Printed in the United States of America
1 2 3 4 5 6 7 14 13 12

To my wonderful family, Alicia, Jared, Kimberley, and Lucas, for all their support.

ACKNOWLEDGMENTS

I would like to thank a number of people who have been involved in the creation of the book. To my wife Alicia and my children, Jared, Kimberley, and Lucas, who have supported me through another book project. To Chris Branch, who wrote the Adventure Game objects, this has made the whole process of creating adventure games easier in Multimedia Fusion. To Adam Lobacz, who made some of the adventure graphics you see in the book. To my good friends, Yves Lamoureux and Francois Lionet, who provided help and support to ensure the book was as complete as it could be. To those people who gave me permission to include their adventure games screenshots and those that are making them for adventure fans across the world. To the professional and friendly staff at Cengage Learning, Emi Smith and Heather Hurley, who again have provided excellent support throughout the whole process.

ABOUT THE AUTHOR

Jason Darby is currently working as a game designer for one of Europe's leading game developers and publishers. Darby is working on a leading AAA game title for the PS3 and Xbox platforms.

Jason is the author of a number of game creation books, including *Wizards and Warriors: MMO Game Creation, Make Amazing Games in Minutes, Power User's Guide to Windows Development, Awesome Game Creation, 3rd Edition, Game Creation for Teens, Going to War, Creating Computer Wargames,* and *Picture Yourself Creating Video Games,* which have all been published by Cengage Learning.

He has also had a number of articles published in the UK press, including a number in *Retro Gamer* and *PC Format,* both leading magazines in their field.

Contents

If you are reading the print version of this title, please download Chapters 15, 16, 17, and 18 from the companion website: **www.courseptr.com/downloads** or the author's website: **www.castlesoftware.co.uk**.

Introduction

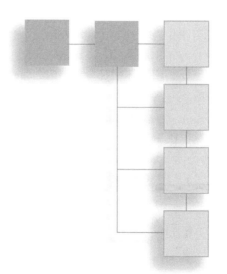

Welcome to *Creating Adventure Games for Teens*. This book is aimed at anyone who wishes to make exciting computer adventure games or hidden object games for Windows. This book will show you how to make a number of different types of adventure games in a drag-and-drop game creation system that requires no programming knowledge. You will learn all the different types of adventure games that you can make as well as all of the different components that make up each game, such as graphics, character movement, text, inventory systems, and recognizing user input such as typing in words and clicking on the screen.

By the end of the book, you'll be ready to make your own computer adventure games and start adding your own features.

Audience

If you've purchased this book or are reading it in a bookstore, then we can assume you're interested in making computer adventure games. You may be interested in text-based adventures or advanced graphical adventures; you may be someone who really enjoys hidden object games and wants to make your own version; you may want to make adventure games for yourself or your friends or maybe you want to make games that you can publish to allow other people to play either for free or for a small charge.

Or, maybe you're someone who hasn't programmed before (you do not need to be a programmer to use this book) or you may have some background in traditional programming such as C++ or Visual Basic. You may have looked at other game creation tools and systems before, but have not been able to get very far.

If you have an interest in computer adventure games, then this is the book for you.

Aim of the Book

The aim of the book is to allow anyone with no programming background to make exciting adventure games for Windows. The tools that we use in this book also allow you to convert your games to other systems with the right plug-in. Even though we are focusing on the Windows platform, you may also be able to create your games for Mac, iPhone, and Android.

Some of the things that are covered in this book are:

- History of adventure games
- Different types of adventure games
- Introduction to MMF2 and S.A.M
- Programming basics in MMF2
- Creating text-only adventures
- Allowing a player to enter text and what to do with what they have typed
- Creating adventures with graphics
- Point-and-click and how to use it within your games
- Inventory systems
- Creating hidden object adventure games
- Using S.A.M to create your own adventure games

By the end of the book you should be very comfortable with the Multimedia Fusion 2 software and then begin to make your own adventure game ideas a reality.

This book does not:

- Teach you more complex programming languages like C++, C#, or Java and isn't meant to. This book is aimed at those who want to make games easily without needing to learn those more complex languages. If you are interested in C++ then consider *C++ Programming Fundamentals* by Chuck Easttom.
- Teach you how to be a graphic artist or music creator. Look at *Composing Music for Video Games* by Andrew Clark or *3D Graphics Tutorial Collection* by Shamms Mortier if you are interested in those topics.

- Show you how to become an indie developer or build a team (if you want more information on being an indie developer read *The Indie Game Development Survival Guide* by David Michael).

- Assume you are an expert at game creation. This book is aimed at those with little or no knowledge of game creation but also those who might have an idea how things are put together but need more information.

Chapter Overview

This book runs in a simple yet effective order to allow you to get the most out of reading it. As many of the chapters build on the previous example files, it is not recommended that you skip chapters.

Chapter 1 Adventure Games Through Time: An introduction to the different types of adventure games and how they made their arrival on the home computer.

Chapter 2 Introduction to Multimedia Fusion 2 and SAM: Learn all about the software that you will be using to make your adventure games and what other tools you will be using throughout the book.

Chapter 3 Choose Your Own Path: Learn all about adventure game books and how you can create your own computer-based version called *Moon Traveller*.

Chapter 4 Adventure Game Objects: Learn about the special objects for Multimedia Fusion 2 that have been created specifically for this book.

Chapter 5 Dungeon of Text: Learn how to make a text-based adventure game system. This will introduce some very basic concepts as well as introducing you to various object features.

Chapter 6 Text Adventures in Depth: Learn more advanced features for creating your very own text adventures.

Chapter 7 Graphic Text Adventures: Learn all about graphics, and how to load and display them on-screen in Multimedia Fusion 2.

Chapter 8 Wild West: Make a Wild West adventure game with graphics and features discussed in the previous chapters.

Chapter 9 Editors: Learn how game editors can make creating adventures games easier.

Chapter 10 Creating an Editor: Create an editor in MMF2 that can store and retrieve game-based data.

Chapter 11 Point-and-Click Adventures: Learn features that comprise a point-and-click adventure game.

Chapter 12 Sherlock Bones Underworld Detective: Create a simple point-and-click adventure with a skeleton character.

Chapter 13 Hidden Object Games: Learn all about hidden object games and what features they contain.

Chapter 14 Lost and Found: Create a hidden game adventure called *Adventures in Endapur*.

If you purchased the print version of this book, Chapters 15, 16, 17, and 18 can be found on the companion website www.courseptr.com/downloads or the author's website www.castlesoftware.co.uk.

Chapter 15 Graphic Adventure Games: Learn all about other types of adventure games including those made in the first-person view.

Chapter 16 Story Adventure Maker: Learn all about a set of editors that you can use and improve to make creating your adventure games much easier.

Chapter 17 Compiling Games: Learn how to create your games in a format that will allow other people to play your games.

Chapter 18 Help and Support: Learn where to get help once you have finished reading the book and following the example files.

COMPANION WEBSITE DOWNLOADS

You may download the companion website files from www.courseptr.com/downloads. Please note that you will be redirected to the Cengage Learning site.

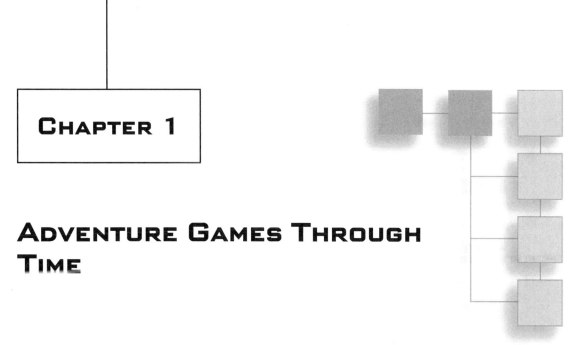

CHAPTER 1

ADVENTURE GAMES THROUGH TIME

Welcome, traveler. We are about to embark on the adventure of a lifetime, whereby you will be tasked with making your very own exciting computer adventure games. The journey is dangerous, but by the end of the quest (reading the book), you will have become a detective, escaped from a dangerous dungeon, traveled into space, and, finally, visited the Wild West.

Using this book and the demo version of Multimedia Fusion 2 software, you will learn how to create the various features found in computer adventure games. By the end of the book, you will be ready to design, program, and distribute your very own adventures to friends and family—or, in fact, anyone.

Don't worry if you don't know how to program a computer, design games, or come up with story ideas—all will be revealed. I will be covering many different types of adventure games within this book, with different levels of difficulty and complexity, so by the end of the book, you can choose which adventure game types you find most interesting or best suited to your skill level when you start making your very own games.

In this chapter, we will look at what constitutes an adventure game and what types of adventure games currently exist. So let's get started!

Note

Multimedia Fusion 2 is also called MMF2 for short and will be used throughout this book to describe this product.

What an Adventure

The word *adventure* should make you think of an exciting, action-oriented journey that a character makes to complete a specific goal. Maybe you are thinking of a movie or story that contains spies, pirates, a medieval knight, or an archaeologist. Within this story, the character will need to face a number of enemies, travel through dangerous places, and maybe even have to navigate through or around traps or puzzles.

In general, the following will be true of an adventure game (be it computer or otherwise):

- You are normally the central character (or hero) of the game.
- The game takes the form of a story that evolves throughout the game—using a particular character or story theme, such as an evil wizard, an invading army, a disaster, or the discovery of a particular item of great power.
- The game contains some form of puzzles or traps.
- The game contains items for the player to collect and use—some may be special while others may be less beneficial.
- The player will have a backpack or bag to store collected items (this may be a virtual backpack that the player does not see)—this is usually called an inventory.

So now that you have an idea of what constitutes an adventure game, let's take a look at where computer adventure games have come from and the types that are available.

Note

Chapter 4 of this book provides more information on the features that you will see in an adventure game.

A Brief History of Adventure Games

There are many different types of adventure games, ranging from board games and books to computer games. In this section, to help you get a better idea of how the market has changed, we will look at different technologies that were used to create adventure games throughout the years. You should come away with a good idea of where you can look to gain inspiration for your ideas.

Note

There are many different types of adventure games, with hundreds of different products released over the last 50 years. Many of the game types overlapped in terms of when they were released, and so a true timeline of events cannot be accurately presented in the following text. What is documented here are the key events, technologies, and games and those products that had an impact on me as I was growing up.

Board Games

Board games in many different forms have been around for thousands of years. Some of the early games were strategic and based on conquest, such as chess or checkers. It wasn't until the twentieth century that board games began to branch out into more commercial concepts.

Board games such as *Clue, Monopoly, Risk*, and *Escape from Colditz* showed that you could take a simple concept and make it extremely interesting for the game-playing public. *Clue* is a murder mystery in which you need to find out which game character used which weapon in what room to murder one of the other characters. *Monopoly* is a city trading game, where you try to bankrupt the other players. *Risk* is a global warfare game in which players can collaborate, lie, and deceive. In *Escape from Colditz*, you play either the soldiers trying to escape (captors) or the German soldiers (guards).

Board games in the 1960s, '70s, and early '80s became extremely popular, due mainly to the lack of home entertainment systems. TVs were expensive and had few channels (which in many cases, aired very few good TV shows). There were no home computers, handhelds, or mobile phone devices on which to play games.

Over the years, the board game market has found new ways to bring original ideas and stories to the player. Sometimes this has been through the use of electronic games such as *Dark Tower*, to complex stories with amazing model figures such as the pirate ships in *Dreadfleet*. Though classic board games still exist and still continue to sell well to the family market, some extremely detailed and complex board games are also available. In the face of stiff competition from computer games and mobile phone entertainment, these story- and visually rich board games continue to attract a wide range of players.

Role-Playing Games—*Dungeons & Dragons*

Board games were (and still are) a great way for families to sit down and enjoy some quality time together. Board games are especially popular at Christmas, when parents are at home spending time with their children.

In the 1970s, the designs of many board games were pretty simple and they didn't provide the level of depth that many people were looking for. It was during that decade that two game designers, Gary Gygax and Dave Arneson, created a fantasy role-playing game (RPG) called *Dungeons & Dragons (D&D)*, which would have a massive impact on the future of games, including fantasy-based computer games. When it was released, *Dungeons & Dragons* seemed to strike a chord with teenagers and adults who wanted to move to the next level beyond board games and tabletop war games.

The term *role-playing* means to act out a story situation with other people. Each person has a particular role in the story and might have notes to act in a certain way. Role-playing has been used in businesses for many years, to train people how to deal with difficult situations or difficult customers. For example, a company might train telephone help-line employees in how to deal with customers who have a complaint. One employee will play the part of the staff member trying to help the caller who has the complaint, while another employee will pretend to be the angry customer and try to disrupt the conversation. Both staff members are given basic instructions about the situation but basically make the story up as they go along. This is a similar concept to RPGs such as *D&D*.

Dungeons & Dragons was set in a fantasy world containing characters such as wizards, mages, clerics, warriors, dragons, and the undead. *D&D* consists of the storyteller called the DM (Dungeon Master) and a number of players. Each player takes the part of a particular character, with a number of stats (statistics), such as health, strength, and charisma. The DM tells the players a particular story, and the players need to decide what to do next. Based on this decision, the DM would roll a set of dice to determine if a particular set of actions, such as looking for a hidden entry to a building, was successful and then tell the players any consequences of their actions.

Today *Dungeons & Dragons* is just one of many RPGs available on the market. They cover a wide range of subjects, from sci-fi to medieval worlds. Movies and TV series have also been made into RPGs, such as *Aliens*, *Star Trek*, and *The Evil Dead*.

Books and Choose Your Own Stories

In the 1980s, the home computer started to become more popular for people who wanted a more interactive game-playing experience. Unfortunately, many families still found the cost of a home computer too prohibitive. A great thing about computers was that, unlike board games and RPGs, they provided a single-player experience, meaning they didn't necessarily require other people to join in.

Even though books had provided a source of adventure in their storytelling, they weren't providing any game-playing experience. Not until Ian Livingstone and Steve Jackson created the *Fighting Fantasy* series of books did people generally consider books a good source for game playing. Ian and Steve, already extremely successful game creators, were responsible for the creation of the U.K. tabletop gaming company called Games Workshop. It didn't take long for the books to become a major success. After the initial book, *The Warlock of Firetop Mountain*, many more books were written and released.

Each *Fighting Fantasy* game book provides readers with an exciting introduction to an adventure, such as needing to enter a dungeon to win a prize or escape a horror-filled house. At the end of the introduction, the player is given a number of options. Each of these options contains a different number. For example:

*You walk into a small wooden barn. On one side of the barn are bales of straw which look like they have only recently been cut from the fields. In the middle of the room is a small sturdy looking wooden table. In the middle of the table are three maggot-ridden apples. You can see a door leads outside to the north. You haven't eaten in a while, so if you decide to eat an apple go to **27**; if you wish to leave the apples on the table and proceed through the door north, go to **196**.*

Each part of the story is broken into sections and then placed in different areas of the book, so unlike normal books, where you read from the start to the finish sequentially, you jump throughout the book to read the next action you have decided to take. At the top of every new paragraph/section of the book, you'll find a number to identify the particular action. For example, a player deciding to eat the apple in the previous example would jump to section 27.

27.

*After removing all of the maggots you can see, you take a big bite out of the first apple. Unfortunately the inside of the apple contains as many maggots as the outside; you start to feel quite ill as you spit the apple out as quickly as possible, washing your mouth out with water from your flask. It seems the apples weren't meant to be eaten. You lose 5 points of health. After 5 minutes of excruciating stomach cramps, you begin to feel well enough to continue on your journey. You go north to **196**.*

The books also contain a simple battle system, where you can fight characters in the story. You use a set of dice such as 2D6 to calculate if your attack was successful. The books cover different systems for different settings, such as fear in the *House of Hell*, while in others you can use magic.

Note

The term *2D6* is a dice-naming system commonly used in role-playing games. 2D6 means rolling two six-sided dice and then using the result to calculate a particular event, such as an attack or a block, or the success of an action, such as trying to pick a lock. You can get different dice with different shapes and number combinations.

For more information on these books, visit http://www.fightingfantasy.com.

The *Fighting Fantasy* books weren't the only adventure books that were available at the time. There were other titles, such as the *Choose Your Own Adventure* series, which were also extremely popular.

Computer Games

This book is all about creating computer adventure games. Now that you have an idea of how people played adventure games on other formats, there's no better time to look at how computer adventure games started and how they have changed over the years.

Text Adventures

Before the home computer revolution, most computers were used in businesses or universities for data processing. Though these machines were extremely powerful at handling data, they had very basic graphical hardware and would only display single-colored text on a black or green background.

Programmers were employed to write special programs that the computer could understand to improve a business's handling of data. This could have been to write code to allow the ordering of equipment and checking how much was in stock or perhaps detailing the company's telephone directory.

Some programmers decided to write simple games on these machines to see how far they could push these computers. These computers generally only accepted keyboard input and displayed text output, so the computer text-based adventures were the perfect platform.

The main issue with these first text adventures was that very few people had access to them. This was about to change with the arrival of the home computer. Even though these early home computers had limited memory and graphical capabilities, they still could produce results that would amaze people who played them. These early computers, such as the Spectrum ZX81, Electron, and the BBC computers, could also be programmed by the end user. Not only could people learn to program their own home computer, but they could also type in instructions found in magazines. This BASIC (Beginner's All-purpose Symbolic Instruction Code) programming language led to many people creating their own games, from which came the term *bedroom programmer*.

So began the release of the first wave of adventure games.

You can see an example of an early text adventure for the home computer in Figure 1.1.

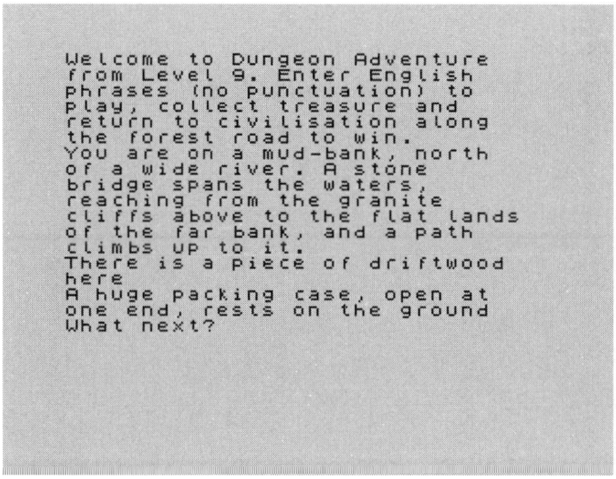

```
Welcome to Dungeon Adventure
from Level 9. Enter English
phrases (no punctuation) to
play, collect treasure and
return to civilisation along
the forest road to win.
You are on a mud-bank, north
of a wide river. A stone
bridge spans the waters,
reaching from the granite
cliffs above to the flat lands
of the far bank, and a path
climbs up to it.
There is a piece of driftwood
here
A huge packing case, open at
one end, rests on the ground
What next?
```

Level 9 Computing

Figure 1.1
Dungeon Adventure.

As text adventures could contain elaborate stories and puzzles, it didn't take long for text adventures to become an extremely popular genre on the early home computer. As bedroom programmers and game companies released more adventure games, they all looked to differentiate their games from the competition by adding colored backgrounds, using different fonts, flashing text, and simple sound effects.

Graphic Adventures

Even though the early computers had very limited memory and very few colors, programmers were still able to get a lot out of the technology. One such computer was the Spectrum 48K, which had only 48KB of memory. When you consider that a simple Word document with a few pages of text can easily reach 48KB, you suddenly realize how little memory programmers had for programming their games. So it's surprising that programmers went so easily from text-based games to adventures games containing graphics.

With text adventures, players had to imagine the world they were traveling in based on the text they were reading, much like people have to imagine the characters in a book. So when graphics arrived in adventure games, the game designers were able to show the player how a particular area in the game really looked. This helped build immersion and made the games even more exciting for the player.

An example of an adventure game with both graphics and text can be seen in Figure 1.2.

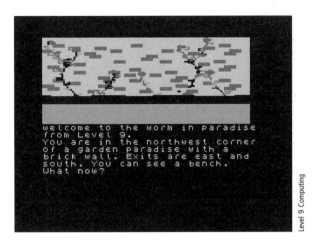

Level 9 Computing

Figure 1.2
The Worm in Paradise.

The Rise of the Game Creators

From the time of early computers, there were always programs you could buy to help you make your own computer games. Some were simple graphic-creation programs; others allowed you to create a complete game, which you could then distribute among your friends. You were even allowed to sell some of them.

Some of the early game-creation systems needed the original creation program for the game to be run, thereby limiting your ability to distribute your games. Other systems allowed you to create a version of a game that you could copy onto a tape without the need for any further input from the original creation system. It is no surprise that those that didn't require the original program ultimately became more popular. Users wanted to create their own games and have the opportunity to sell them.

There have been many different types of game creators available over the years, covering different genres, such as arcade games, pinball, war games, and, of course, adventure games. Some required knowledge of programming while others only required the ability to think about the logic of the game you were creating.

Following is a selection of adventure game–creation systems:

- **The Quill:** This is an adventure game–creation system released for the Spectrum 48K computer (and many other 8-bit computers). The Quill, a very successful adventure game–creation program, allowed users to create and sell their own games. Initially The Quill was only text based, but a program called Illustrator added the ability to incorporate images.

- **Professional Adventure Writer (PAW):** This follow-up to The Quill improved text handling and graphical abilities, such as placement and scrolling of text. Many commercial games were made in both PAW and The Quill.

- **Graphic Adventure Creator (GAC):** This was a competitor to PAW and was considered by some to be less powerful than PAW, especially in terms of graphic management and placement. But GAC was still a competent game-creation system.

Note

My very first (albeit unpublished) adventure game—*The Search for Dracula's Son*—was made using GAC in 1988. The simple idea was that Dracula's son was also a vampire and needed to be hunted down before he created his own army of the dead.

Point-and-Click

With the advent of more powerful home computers, such as the Commodore Amiga, Atari ST, and PC, and with the introduction of the mouse, adventure games went through a gameplay revolution. Text entry was quickly being replaced in adventure games with graphical buttons and menus from which players could pick up, view, and then use objects.

In many cases you could see your character on-screen and control his movements by guiding and clicking the mouse on the location of the screen where you wanted the character to move. *Future Wars: Time Travelers* for the Amiga computer was a highly rated point-and-click adventure. The game started with you cleaning the windows in a multistory building, at which point your boss looks out the window and tells you off. The game had a really intuitive pop-up menu system that allowed you to select from a group of options to view, select, and use items. For example, you could pick up a bucket, fill it with water from the WC, and then place it over a door, so that when your boss next walks into the room, it would fall onto his head, allowing you to escape into another room. One of the downsides of the early point-and-click games was the lack of on-screen precision. Because the screen resolutions were quite low, you sometimes had to click on a location multiple times to get the objects or game to activate.

The Amiga computer and PC saw the release of many point-and-click adventure games, as their increased memory and graphical capabilities meant they were the

Figure 1.3
Broken Sword.

perfect devices for these new games. Programmers could put music, sound effects, animations, and inventory management into a single game.

One very popular point-and-click adventure game on the PC was *Broken Sword*, which has since been rereleased on Mac, Nintendo DS, and iPhone/iPad devices. You can see a screenshot of *Broken Sword* in Figure 1.3. In *Broken Sword* you are on holiday in Paris when a clown sets off an explosion in a café. In *Broken Sword 2* you are back in Paris and have a meeting lined up with Professor Oubier, but it doesn't take long before everything goes horribly wrong. You find yourself tied up and bound to a chair, with a killer spider released from a box in front of you, and the building is on fire.

It is well worth checking out other point-and-click adventure games, such as *Beneath a Steel Sky*, *Monkey Island*, *King's Quest*, *Space Quest*, *The Last Express*, and *Zork*.

Point-and-Click and Role-Playing Games   Adventure games also came together with role-playing games to produce interesting adventure games with a new twist. These games had the player viewing the game in a graphic adventure setting, with text describing scenes or events—but the player had the ability to create characters with complex stats and attack abilities.

Many RPGs consist of various elements of adventure games, such as the *Ultima* games and *Fallout 1* and *Fallout 2*.

New Media   Computers were changing at a fast pace, from cassette tapes to 5¼- and 3½-inch discs to the CD-ROM. This allowed more data to be placed onto media, which meant more data could be streamed to the computer. This allowed game companies to think about displaying some content as video rather than computer graphics. These full-motion video (FMV) games allowed designers to present cut scenes or parts of the story using real actors. Some games had success on various platforms; well-known FMV-based games are *Dragon's Lair*, *Myst*, and *7th Guest*.

Though FMV games were talked about as being the next big step in adventure gaming, and though it did help with CD-ROM–based sales at the time, they haven't been the mainstay of games for the adventure player.

Return of the Adventure Game   Gaming is circular. When something seems "over" in gaming and starts to disappear from general usage, it will generally make a comeback in some form or another sometime down the road. This happened to adventure gaming for many years; it became a bit of a niche market and so companies focused on other genres, such as RPGs as well as first-person shooter (FPS) and real-time strategy (RTS) games.

A combination of things happened that brought adventure games back into the mainstream: first, the advent of the hidden-object game (which we will discuss shortly) and new technology.

Mobile platforms and the massive increase of PC/Internet usage has meant that gaming can be delivered a lot quicker to users than ever before. This has allowed game creators to focus on what users want and directly provide those games rather than having to go through a publisher. It has also meant that many people who might not have found a game genre or boxed product to their liking can now quickly and easily purchase one. This has revolutionized gaming.

With devices such as the iPhone and iPad, adventure gaming has become popular again, but this hasn't been limited to mobile devices. Console gaming services on the PS3 and Xbox have also seen a number of successful adventure games released, and it seems this will continue.

Hidden-Object Adventures   A *hidden-object* game is where you are presented with a situation, a background story, and then a scene. In this scene are many objects. You will also be provided with a list, and from this list you will need to find the object on-screen and then click on it. Once you have clicked on the object, it will be removed from the list, and you will need to locate any other objects that are still present.

You may not initially associate a hidden-object game with an adventure game, but over the years the adventure game format has adapted and changed. From the original text entry to pointing and clicking, the adventure game has adapted to suit different markets. The hidden-object game can contain many features that you would associate with an adventure game, such as an overriding story, a main character (you), a goal that is based on the story—such as finding out who stole the queen's crown jewels—and complex puzzles.

These hidden-object games have become very popular and will continue to push the adventure game in a different direction, much like the point-and-click adventure games that are continuing to be made.

Chapter Summary

You should have a good idea of the history of adventure games and the different types that you can play today. I recommend that you purchase a few different games, so you can get a good understanding of how they work. In Chapter 2, we will look at Multimedia Fusion 2, the program that we will use to make our adventure games.

Note

If you are looking for games that will give you a better understanding of how adventure games look and work, I recommend the iTunes store from Apple (you will need an Apple device, such as an iPhone, iPad, or iPad Touch) or Good Old Games (www.gog.com). There are many adventure games available at these two sites at very good prices. Not only can you learn a lot from the games mentioned in this chapter, but they are also a lot of fun.

CHAPTER 2

INTRODUCTION TO MULTIMEDIA FUSION 2 AND SAM

In this chapter, you will learn how to install the Multimedia Fusion 2 demo and then take a tour of the application, which will help you understand how to create your games. You will learn all about the editors, toolbars, and different screens available, some of which you will use a lot. You will see which key objects you can use to make your games in Multimedia Fusion 2; these objects are the cornerstone to any creation within the program and are essential to getting features like text, graphics, and buttons in your adventure games. Finally, you will take a look at SAM, which is an application in MMF2 for making adventure programs. It will show you how to take the code used in this book to make a program that can create editors that can generate user-based adventures.

WHAT IS MULTIMEDIA FUSION 2?

Multimedia Fusion 2, or MMF2 for short, is a powerful but easy-to-use game-creation tool that allows you to concentrate on making games (and designing them) rather than having to worry about learning complicated programming languages.

The great thing about MMF2 is that you don't need to have any previous programming knowledge; you only need a passion for wanting to make computer adventure games, a Windows PC, and some ideas. MMF2 uses an event-based programming system. By using the mouse and keyboard, you can create your code. This code is logic based, so as long as you have a good idea what you want your game to do, then you can easily create your code. You will learn more about how to code your game later on in this chapter and throughout the rest of this book.

Installing MMF2

In this section of the book, we will go through the process of installing MMF2. First you need to download the MMF2 demo installer from the Internet. You can download the MMF2 demo from http://www.clickteam.com/webftp/files/mmf2/Demo/MMF2Demo_En.exe.

1. Once you have downloaded the file, select Run. A User Account Control dialog box may appear asking if you want to run this application (see Figure 2.1). Click on Yes to continue.

2. Once you have clicked Yes, this will open up the MMF2 Welcome dialog, as shown in Figure 2.2.

3. Click on the Next button.

4. You will now be presented with an Information screen (see Figure 2.3); read the information about the demos, and when you are happy, click on Next.

5. Now you will see a license screen (see Figure 2.4). Click the "I agree with the above terms and conditions" button if you agree to the terms. If you do not agree, then click on Exit; however, you will not be able to install the software and follow the examples in this book if you do not install the demo.

6. When you are happy with the license agreement, click on the Next button.

7. A screen like Figure 2.5 will then appear asking you in which directory you want to install MMF2. You can leave it as the default Program Files directory or click on the three dots to select a new location. Click on the Next button when you are ready to proceed.

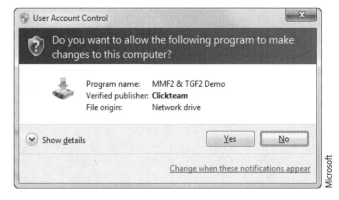

Figure 2.1
The User Account Control dialog box.

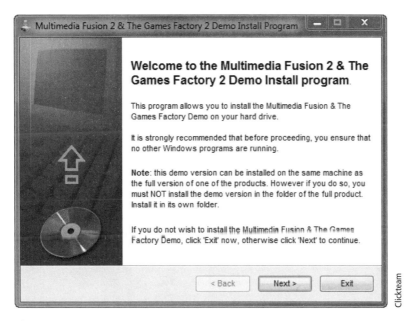

Figure 2.2
The MMF2 Welcome screen.

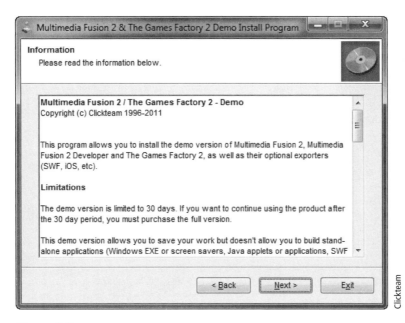

Figure 2.3
The Information screen.

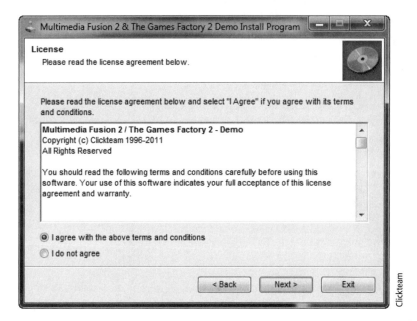

Figure 2.4
The License screen.

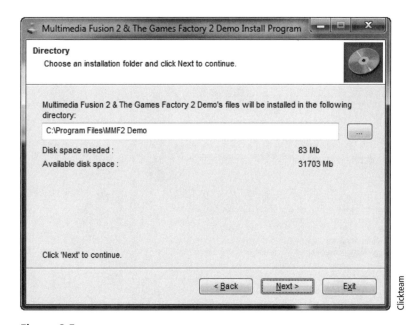

Figure 2.5
The Directory installation path.

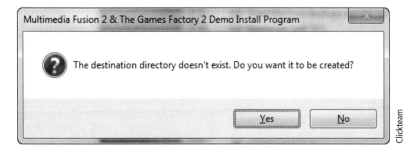

Figure 2.6
Confirm directory path creation.

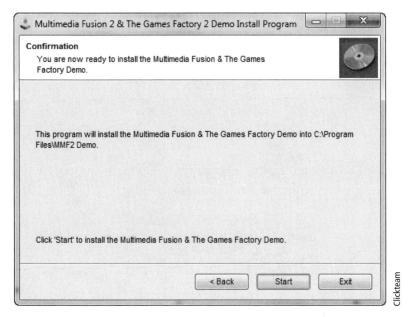

Figure 2.7
Confirmation page.

8. You will be asked to create this directory if it doesn't already exist (Figure 2.6), so click on Yes to create it.

9. You will be presented with the confirmation dialog box, which confirms the location where you will install the demo (see Figure 2.7). Click on the Start button to begin the installation or Back to make changes.

10. Once you have clicked Start, installation will begin.

11. Once all of the files have copied to the PC, you will see an End dialog box (see Figure 2.8). The end screen advises whether the installation was successful and

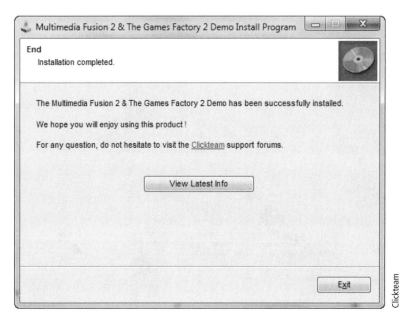

Figure 2.8
Installation complete.

provides a number of additional links, such as the Clickteam Support page, and the ability to view the latest information about the products. Click on Exit to continue.

12. To start the demo, you will need to locate the demo launcher from the Start bar or from the Desktop. Click on the Start bar (Windows 7) and you will see Multimedia Fusion 2 and The Games Factory option. Click on this to start the application. If you are not running Windows 7, you may find it easier to launch the app from the Desktop under the same name. See the desktop icon shown in Figure 2.9.

Figure 2.9
The Start Demo icon.

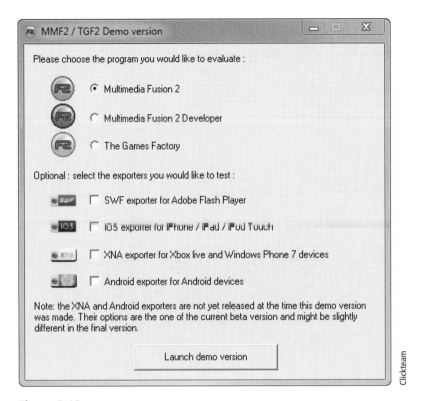

Figure 2.10
Select the version to evaluate.

13. Once you have double-clicked the desktop icon or launched it from the Start menu, you will be presented with a special dialog box; pick the features you would like to test in the demo (see Figure 2.10).

14. The games we will be making will be primarily for the PC platform, but if you want to create an adventure game for Flash or the iPhone, you can select those options to get an idea of the features available for that platform. For this book we will be using Multimedia Fusion 2 and no additional exporters. Once you have selected the required options, click on the Launch Demo Version button.

15. You will now get an overview of the different features available in each product (see Figure 2.11); it would be beneficial to read these because, if you intend to work on your adventure games in the long term, you will need to purchase a version of the software. Click on the Continue button to start MMF2.

16. You will now see MMF2 launch (Figure 2.12).

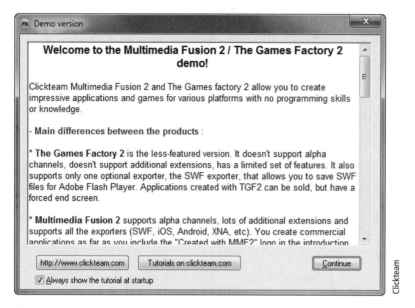

Figure 2.11
The Demo features dialog box.

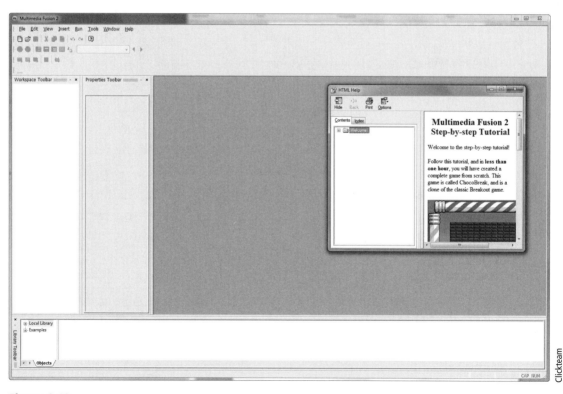

Figure 2.12
The launched MMF2 application.

CREATING GAMES IN MULTIMEDIA FUSION

Several stages are involved in making a game in MMF2; these can be categorized as:

- **Creating a new application:** Each MMF file/game is called an application.

- **Creating the structure:** Games created in MMF2 comprise a series of frames. You can think of these frames as screens or areas of your game, perhaps the main menu, a loading screen, the game itself, or a frame for the high scores. The frame system provides a simple and easy way to break your game into sections; for example, you could create a frame for every level in your game, so each frame could be a different world in your game.

- **Setting the scene:** Every game needs graphics or content, and you will need to draw, create, or import this content into your MMF2 application. Everything you place in MMF2 is an object. The object could be a piece of text, an object to display the player's current lives and score, or a graphic object.

- **Setting object properties:** All objects that you place in MMF2 have a set of properties; these can be anything from its position on-screen, its size, its visibility, or its movement.

- **Programming the logic:** Once all content is in place, then it's time to create the logic for the game using events. This is called the programming stage.

- **Testing:** You will need to test your game to make sure it is working as expected.

- **Compiling:** Compile all the elements into a final file that you can give to other people to play. This changes the MFA file that can only be used in MMF2 to a format that is accessible on the platform of your choice, such as Windows executable.

- **Distribute:** Once your game is compiled, then you need to get it to all of your fans (or perhaps just your friends) who are waiting to play the game.

Note

Because much of the content of a text adventure game is text, we will be placing the game's content on one frame, rather than separating locations into frames.

Note

If you are using the trial version of MMF2, you will not be able to compile the file into a format that you can distribute. To do this you will need to purchase the full version of the software. Don't worry though; you can create, test, and play your creation all within the demo software.

Program Walkthrough

Now we will tour the MMF2 interface and the screens you will encounter when using the product (the different screens are called *editors* in MMF2). You will learn when you might use different parts of the application for future reference.

Note

If you forget which part of the application does a particular task, you should refer back to this section for advice on which editor to choose.

MMF2 has several editors and toolbars that you will use to create your programs. In this section, you will learn about each of them and when you might use some editors and toolbars and not others.

Note

An *editor* is a special screen in MMF2 for completing a specific task. The task could be creating a picture, programming some interactivity, or placing your images on-screen. A toolbar is used for accessing specific information and data in MMF2.

The following sections contain more details about the individual toolbars and the editors that are available.

Program Areas

Figure 2.13 displays what you see when you first load MMF2.

1. Menu toolbar
2. Menu Button toolbar
3. Workspace toolbar
4. Properties toolbar
5. Library toolbar
6. Workspace/Editor Area
7. Layers toolbar

Note

The actual layout of the screen may differ slightly in the trial version of the software. The Layers toolbar may or may not be automatically displayed.

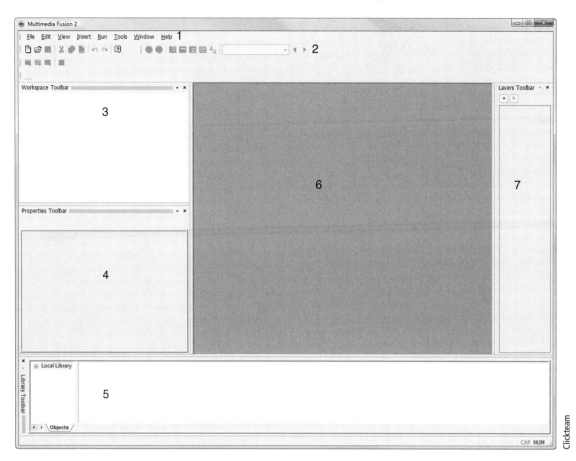

Figure 2.13
Various editors and toolbars highlighted in MMF2.

You will come into contact with the majority of these toolbars throughout the use of the product and will use some more than others.

- **Menu toolbar:** This is the text menu at the top of the MMF2 program, which configures the general layout and program preferences. From the Menu toolbar, you can also load and save programs. An example of the Menu toolbar in action can be seen in Figure 2.14.

- **Menu Button toolbar:** Just under the Text menu is the Menu Button toolbar. Depending on which editors are open, different buttons will be present. These buttons provide quick access to various settings and other editors. An example of some items in a Menu Button toolbar can be seen in Figure 2.15.

- **Workspace toolbar:** The Workspace toolbar provides a view of your program and its contents. In the toolbar you will see objects and frames; these are

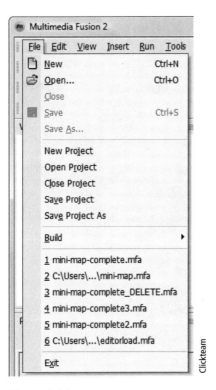

Figure 2.14
The File option from the Menu toolbar has been selected.

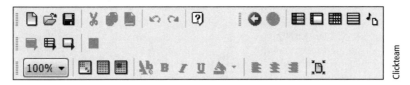

Figure 2.15
A selection of menu buttons.

discussed later in this chapter. An example of an application structure in the Workspace toolbar is shown in Figure 2.16.

■ **Properties toolbar:** Different items within MMF2 contain properties. The Properties toolbar provides a quick way of accessing them. The Properties toolbar is shown in Figure 2.17.

■ **Library toolbar:** From the Library toolbar you will access premade objects and graphic libraries; you can use those that come with the product or create your own. An example of a library already selected is shown in Figure 2.18.

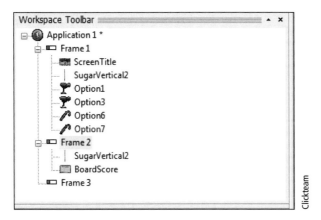

Figure 2.16
An example application loaded into the Workspace toolbar.

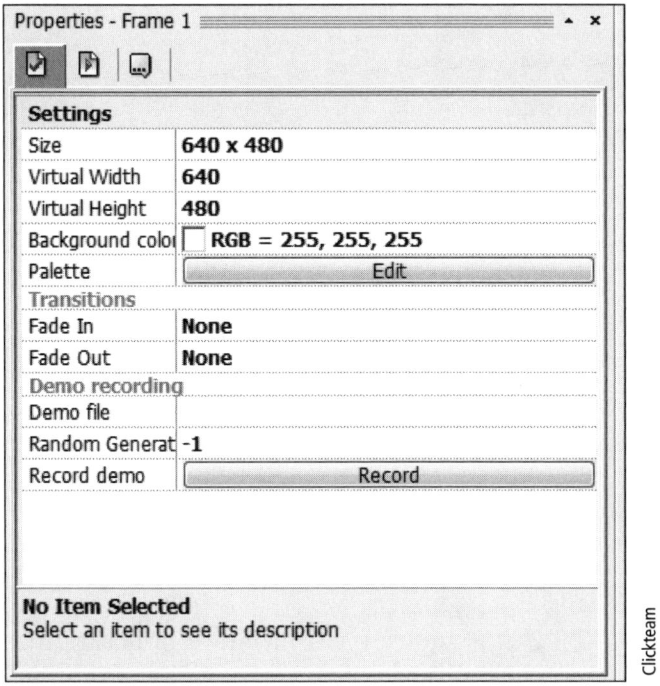

Figure 2.17
An example of frames properties.

■ **Workspace & Editor Area:** This is where a number of the editors will appear (one at a time), allowing you to make your creation (by placing the graphics on the screen) or to program it. Examples of the editor are discussed in the next section, "The Editors."

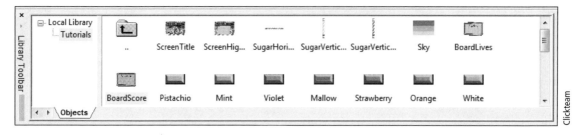

Figure 2.18
A set of game items loaded into the Library toolbar.

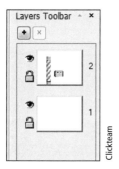

Figure 2.19
A two-layer program.

■ **Layers:** The Layers toolbar allows you to create multiple layers to place your objects and graphics on-screen. This is very useful for graphical effects or for grouping graphic items. An example of two layers in use can be seen in Figure 2.19.

THE EDITORS

The editors within MMF2 are:

■ Storyboard editor

■ Frame editor

■ Event editor

■ Event List editor

■ Picture editor

■ Expression Evaluator

Storyboard Editor

The Storyboard editor allows programmers to see the structure of all the screens within their games; these screens are called frames in MMF2. These frames could be levels of a game, different pictures in a screensaver, or various screens within a multimedia tutorial (an example of a three-frame program can be seen in Figure 2.20). The Storyboard editor allows you to visualize the order of frames within your program. The editor also gives you the ability to drag and drop frames into a specific order or to insert additional frames. The Storyboard editor can help provide useful insight into understanding the amount of work you still have left to do to complete your program (for example, working out the percentage of the frames still left to program).

If we take a closer look at the Storyboard editor (see Figure 2.21), you will notice a number of configurable options are available from this screen. These include the name of each frame, the size of the frame, the password, and transitions for the start or end of each frame.

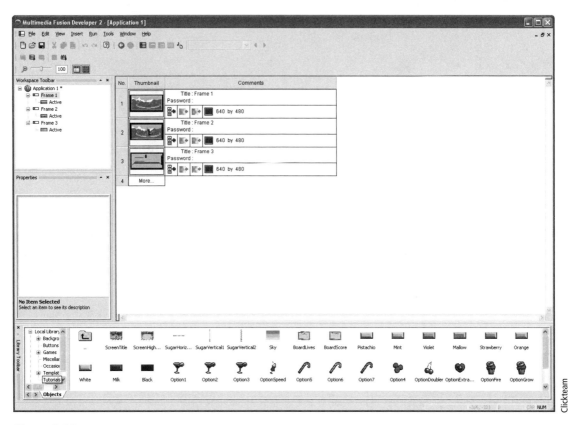

Figure 2.20
Example program displayed in the Storyboard editor.

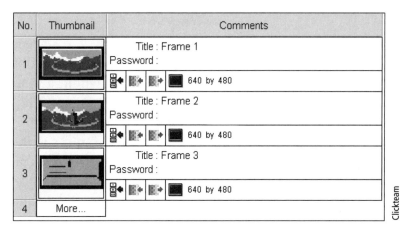

Figure 2.21
Storyboard editor close-up.

If you were going to change the frame size or the title of a frame, you probably would do this in the Workspace toolbar, and you would generally only use the Storyboard editor to assign a password, add a transition, or change the order of a frame.

Frame Editor

The Frame editor is one of two core editors that you will spend the majority of your time working in (the other one is the Event editor). The Frame editor is where you place all of the graphical objects for your program. Within the Frame editor you may also add any other objects that are required for the frame to function. These objects could allow you to display a picture, open a file, and create a text file. These objects will be covered shortly.

After you drag the items from your Library toolbar to your frame or import them using the built-in Picture editor, you will see them in the left-hand pane. This window pane allows you to select individual objects, which can be quite useful if you have a lot of items placed on top of each other. You can also create object folders, which allow you to organize relevant items in one place. (See Figure 2.22.)

Event Editor

The Event editor is where all the coding is done in MMF2. The coding is not what you might normally expect of a programming language because you won't need to enter much text. The majority of the programming within MMF2 takes the form of left- and right-clicking of the mouse buttons. The Event editor is based on an eventing system, which makes it an easy system to understand for anyone with no

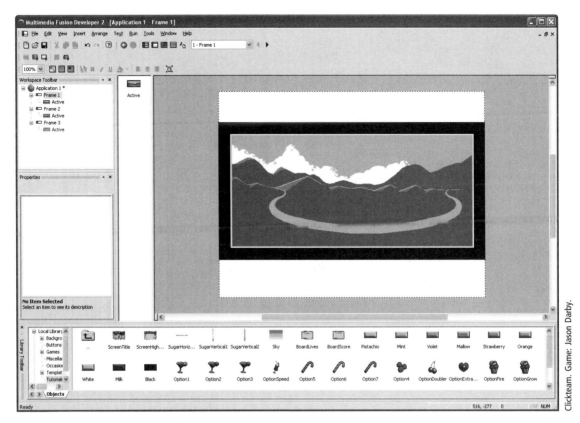

Figure 2.22
A program displayed in the Frame editor.

programming background. The programming side is simplistic and quick. Because of the work already done by the programmers of MMF2, there is a lot of power in the product. You will not sacrifice the power of the program because of its ease of use, which is very important when you start getting into very complicated programming projects.

An in-progress project displayed in the Event editor is shown in Figure 2.23. A closer look at the Event editor can be seen in Figure 2.24.

The Event editor is split into several rows and columns. Down the left-hand side, as shown in the gray shaded boxes in Figure 2.24, you'll find several events. These events contain conditions. Across the top are objects (these are our programs' required core components, such as graphics, multimedia, and text video), and the gridlike area between those two areas is where the actions are placed (where a checkmark is displayed). The first seven objects across the top, called System objects, are always present in your creations. Listed after these seven System objects are any

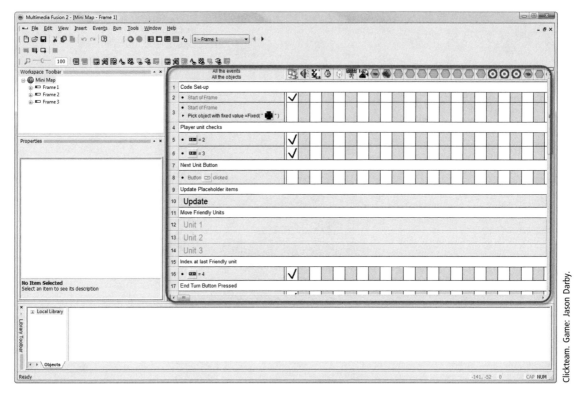

Figure 2.23
Event editor within the MMF2 interface.

additional objects that you have added to that specific frame. To the right of the events and directly below the objects (the white boxes) are action boxes. Where you see a checkmark in Figure 2.24 is where actions have been assigned to a condition.

An event is simply a container that holds one or many conditions that tell the program to wait for something to happen. Some examples of possible single conditions are:

■ Program has just appeared.

■ Ball graphic stops moving.

■ User exits program.

■ Music is playing.

■ Internet is loading.

■ User clicks on a button on a CD-ROM menu.

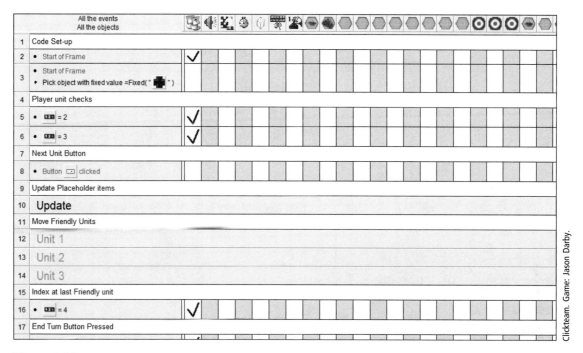

Figure 2.24
Close-up look of the Event editor.

Clickteam. Game: Jason Darby.

Note

These are example conditions to illustrate what you might find within your games and are not examples of conditions shown in Figure 2.24.

You can also use multiple conditions in MMF2:

■ Music is playing and user clicks on button.

■ Ball graphic hits bat graphic and current score.

■ Graphic has disappeared off-screen and player's lives equal zero.

Note

You can create more than two conditions in an event.

Having defined a condition, you will then want something to happen, and this is where actions come into play. The whole reason you are trapping conditions is because you want something to happen at that point.

Table 2.1 Conditions and Actions

Condition	Action
User clicks on button.	Go to different screen.
User clicks on exit button.	Exit that screen or exit the program.
Ball goes out of play.	Remove one life from player's life total.
No lives are left.	Display high score.
Song has finished playing.	Play next song.
File has downloaded.	Display a message to say that the download is complete.

Some examples of action are as follows:

- Lose a life.
- Add 20 to player score.
- Exit the program.
- Play a sound or music.

Some examples of how conditions and actions work together can be seen in Table 2.1.

The important thing to remember about the action box is that it is directly under a specific object. Perhaps we have a graphic of a plane, and when it gets to the edge of the screen we want that plane to bounce back so that it doesn't leave the frame. The condition might be as follows:

Is the "Plane" object about to leave the playfield?

Note

This is an example of a condition and action of a particular object and not the actual text that will appear in your MMF2 games.

When placing the actual action, we need to place it in the action box that directly relates to what we want to happen. In this case we want the Plane object to bounce back. So moving across from the condition, we would ensure that we are directly below the Plane object and then find the action Bounce. You can see an example of this code and what it would look like within the Event editor in Figure 2.25.

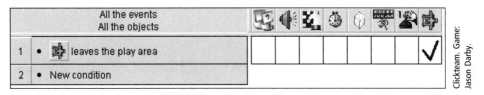

Figure 2.25
Plane object with action.

Event List Editor

The Event List editor is a refined view of the Event editor that allows you to see your conditions and actions in a list. Figure 2.26 shows where the Event List editor is displayed in the MMF2 application. Figure 2.27 shows a close-up view of this screen.

One of the things you need to consider in an event-based programming system is that the code is executed in the order that it is placed in an event or action box. This is fine for conditions because in the Event editor you can change the order of the conditions, but for actions, you can only add new ones, which are then displayed

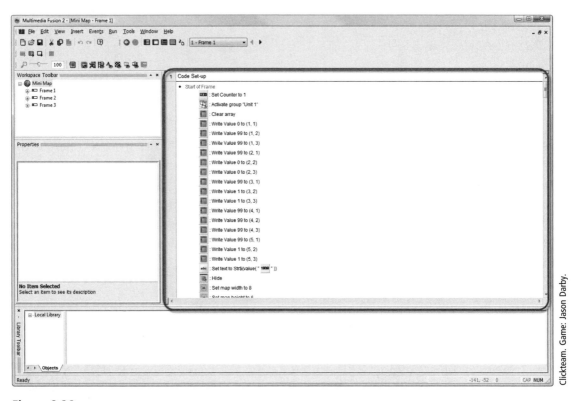

Figure 2.26
The Event List editor.

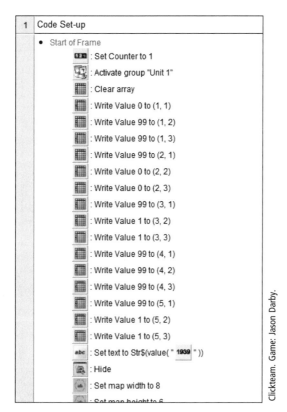

Figure 2.27
Close-up view of the Event List editor.

as checkmarks or colored blocks. The Event List editor allows you to change the order of created actions (by dragging and dropping them in the order that you want them). Another advantage of the Event List editor is that it is graphically stripped down, which is perfect for printing your events out so you can study them away from your computer. Except for printing or ordering actions (conditions and events can be ordered easily from within the Event editor), you will not need to use the Event List editor.

Picture Editor

When you want to import graphic images or perhaps draw your own, you will use the Picture editor, as shown in Figure 2.28. To use the Picture editor, you must first have placed an object of a graphical nature onto the frame play area. Once you have done that, you can then double-click on the object to edit it (more information about objects is available later on in this chapter).

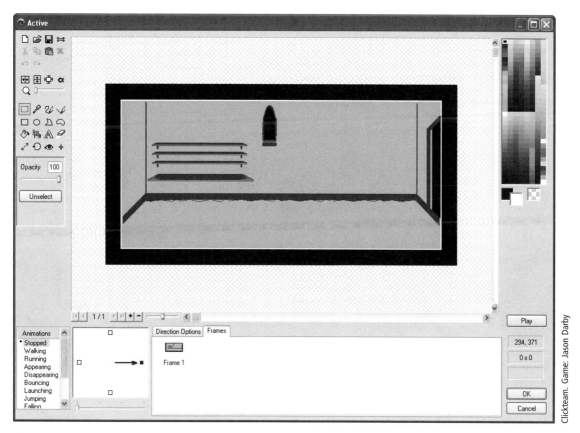

Figure 2.28
Picture editor for drawing or importing graphics.

The Picture editor contains similar tools that a normal drawing program might have, including Pencil, Paintbrush, Fill, Text, and Shapes. You also can select different colors to apply to your images as well as implement picture transparency.

Included within the Picture editor is an Animation editor which allows you to create multiple pictures in a single animation and also set the speed of that animation. You can create multiple animations for the same object, so you could, for example, create a robot with walking, jumping, and running animations. This would all be kept within the same object, and you would then use MMF2 to select which animation you want to play at a particular time.

Expression Evaluator

The Expression Evaluator resembles a scientific calculator with a selection of numeric- and calculation-based buttons. You will use the Expression Evaluator when you want to compare different types of data, do calculations, or set data into a specific object. An example of the Expression Evaluator can be seen in Figure 2.29 and Figure 2.30. You will notice that the buttons are the same but the expressions are different. The type of calculations you are trying to do will depend on the Expression Evaluator that is displayed.

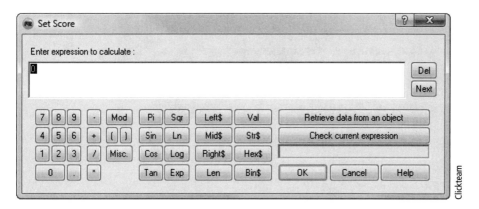

Figure 2.29
The basic Expression Evaluator.

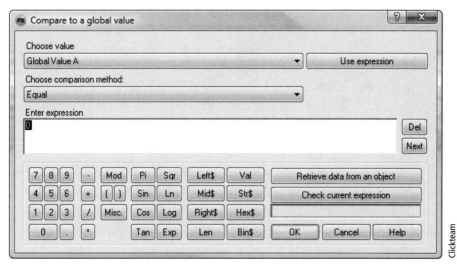

Figure 2.30
More complex Expression Evaluator.

Some examples of when you might use the Expression Evaluator are as follows:

- Set a number into the score object.
- Set a text word—for example, **Hello**—into a text object.
- Compare two numbers and see if one is greater than, less than, or equal to the other number.
- Compare two pieces of text.
- Find the location of a file (the current drive where the application is installed).
- Obtain specific information from an object.

OBJECTS

Objects in MMF2 are the core components for creating your program. When you look closely at any program in MMF2, you may notice that every item on the Frame editor is a separate entity. These entities are all objects. Some examples of objects being used within a program could be:

- A score counter
- A background graphic
- A player-controlled graphic
- A button for clicking Next
- An animation
- A high score table
- A drop-down menu box
- A video box

It makes no difference if you are making an adventure game, a multimedia application, a video player, a kiosk system, or an arcade game; every program will utilize objects. Objects are what make MMF2 extremely powerful because, not only does MMF2 have a large number of already included objects, but anyone with a knowledge of C++ can also create additional objects. If you purchased the full version of the product, you can download the Bonus Packs to gain added functionality.

Note

The demo comes with a standard set of objects and will allow you to make all of the programs detailed in this book as well as a wide and varied number of other programs you might want to make yourself.

Note

Objects are also referred to as extensions or extension objects.

The trial version of MMF2 makes available approximately 70 objects, some of which will be covered in more detail throughout the book. You will learn how to add an object in Chapter 3. Until then, here is a quick rundown of each of the extensions:

- **Active:** The word is appropriate for this object type because it is associated with any graphic object that is going to move across the screen or be animated.

- **Active Backdrop:** The Active Backdrop object is used for any images in the background (at the back) of your game that might be moved or modified, such as a scrolling background. The most important thing to remember about the Active Backdrop is that it does not handle collisions, so you cannot check if another object has collided with it. This means that the Active object does not have to perform complex calculations and is better for performance.

- **Active Direct Show:** Direct Show, a media format from Microsoft, allows you to play formats such as AVI, MIDI, MPEG, MP3, WAV, WMA, and WMV.

- **Active Picture:** You can load a picture from the hard disk and then rotate, resize, and manipulate it in real time. You can either load the picture into the program you are developing or get the object to ask the user to specify a file when the program has been compiled.

- **Active System Box:** This object is generally used for application toolbars or toolbar buttons and can contain checkboxes and hyperlinks.

- **Active X:** Active X objects are a specially formatted file created by Microsoft and other software vendors. Using Active X gives you the ability to add functionality from applications that the user might have installed. For example, it is possible to use Internet Explorer Active X to create a web page display within an MMF2 application. To be able to create a web browser within MMF2, you would need to have IE installed; this will allow you to insert the IE Active X control within your own programs.

Note

Not all Active X objects are available on every user's machine; the number of objects is dependent on the applications the user has installed. Additional license restrictions or requirements may be assigned to an Active X control, and care should be taken when using them. If you create an application with an Active X control that is not available on the end user's PC, the application will fail to work.

■ **Analog Joystick:** This object reports specific information about the movement of the joystick and which buttons are pressed. Support for standard joysticks is built into the Player object.

Note

The Player object is part of a special group of objects that are always present in an MMF2 program and will be discussed shortly.

■ **Animation:** The Animation object is used to display FLC and GIF still images as if they were animated; it does this by showing each of the images quickly to give the illusion of a smooth animated movie. If you are going to animate BMP or other file formats, you should use the Active object.

■ **Array:** When you want to store information that you might want to retrieve in your creation at a later stage, you can use the Array object. Arrays store either numbers or text. You can write to and read from the array file at runtime. The array is an efficient way to store and retrieve information that is used regularly.

■ **AVI:** AVI, a video format, is used to display and play video files within the MMF2 application.

■ **Backdrop:** This is used when you want to display a graphic or background image that you don't need to animate.

■ **Background System Box:** This is used in conjunction with the Active Background system object. Used if you want to attach buttons and move the object with the active buttons attached to it. This object is also used for toolbars like the active system box.

■ **Button:** Use this object when you need various button types, either standard ones within Windows applications or your own buttons using your own images. It contains standard Windows checkbox, radio, and push-button types.

■ **CD Audio:** This allows you to play audio CDs from within an MMF2 program. You can also use it to open and close the CD-ROM door. We will be using the CD Audio object later for one of the practical projects.

■ **Click Blocker:** When you want to prevent the left, right, or center mouse button from being registered as clicked in MMF2, you can block it (prevent it) by using the Click Blocker.

■ **Clickteam Movement Controller:** The Clickteam Movement Controller is a special object that can be used on any Active object to provide special movement types, such as creating presentation movements similar to PowerPoint or creating alien attack waves seen in games such as *Space Invaders.*

■ **Combo Box:** This standard Windows control is used for displaying lists in a drop-down box.

■ **Counter:** This number or graphics counter can be used in a variety of ways: for keeping track of a calculation or scores or to display a health bar in a game, and so on.

■ **Cursor:** This object allows graphical changes to the mouse cursor.

■ **Date and Time:** This object gives you the ability to add a date and/or time to your programs or do comparisons of the computer's current settings. The time can be displayed in analog or digital format.

■ **Direct Show:** This object allows you to include, within your own creations, a wide variety of sound and video file formats, such as AVI, MPEG, and MP3.

■ **Download:** This object allows you to download files from the Internet using the HTTP protocol.

■ **Draw:** The Draw object creates an area of the screen that acts like a paint program where different Pen, Paint, and Fill options can be applied.

■ **Edit Box:** This object allows you to create a way for the end user to enter text. The object also has the ability to save and load text.

■ **File:** Using the File object, you can load, save, append, and delete files. It features a host of other file- and folder-checking capabilities.

■ **Formatted Text:** With this object you have the ability to add text to the screen, which can be given formatting features, such as bold, underlined, and italic.

■ **FTP:** FTP, which stands for file transfer protocol, is used to download or upload files to the Internet.

■ **Hi-Score:** This object adds a Hi-Score table, which can be configured with a predefined set of scores and names.

■ **InAndOut Movement Controller:** The InAndOut Movement Controller object is useful for presentations or screens with scrolling text.

■ **INI:** This object is a special type of formatted file, in which MMF2 can store information and from which MMF2 can read at runtime. It is used for storing basic program configuration information.

■ **Layer:** The Layer object allows you to change the order of objects on the screen so you can move items in front of or behind other objects.

- **List:** This object creates a list that can be sorted. This is a standard Windows control object that you will see in dialog boxes and applications.

- **Lives:** The Lives object displays the number of lives that a player has in a game, in text, in numbers, or in image format. When a player loses a life, you can subtract a number from the number stored in the Lives object, which will then update the display to reflect the current state of play.

- **MCI:** This object allows the MMF2 to control any multimedia device that is connected to the computer. It works by sending a string (text) command to the MCI object. There is a large selection of commands to choose from, and you can find advanced documentation on the Microsoft website.

- **Mixer:** The Mixer object allows you to change the volume control of your sound and MIDI-formatted files.

- **MooClick, MooGame, and MooSock:** This selection of network-based objects allows the creation of multiplayer games, chat programs, and special network protocol-based applications.

- **MPEG:** MPEG (Motion Picture Expert Group), a common video format, allows you to play these files within MMF2.

- **Multiple Touch:** This object is used for touch screens and touch devices, where it can identify the number of touches that have been made.

- **Network:** This is a basic local area network (LAN) communication where two machines can communicate with each other.

- **Object Mover:** The Object Mover allows you to assign objects to the invisible object, so when the invisible object has been moved, all objects assigned to it will also move. This is very useful for items such as moveable menus or menus that resize.

- **ODBC:** Standing for open database connectivity, ODBC allows communication with a variety of database files, such as Access, Dbase, SQL Server, Oracle, and Excel. Using the object, you can access, update, edit, and create new tables within the database using SQL language.

- **Picture:** Load this object to display a picture that can be resized within MMF2 at runtime.

- **Pop-up Menu:** You can see the pop-up menu in use in the Windows operating system when you right-click on the Windows desktop. This object allows you to create your own pop-up menus in MMF2.

- **Print:** This object allows you to use specific print options and printer settings.

- **Question & Answer:** If you want to create a program that asks the user a selection of questions, a quick way to create them is to use the Q&A object.

- **Quick Backdrop:** Using this object, you can create a simple background image for your program, which can include gradients or a solid color.

- **Quicktime:** This object allows you to implement Quicktime movies in your creations.

- **Quiz:** An improved Question & Answer object with multiple choice, Likert scale and matching items quiz system.

- **Registry2:** This object allows you to access, write, and update the Windows registry.

- **Rich Edit:** Rich Edit is a special kind of object that allows advanced text formatting as well as the loading and saving of text files.

- **Score:** This object keeps track of a player's score and displays it as a graphic object.

- **Screen Capture:** With this object, you can capture (take a picture of) an area of the screen and save it to a graphic formatted file.

- **Search:** Search gives you the ability to search text files for a phrase or word as well as to use wildcard options.

- **Shared Data:** This object allows you to share data between several files that have been created in MMF2.

- **Static Text:** This is a basic text display object.

- **String:** This is another basic text display object.

- **Sub Application:** This object allows you to insert another MMF2-created application into the frame of another MMF2-created application.

- **Text Adventure Map:** Use this object to create your adventure games locations and maps.

- **Text Adventure Messages:** In adventure games, this object can send messages to the player, such as "You are not able to do that right now."

- **Text Adventure Pages:** This is used for creating branching stories, such as the Choose Your Own Adventure/story-type books/games.

- **Text Adventure Words:** This is used to figure out what the user has typed and provide him with the correct response.

- **ToolTip:** This creates rectangular tooltips when a user moves the mouse pointer over a particular object or zone. These are common in Windows applications but can also be used in games to provide additional help comments on a particular feature.

- **Tree Control:** This object allows you to create application-based trees, such as seen in standard Windows applications, using folders and items.

- **Vitalize Plug-in:** You can open a URL or download a file using this object.

- **War Game Map:** This object will create war game maps and unit movement.

- **Window Control:** This controls the size, visibility, and position of the current MMF2 application.

- **Windows Shape:** Use this to create an application with a rounded shape or use another object (graphic picture) to create the shape of your application.

SYSTEM OBJECTS

The objects just described are those you will add to your program for a specific set of features. If you do add these objects, they will not appear in your program or the Event editor object list. A System object is present in every MMF2 file. These seven objects are not displayed within the Frame editor but are instead in the Event editor. Figure 2.31 shows a blank Event editor with no code written in it but with the seven objects already present.

The seven System objects can be used in the same way as normal objects and can create conditions or actions. These System objects have the following capabilities:

- **Special conditions:** Used when comparing numbers and strings, running external programs, enabling and disabling groups, and checking the clipboard contents.

- **Sound:** Used to determine whether a sound is playing or to apply a sound to be played.

- **Storyboard controls:** Used to handle movement between frames and to check to see if the frame has started or finished.

- **Timer:** Used when you want to do comparisons on the current time or determine the amount of time that has passed since the application was first started.

Figure 2.31
The System objects present in the Event editor.

- **Create New Objects:** Used when you need to create copies of already-created objects or to pick or count objects that are already in play on the frame.

- **Mouse Pointer and Keyboard:** Used to check if the player has used the mouse or keyboard.

- **Player 1:** Used to set up the player controls (joystick or keyboard) and also to configure the lives and score of the current player.

GAME DESIGN PROCESS

There are a number of processes that you can follow that are similar for every game that you will ever make. Understanding this process will help you when you are ready to start making your very own games.

The processes for making a game can be categorized into the following:

- **Team, Tools, Skills, and Budget:** Determine who is helping to make the game, what tools you will use, what skills are required, and whether you have a set budget to spend (and what it is).

- **Ideas and Brainstorming:** Determine the ideas you want to develop.

- **Market:** Determine your game's market—for example, the end user and the platform (device).

- **Idea in More Detail:** Create more detail about the game you are going to make.

- **Design Document and Storyboarding:** Create both a design document, which details your game's components (e.g., characters, places, locations, game mechanics, and scoring), and a storyboard, or a graphical representation mapping out your game's structure.

- **Programming Process:** Create the game using MMF2.

- **Testing:** Test the game to make sure it works as you expect.

- **Alpha and Beta:** Follow standard game-making milestones to ensure your game gets made.

- **Release:** Release your game to your users.

- **User Feedback and Changes/Patches:** Find out how things go after the game has been released, and consider a patch to correct any problems.

We will now go into more detail about some of these items, so that you will have a greater understanding of what will be involved in making your game.

Note

You do not need to follow every item or process; they are listed so that you can pick and choose which ones you think will be useful in creating your game.

Note

The items in the game-making process may overlap, and you may have to go back to an earlier process and make changes if you discover an error.

Team, Tools, Skills, and Budget

Before you start making any game, even a game for fun, you should take a moment to consider what you have at your disposal. This will help you understand what type of game you can actually make. Perhaps you love point-and-click graphic adventures but you can't draw; you will need to make a decision if you are going to make this type of game using your own art, find a friend/someone else to draw it for you, or consider a different type of adventure game.

Note

Remember, you don't need to jump straight into making a particular game type; it may be more beneficial to learn the process of making an easier game to get some experience first.

Team

So let's start with the team you are putting together to make your first game. Following are some questions you may want to think about:

- Will you be making the game on your own?

- Do you have some friends who can help you with certain aspects of game creation? What skills can they bring to the project?

- If you are getting people to help with your project, will they be working for free or will you be paying them?

- If you have a group of people helping you, who will own the IP (intellectual property) once the game is released?

- How will you communicate with your team (face-to-face, e-mail, or online chat systems such as MSN)?

In most cases, it's sometimes easier to start on your own to get an idea how to use the software and to gain some knowledge before trying to bring friends in to help you.

Tools

Tools are an important aspect of making any computer game. For the games in this book, we will be using MMF2 and Adventure Game objects. MMF2 is perfect for the games we will be making. Programming knowledge is not required, and it's a tool that can get a game up and running quite quickly, meaning you can spend more time on adding more features.

But you will need to consider what other tools you will need to create your game. Some examples are as follows:

- **Design:** When you are in the process of creating a game, it is a good idea to document what you want your game to do. This is especially useful if other people are involved in the process. MMF2 puts your game screens together by placing graphics within the correct sized game window. You might also use a pen and paper and draw out what you want. Many game companies use MS Word to write their design documents (ideas) and MS Excel to set out gameplay mechanics (how the game works mathematically). I like to use Balsamiq (www.balsamiq.com) to lay out my screen design when I make UI (user interface) game screens.

- **Graphics:** Although MMF2 has its own built-in Picture editor in which you can create your own images, you may prefer to draw your favorite art package before importing into the game creator program. You could use Windows Paint, Photoshop, or any of a number of other products.

- **Sounds:** An important aspect of any game is the sound and music effects. In a text adventure, this may be simple music and sound effects, whereas a point-and-click adventure will have sound effects that relate to what's happening in the world, such as footsteps, doors opening, and characters talking. To create these sounds, you might need to record your own noises, purchase sounds from an online sound library, or import selections from a CD-ROM library of sounds. You may also need a tool for editing sounds. If you intend to create a game for the iPhone, the sound samples need to be as compact and small as possible to save space and reduce the loading time (which is less of a problem on the PC platform), so I used specific tools, such as Adobe Soundbooth, to change the format or reduce the quality, which won't be noticeable to the player but will save a lot of hard disk space.

Note

There are many different tools that people can use when creating a game's art, design, and music. There are many free alternatives available on the market if you do not own some of the more well-known commercial products.

Job Roles

When creating adventure games, you will need to either be able to do the following job roles yourself or obtain these skills from other people:

- **Writer:** Every game has a story and characters as well as places that the players will visit. You will need descriptions of the locations that the players can visit and also the objects they can interact with.

- **UI artist:** The UI (user interface) consists of the graphics that help the player navigate the screens/game. In a text adventure, the UI will be pretty much non-existent, but in graphic adventure games and point-and-click, it will be essential.

- **Background artist:** Will you be creating a graphic adventure? If so, you will need graphic backgrounds. Perhaps you will use photographs or will want to have your backgrounds drawn.

- **Animator:** If you are creating a point-and-click adventure, your character will move (animate) in the game. The animator can be the person who is responsible for drawing or someone who specializes in animating characters.

- **Sound creator/musician:** Sound is a very important aspect of any game and will require specific samples. For example, if you are opening a door, you might want to add a door creaking noise. For music, you may want something intense when the player is in immediate danger or more peaceful when the player is safe.

Note

If you don't have the skills to fill these roles, then don't worry; you may be able to find a friend who can help you with the parts that you don't feel you can do yourself.

Budget

The budget you have to make your game will depend on what you have at your disposal. If you can already draw, you may, for example, be able to make the game yourself without any further help. If you cannot draw, you may be using the royalty-free art that comes with the MMF2 product. But in some cases, you may

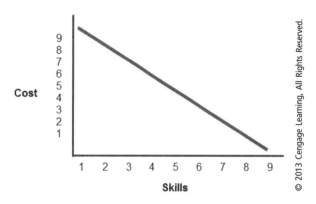

Figure 2.32
Skills vs. cost graph.

decide that you want to spend money on certain aspects of your game so that you can improve the overall quality.

The budget of your adventure games will entirely depend on how high quality you want the game to be, defined by the amount of skill that you have.

As you can see in the very simple diagram in Figure 2.32, the cost of any game will be significantly reduced the more skills that you and your team have. Of course, you could still make a game with your friends at no cost. This figure shows that the more jobs you are able to fill at no cost, the less likely you will need to finance any part of the game, such as paying a third-party artist or musician.

If you are uncertain of what skills you or your friends have, then you should start with the text adventure and work toward more complex games when you feel you are ready.

Ideas and Brainstorming

So you now have an idea who is working with you on your game and what roles they will take, or you may have decided you are making the game yourself. Now that you have a basic plan on who is doing what, you now need to consider what type of adventure game you want to make. It's easy to come up with an initial idea; in fact, it's quite common for designers to have multiple ideas in mind at the same time.

First, you need to gather all of your ideas. You can keep track of them in a simple Microsoft Word document or Excel spreadsheet, or perhaps you would prefer placing all your ideas on a board or a wall.

For example, here are some basic ideas:

1. Text adventure game based on the *Titanic*.

2. Text adventure game where the player travels through time. The map is the same but changes depending on the timeframe.

3. Graphic adventure game set in the 1980s Cold War era where the player has to steal some secret plans.

4. Point-and-click adventure game in space.

5. Hidden object game where the player must find the golden sword of Avalon.

You shouldn't worry about going into too much depth at this time. A number of factors will influence your decision to make a particular game, such as which game is most exciting to you, the difficulty level to make a particular game, people needed (if any) to help you make the game, and the market you are making the game for.

Market

The market refers to the actual users and platforms you will be making the game for. In many cases, the market is usually an age group, a genre or niche, a particular gender, or a particular technology (such as a mobile phone or PC).

If you are making a game for fun, then the market for your game is you. Here are some other markets that you may be looking to gear your game toward:

- **Age:** Are you thinking of making a game for kids? Or a game that is aimed at players over 40?

- **Gender:** Are you aiming your games at male or female users? Some games are weighted toward a particular gender. For example, more males than females are interested in games involving boxing. More females play hidden object games.

- **Genre:** What type of genre are you considering? Perhaps you are going to focus on a horror game or perhaps an action-adventure game. The genre will define a lot about your game.

- **Platforms:** What platforms are you going to release your game on? The technology you are using will define the features that you can use in your game. For example, are you going to release on PC or iPhone? The differences between the two platforms are obviously differences in screen resolution, keyboard, and mouse usage (will it require touch screen game mechanics).

Idea in More Detail

So now that you have a clearer picture of the type of game you want to make, it's important to flesh out that idea with more details before you begin the process of designing it.

For this example, we have created a game idea called *Cold War*. This is a text-adventure game in which the player is attempting to retrieve the government's plans for a top-secret weapon. The plans were stolen by a rival government; you must recover the plans before they can be sent back to the rival country.

To help us with our idea, we create a simple introduction document that details the basics of the game. The document contains the following information:

- **Game name:** This is the name of the game, and if you haven't decided on the game name yet, the codename. In our example we will be calling our game *Cold War*, but if we hadn't decided on a name, we might call it *Game1* or *Spy Game*.

- **Game technology:** We have already discussed in Chapter 1 the different types of adventure games that you can make, so will it be a text adventure, a graphic adventure, a point-and-click, an FMV, or a hidden object game?

- **Basic concept:** What is the idea behind the game? This provides you with a brief reminder of what the high level concept is for the game.

- **Characters:** Who are the key characters in the game? What are their names and what are their roles in the game? As this is only a brief document, you should not go into detail about these characters yet.

- **Locations:** What are the key locations within the game? You can also provide a brief description.

- **Objects of importance:** What are the key objects that the player can collect or use that are important to the story or game?

- **Price:** Will the game be sold? Or is it something you are just making for your friends?

- **Platforms:** What platforms will you release the game on?

- **Team:** Who is involved in making the game?

- **Release date:** When do you think you will complete the game?

- **Resources:** If they are needed, what resources, such as picture and sound libraries, will you be using?

So if we use *Cold War* as an example, we would have the following:

Game name: *Cold War.*

Game technology: Text-based adventure.

Basic concept: As one of the government's top-secret agents, you have been brought out of retirement to retrieve the stolen plans of weapon X, a new super weapon that can slow down time. You only have 24 hours to retrieve the plans before they are sent back to the Soviet Union.

Characters: You are John Ryan, a spy brought out of retirement to help the government retrieve secret plans. Mr. W is your boss and not a particularly happy one at that. Agent Jones, your contact back at base, provides you with your mission objectives.

Locations: The game starts off in London and like the main character in any good spy movie, you get to travel to locations around the world. Your starting location is your flat in London. Your first mission is to get to the MI5 base.

Objects of importance: There will be many spy objects that you can use within the game, but the most important will be your pick-lock kit, decrypter device, gun, and obviously the secret plans.

Price: $0.69.

Platforms: PC, iPad, and iPhone devices.

Team: Writer and Designer—J. Darby.

Release date: 2012.

Resources: Graphic resources provided by stock graphics library or graphic artist.

Now that we have our basic concepts and project information written, we can now begin to expand on this in the game design document.

Design Document and Storyboarding

We have a good idea of what we want to create in the text adventure *Cold War*. So the next stage is to expand the ideas and create a full design document and storyboard.

A game design document should contain as much information as possible for you (and others, if you are having people help you) to understand what you need to put into the game. This will contain detailed information on characters, locations, game mechanics, and scoring.

It is sometimes more interesting to jump straight into making a game, but doing so will most likely cause you more problems later on in the game's development. Even a simple game requires a basic set of rules and a reason for existing. You don't need to write pages and pages of text to design your game, and you may only require a single page of paper. As long as the design document contains enough information for you to make the game without struggling later on to understand why you did something a certain way, then that will be sufficient. Obviously, the more complicated the game, the more likely that you will need more extensive design documentation.

Note

A storyboard is a graphical representation of what each screen in your game or frame in a video sequence will look like. It is totally up to you which methods you use to map out the structure of your game; you should use what helps you get the game made.

Text adventures will be easier to design than a point-and-click adventure or a hidden object game. Adventure games in some respects can be easier to design than a traditional game such as a shooting or real-time strategy game, but they can still become quite complex. For simple text adventures, you might want to start off mapping out your game world. This will provide you with a good starting base for your adventure. More complex adventures may require more detailed information and storyboards.

Note

Game mechanics are the rules that govern a game; for example, if you were making a soccer game, you would detail information on things such as the game consists of two halves, both 45 minutes long, injury time, offside rules, and player substitutes.

The game mechanics of your adventure game might be that the player can place objects into his inventory, but he is restricted by a particular number or the total weight of the objects.

In Figure 2.33, you can see a simple map of the first area of the game. You will notice a map letter on the top-right corner. This allows us to link maps together. We also have labeled each room with a number; these numbers are effectively A1, A2, and so on.

You can then create a second document that links to Map A, which details each particular location. So for the starting location:

A1: Living Room

Location Description: The starting location for the player. The player awakens to a telephone ringing. The room contains various clues and items about what is happening in the world. This provides a backdrop to the current headlines. The player is asked on the telephone to come into MI5 (the British Intelligence)

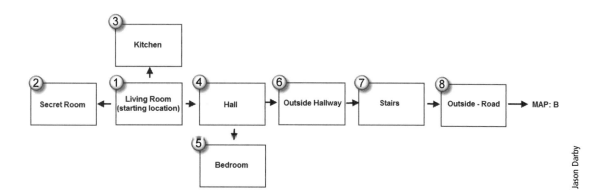

Area 1 - Starting - Safe House

MAP: A

Jason Darby

Figure 2.33
The starting map for our spy game.

because they need the player to help with an urgent intelligence matter. The player can then look around the various rooms in the house and proceed downstairs to where he can jump into a taxi that will take him to MI5.

Objects in Room: Passport; newspaper (with current headlines); TV; picture on wall (which hides a secret panel that activates a secret door); half-eaten sandwich; selection of books; a table that contains two wine glasses, an empty bottle of wine, and a corkscrew.

Exits: North to Kitchen, West to Secret Room, East to Hall.

You may decide to break down the objects in the room further, with such details as those shown in Figure 2.34. Of course, you can add further details to your tables if you require them.

Item	Location	Cost	Weight
Passport	A1 – Living Room	0	0
Newspaper	A1 – Living Room	50 cents	1
Sandwich	A3 – Kitchen	0	0
Book – Car Mechanics	A5 – Bedroom	$5	3

Clickteam. Game: Jason Darby.

Figure 2.34
A graphic showing our objects, locations, and basic details.

Alpha and Beta

These are two terms commonly used in software development and game creation. *Alpha* is used in regard to a game that has become feature complete—all of the key elements of the game, such as the inventory system, objects, and mapping system, are in place. These items may not necessarily be data complete (i.e., you may not have all objects added) and there may be bugs, but in terms of the core functionality, it should be in place.

Beta is used to describe a product that is generally both feature and data complete, and the only thing left to do is test and fix bugs. The reality is usually far from the truth in many games, especially indie-made games, where developers may continue to add features up until very late in the product's release.

When making any game, you should set some basic timeframes for when you will complete various stages of your game. Once you have created your design documentation, you should begin to break this down into key features. For our spy game, it could be broken down into very basic groups such as:

- Main menu graphics
- Menus and user interface
- Inventory system
- Text display
- Text entry
- Objects and their properties
- Map creation and storage
- Game content

You would expect to finish all key systems by whatever date you decide to set as your alpha date.

Release

Once your game is complete and has been tested, and all seems to work fine, then you will be ready to release the game to the general public (or just your friends and family, if you prefer).

First be sure to consider these few issues:

- **Price:** Are you going to charge for the product? If so, how are you going to take payment? Do you use services like PayPal? Do you have a method for asking the user for payment and then providing him with the game after he has purchased it? Do you have a bank account that can be used to accept any funds? Additionally, if you are receiving payment, you may need to consider your local tax requirements. If you are creating a product for free, then you don't need to worry about any of these issues.

- **How to distribute:** How are you going to distribute your game? Will it be available on your own website? Or will it be available on a game portal site? Will your game be in a single executable or will you need to create an installation file so that the player can be given an automated process to install it onto his PC? If you are making a Flash game and will be placing it on a website for people to play, do you have a website to host the game? If you are releasing it on phone platforms such as iPhone, do you have an account created and have you gone through the approval process?

- **Advertising:** Are you going to advertise your game to get more people to download it? Will you use services such as YouTube, Twitter, and Facebook to get your product out there?

Once you've got your game out into the wild, you should be looking to see what went right and what went wrong when making the game. Maybe you'll want to make a follow-up game, or just another game. You'll learn from your mistakes and get better. Perhaps you made some mistakes that delayed the release of the game, or you had issues with programming, graphics, or design that you wish to improve on the second time around. The easier it is to make your game, the quicker you can complete it, which in turn will prevent you from a long, drawn-out development time. This is a common issue when making games on your own or on a small team, and if it takes too long to release, you might find yourself getting bored of the project and stopping work on it altogether.

We discussed Alpha and Beta in the previous section. Releasing Beta versions of games to the public is becoming a common occurrence. This way you can get feedback from your user base and make changes to the gameplay before it is complete, which in turn should provide a better game experience for anyone else who comes along after the game has been released. Some products, such as *Minecraft*, spend a large amount of time in Beta, but the creators have been able to add a large amount of content that users have requested.

If you intend to complete your game and then release, you may discover that users find bugs that you never considered while creating the game and, in fact, that you never spotted when testing the game yourself. You should always consider giving the game to friends or other people who have not been involved in the development of the game, as these people are likely to find bugs that you didn't think of.

Patches are very useful for fixing issues with games after they have been released. You should, however, try to ensure that your game is in a working state before being released and not rely on releasing a patch to fix it. As an indie developer, you may feel the need to just get the game released even though something may not be working as expected. Reject this urge because often only another few hours or days of development will make all the difference to the quality of your game.

What Is SAM?

SAM stands for Story Adventure Maker, and is an application/tool written in Multimedia Fusion 2. The program was written to handle a set of data from Multimedia Fusion's Adventure Game objects and save this data into external files. Using the editors, we can create data that can be quickly compiled to be used in a set of adventure games.

An editor is a special program that has been written to complete a specific task. The editor will allow the user to create settings/values and properties and save them to a file, which would then be loaded into a game/application. The main benefit of creating an editor is that you can change values without needing to go into the game's code to make changes to the data.

For example, perhaps we want to write an editor that stores information—such as name, weight, and cost—about all objects in any of our games. We could specify all objects individually within code, but this is very slow, and if you decide to change a particular bit of data, you would have to go into the code and change that line of data. If we create an Objects editor, we could then create a nice-looking application that would allow the user to enter the data as records, move through records, delete, and update. Once the user has completed adding his data, he would then save this data into a specially formatted file. The user does not necessarily need to know the format of the file.

In PC and console games that are released on the market today, you may find game designers and level designers using tools to edit game data, without knowing what the data would look like in code. They may change the way a person looks, how much health a character has, or the weight of a sword. Designers can change things quickly without needing to ask a programmer to change the data for them.

I have used SAM to create data such as a Map editor and an Objects and Inventory manager. Though this initially slows down the development of your game (you need to create an editor, create a file format, and then hook this up to any game you create), once you begin making your game, it will save you many hours of development.

The great thing is that you can use these editors in future games and add further features to them.

We will learn more about SAM in Chapter 16 of this book.

CHAPTER SUMMARY

In this chapter, you learned about Multimedia Fusion 2 and how to install it. You learned about all the different editors within MMF2 and what they are used for. We discussed objects and how they are the basic building blocks for any program written in MMF2. We covered the basics of how you might start to think about designing your game and the types of skills you need to make a game. Finally, you learned that by using MMF2, you can also create editors that will make game creation much easier than coding all of the game's data directly into the application. In the next chapter, we will look at creating a very basic choose-your-own adventure game called *Moon Traveller*.

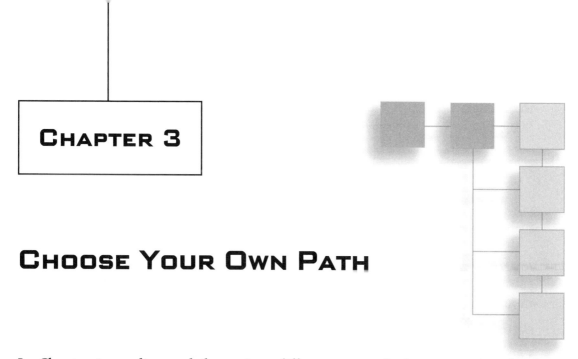

CHAPTER 3

CHOOSE YOUR OWN PATH

In Chapter 1, we discussed the various different types of adventure games that have existed over the years. We discussed the *Fighting Fantasy* and *Choose Your Own Adventure* game books—you read a paragraph and can choose from a number of options. Depending on your selection, you might carry on with your adventure, get into a battle, lose some health, or ultimately the book could end because you have won or lost.

In this chapter, we will be looking at making our very own storybook as a computer game. We will cover details such as what type of features are involved, how to program them into MMF2, and what features you could add to extend it further.

FEATURES OF AN ADVENTURE BOOK

In paper adventure books, there are a number of features that are common, as well as expected by readers. Among these are:

- **Rules:** To explain what the book is about and how it works, there are usually a number of chapters describing how to play. This is because the person who is reading the book may not already know the rules. It's quite possible that this book has a different set of rules than do other books, so it is always important (in any type of game) to explain what the game/book is about and how it works.

- **Introduction:** There is an introduction to the story, which explains the current player's predicament. This gives the background to what has happened and how the player came to be where he currently is. This could be a few paragraphs or a few pages, depending on the story.

- **Topic Numbers:** Every section in the book, except for the rules and introduction, has a topic number. This is the number that is referenced when the player is making a decision. Once the player has selected a decision, he would turn to that numbered topic to continue reading.

Note

Do not confuse topic numbers with page numbers, as they are two different features of a book. In some books, the writer might use a single page per topic; others might have multiple topics per page. For the computer game version, we will not require page numbers, but they are mentioned here for reference.

- **Decision Numbers:** Each section of text has a topic number; at the bottom of each topic will be the decisions a player needs to make with the relevant topic number to go to—for example, eat the apple, turn to 27; leave the apple, turn to 7.

- **Pictures:** Some topics contain pictures.

- **Dice:** To make the books more interesting, there were times when a reader would be required to roll a pair of dice to work out a particular result. Perhaps the player has a luck value and has fallen over; the reader would then roll the dice and compare the result to his luck value to see if he was successful. If he failed, he might lose some health points.

- **Dice2:** Some books—in particular, the *Fighting Fantasy* books—display a set of dice printed on each page; this allows people who don't have two six-sided die to be able to work out their luck/battle results without having to search around for dice. From a program point of view, you would need to create some way for the player to roll results.

- **Battle/Health Mechanic:** Many books had fighting, magic, or even fear (for horror) mechanics. This really helped make the books much more interesting because the story now contained these additional gameplay mechanics. So rather than just telling a simple story with selections, you could battle a troll or wizard.

MOON TRAVELLER

Now that you have an idea of some of the features of an adventure book, we are going to make our own version, but for the PC. The game, called *Moon Traveller*, is an adventure where you are going into space to set up a moon base. Unfortunately things don't go as planned and disaster strikes.

The aim of the game is to reach the moon base successfully; in your way will be a number of issues that may prevent you from reaching this goal. Remember it is very common in these types of books/games to fail or not reach the final goal, which in doing so affords the user the chance to play again; the player may also map out the game world so as not to meet the same fate the next time.

Note

Though we are making the game for PC, you could also convert what you have done to a printed/text-based format if you require.

Note

Due to the possible size of such an adventure book–based game, we have made it particularly short with only a few possible options. This is just for the sake of time and space in this book, but everything you need to make a larger game is covered in the following example.

How to Map Out Your Game

In Chapter 2, we talked about creating maps and storyboards as you create your game's design. The process for creating a PC adventure book is the same, with some additions to allow for particular design needs for this type of game.

A good way to create a basic adventure book for the PC is as follows:

- **Ideas:** Come up with your story idea, detailing the main characters, why they are there, and what the aim of the story is.

- **Maps/flow:** Create a number of maps to help define your adventure story. These can be maps of the country, giving you an idea of how the world fits together story-wise (the main places to visit, including historical or geographical), or more detailed such as a town, or in the case of *Moon Traveller*, a close-up map of the adventure. You may also find it much more helpful to create an adventure flow map; this shows how the game all links together.

- **Text:** Your adventure needs lots of text, but this is also text that links to other text (topics). You need some method of documenting this.

- **Topics and links:** You need a way of tracking the different links between topics for when you convert the story into a computer program.

Now that you have an idea of what you need to do to get this game idea up and running, I will show you how this applies to *Moon Traveller*.

- **Story concept:** Your job is to take your space rocket to the Earth Space Station and recover the supplies before flying off to the moon and setting up the moon base.

- **Characters:** You are the main character (unnamed) and the only other person you will meet on this journey is Captain Ryan, who is in charge of the ESS.

- **Locations:** You will be in the following locations: spaceship, ESS (Earth Space Station), and the moon.

Note

The locations are the key places in our story; they may only exist as one area, which you cannot move around in. An example of this is the ESS, which effectively consists of one room, which you can visit. You may decide you want to increase the areas to visit, but as this is a small example we have kept the locations very small in size.

Story Flow and Map

If we take our story and concept to the next level, we need to draw out the locations that the player can visit and begin to build up a diagram of how the game world fits together. This will help you when writing the story for your game.

If we were to draw the locations and links between different locations in *Moon Traveller* it wouldn't be much help in this instance, because it's effectively a row of connections. In a more complex game, it might have the player moving between locations and returning to other locations, branching off in different directions. But in Figure 3.1 you can see this basic map, which still will help us understand the locations involved in the game.

If we now start to put together a basic flow of our game, we can start to think of the different issues that the player will face while playing. Figure 3.2 shows an example

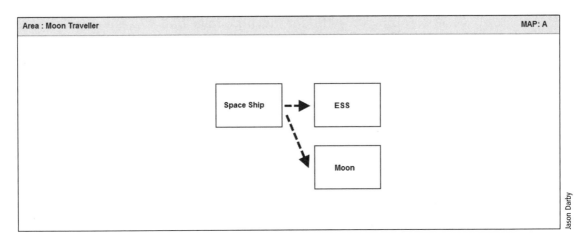

Figure 3.1
The *Moon Traveller* locations map.

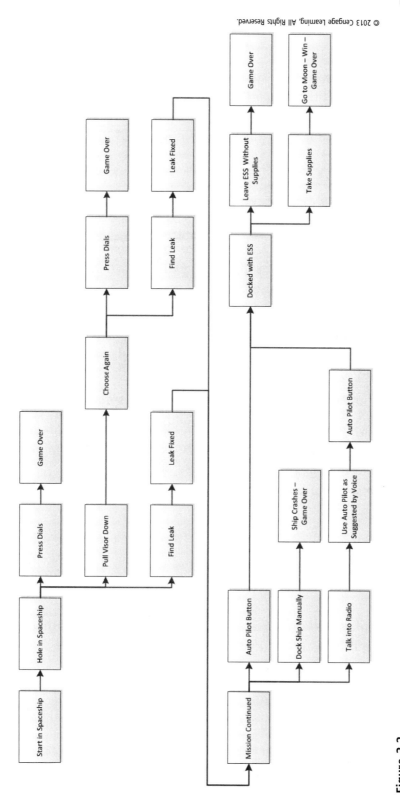

Figure 3.2
The flow of *Moon Traveller*.

flow of the *Moon Traveller* game. As you can see, there is a lot more going on in this game when you compare it to Figure 3.1's location map.

You can make this flow as complicated or as simple as you want—whatever you need to be able to understand how your game will ultimately work. The bigger the game, the more complex it is to design or create your game as you work, and so you should get into the habit of creating flows for your games even if they are simple.

Links and Story Text

Now that we have an idea of what our game will do and what challenges the player will face, we can move on to writing the text to our story.

Writing the text to the story will probably take longer than making the game itself, but it's important to create a system that is easy to follow and that will make putting the data (i.e., the text and links) into the game as easy as possible.

For this process, I have come up with a simple way of creating the text in a Microsoft Excel spreadsheet. The box formatting of Excel is very useful when sorting out data, but you can use any tool that you have at your disposal, as long as you can break your content up and it is easily readable.

You can see an example of the data placed into an Excel spreadsheet in Figure 3.3. In the spreadsheet are a number of columns, as follows:

- **Topic:** The topic number for this particular text. The topic number is the number that the reader jumps to after making a decision.

- **Topic Text:** The text that this particular topic is associated with. This will explain the story.

- **Num Links:** The number of links that each piece of text/topic will have. These links are at the end of the paragraph/topic, providing the user with what to do next. For this story/program, we are going to use three as the maximum number of links in each topic.

- **Link 1:** The link number for link 1. This is the topic number that the player would jump to if he wanted to perform link 1's action.

- **Link 2:** The link number for link 2.

- **Link 3:** The link number for link 3.

- **Link 1 Text:** The text that will be used for link 1. This would include the number detailed in link 1.

- **Link 2 Text:** The text that will be used for link 2.

Last Name

G
r
e
e

Last 4 #s Library Card

3
4
0
1

Pull Date

05	14

Mo./Day

Topic	Topic Text	Num Links	Link 1	Link 2	Link 3	Link 1 Text	Link 2 Text	Link 3 Text	End
1	The noise of the engines was terrifying, but this is what you had been trained for over the last two years. Over the comm's you can just about hear someone shouting, "3..2..1.. lift off, we have a lift off." / This is it, the moment everyone had been waiting for, you were finally off to the moon. The first manned mission since the end of the Apollo missions in the 1970's. / Your first stop on the way to the moon is the ESS (Earth Space Station) to pick up your cargo, some food and a set of building materials to create the first moon base. Once your equipment has been packed you will then spend two days travelling to the moon, before landing on the moon and setting up AlphaBeta Base.	1	2	-	-	Now turn to 2.			
2	Now you are out of the earth's atmosphere you press the auto pilot button. This begins to turn the spaceship in the direction of the ESS. / Suddenly, without warning, you hear a loud crashing noise toward the back of the craft, and then a fizzing noise. You see a dial on the instrument panel decreasing - it's the pressure dial. The ship is losing air and fast. If you don't do something soon, you will run out of oxygen in the cabin.	3	10	4	15	You decide to pull your visor down, turn to 10.	You try to locate where the leak is coming from, turn to 4.	If you decide to press as many dials as you can in the hope it will fix the problem, turn to 15.	
3	Except for a small number of radio transmissions, not a lot to note happens. A small object in the distance gets bigger and bigger, until you can see the ESS.	3	14	7	5	Do you press the auto pilot button, if so turn to 14.	Do you decide to dock the ship manually, if so go to 7.	You decide to pick up the radio handset and talk into it, go to 5.	
4	The leak could be anywhere and the hole could be microscopic. You decide to open a bag of liquid food, as soon as you rip open the bag, the liquid yoghurt immediately starts to move towards the rear of the ship and to a tiny hole. Grabbing the sealing device you quickly seal the hole and the cabin pressure begins to rise.	1	9	-	-	You can now carry on with your mission. Go to 9.			
5	On picking up the handset it crackles to life...before you can even say hello, you hear a voice saying, "Use the auto pilot.. You don't need to get authorisation, we know you were coming"	2	7	14	-	Do you decide to dock the ship manually, if so go to 7.	Do you press the auto pilot button, if so turn to 14		
6	You move back to the ship.	2	11	8	-	You decide to go back and take the supplies, go to 11	You decide to leave for the moon, go to 8		
7	You take control of the joystick moving it slowly towards the ESS docking bay. A voice suddenly shouts out "What are you doing, you cannot manually dock the ship...watch out". Before you can react one of the solar arrays catches the side of the ship, a loud scraping noise can be heard from the right of the ship. / You quickly press the Auto Pilot button, but it's too late, the ship has been too badly damaged, and you will have to return to Earth. I don't think you will be in the next ship to the moon. The End.	0	-	-	-				Y
8	Leaving the ESS behind you begin your two day journey to the moon. After one days travel you realise you needed the supplies. You have to turn back or it could be a disaster.	2	11	12	-	You go back for the supplies, go to 11.	You carry on your journey. Go to 12.		
9	The journey to the ESS is slow and boring. All of the dials are green and there is nothing for you to do at the moment.	1	3	-	-	You sit patiently, go to 3.			
10	You can feel the lack of oxygen in the cabin getting serious, grabbing the visor on your helmet and locking it into place. Suddenly you breathe a sigh of relief as you remember that the space suit you are wearing is connected to it's own tank. You still need to fix the issue with the hole.	2	4	15	-	You open a liquid food container, turn to 4.	If you decide to press as many dials as you can in the hope it will fix the problem, turn to 15.		
11	You take the required supplies back to the ship, and click on the launch button to move away from the ESS. Once the ship is ready you turn it towards the moon and begin the long 2 day journey to its orbit. On arriving you land the ship and successfully set-up AlphaBeta base. Congratulations you have completed your mission.	0	-	-	-				Y
12	You decide to continue your journey. As you reach the moon, you land the ship.	1	13	-	-	Now turn to 13.			
13	Without the supplies there is no way you can build the moon base, what were you thinking leaving the supplies behind. The space agency is not going to be very happy with you. You launch the lunar module back into space and head back to Earth. The End.	0	-	-	-				Y
14	On pressing the auto pilot button the ship effortlessly moves into position and docks with the ESS. You see the red light above the docking door turn from red to green. So you open the door. You move slowly into the corridor and then into the main docking bay room on the ESS, waiting for you is Captain Ryan. "Welcome aboard the ESS, the supplies you need are right over there, help yourself and good luck". Ryan points to a pile of boxes in the corner, and proceeds to go back to whatever task he was performing before you turned up.	2	11	6	-	You take the supplies, turn to 11.	You decide that Ryan is particularly rude and go back to the ship, go to 6.		
15	In desperation you press as many buttons and turn as many dials as you can to solve the problem. Unfortunately you press the abort mission button by mistake. The spacecraft takes a u-turn and heads back to Earth. Your mission to set-up a moon base has failed. The End.	0	-	-	-				Y

Microsoft

Figure 3.3
A Microsoft Excel formatted spreadsheet containing our book game data.

- **Link 3 Text:** The text that will be used for link 3.
- **End:** The end of the story from this topic. This will be because the player has either won or lost the game.

If we take the example of the second topic in our story, what you would normally see in a book would be:

2.

Now you are out of the earth's atmosphere. You press the auto pilot button. This begins to turn the spaceship in the direction of the ESS.

Suddenly, without warning, you hear a loud crashing noise toward the back of the craft, and then a fizzing noise. You see a dial on the instrument panel decreasing—it's the pressure dial. The ship is losing air and fast. If you don't do something soon, you will run out of oxygen in the cabin.

You decide to pull your visor down, turn to 10. You try to locate where the leak is coming from, turn to 4. If you decide to press as many dials as you can in the hope it will fix the problem, turn to 15.

If we break that down into the different groups we've created within our spreadsheet, you will find that the number at the top of the text is the topic number and the first two paragraphs are the topic text. The three sentences in the last paragraph are the text for links 1, 2, and 3, while the numbers 10, 4, and 15 within the text are the links. Finally, the number of links within this topic is three, as they are 10, 4, and 15.

CREATING THE GAME

The game text and its links are all ready to be put into MMF2, so now we are ready to make our game. The game will take the form of a simple adventure book. It will contain the topic number, the topic text, and up to three buttons. The buttons will contain the link text and when pressed will take the player to a new page.

Note
_____

You can get access to all of the book's example files and text items by downloading the file from www.castlesoftware.co.uk under the section books.
_____

Creating the Application File

Our first task is creating a blank application file to contain our game. In this application file will be a single frame. This frame will contain our game, and we will need no further frames.

1. Start up MMF2. If you are using the demo version of MMF2, you will need to select this from the demo list before the application will load.

2. Once the MMF2 application has loaded, click on the New button (which looks like a piece of paper on the button toolbar) or click on File | New option. This will open up a new application at the screen size of 640×480.

3. Double-click on the text Frame 1 in the Workspace toolbar to display the frame as shown in Figure 3.4.

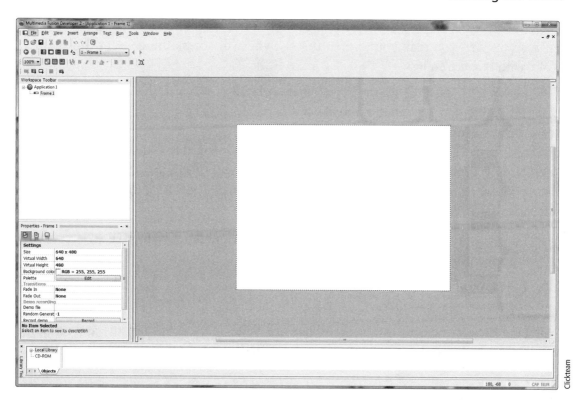

Figure 3.4
A blank frame of a new application.

Now that we have our blank frame that will contain our whole game, we need to drop the objects that we need onto the frame. We need the following objects:

- **Counter:** This will be used to display the current topic number.
- **String:** This will be used to display the topic text.
- **Buttons:** Three buttons will be used as the link to other pages. When the player presses the button, it will automatically display that page's information.
- **Text Adventure Pages:** The Text Adventure Pages object is used for any game you create that is using the choose-your-own-path genre.

We will now drop these objects onto the blank frame and create them in a particular size and position on-screen.

Placing of Objects

In this section of the book, you will learn how to place objects within the game world. Some objects, such as text or images, will be displayed when you run your game, while other objects are used to store results or data and will not appear directly on-screen when you play your game. Instead you will access the content they contain from within your code.

The white area within a frame is called the playfield. This is the area of the screen that the player can see when running the final game. The gray area is an off-screen area; objects can move in and out of this area. We will be placing objects both in the playfield and outside of it. We will place a Data object outside of the playfield, because any objects that will not be seen when the game is playing can still get in your way when you are working on your game graphics, so it's best to keep off to one side any items that do not display content.

1. To place an object in MMF2, you can either double left-click on an area in the Frame editor or use the Text menu and select Insert | New Object.

2. When you have used either of these methods, a Create New Object dialog box appears (see Figure 3.5).

3. Double left-click on the Text Adventure Pages object. All objects are in alphabetical order, but if you have trouble seeing the whole name of the object, you

Figure 3.5
The Create New Object dialog box.

Figure 3.6
The objects displayed as a list.

can change to text view by selecting the List option on the right-hand side of the dialog box (which you can see in Figure 3.6).

4. Once you have double-clicked on an object, the dialog box will disappear, and you will be left with a crosshair cursor. Left-click anywhere in the Frame editor to place the object.

In the instance of the Text Adventure Pages object, it will place a small graphic icon on the frame. The object is used to store information about the adventure game. We don't need to place this object on the playfield as it's not a graphic object, and all data that it contains will be loaded directly into other objects. In this instance, we are going to place the object in a particular location off the playfield.

Note

The Text Adventure Pages object keeps track of the number of links in each topic. It can also do other things, such as look after the topic text. But for this example, we will only be using a few of its features.

You can move any object on the frame by single left-clicking on it and then holding down the left mouse button as you drag the object across the frame. Release the left mouse button to drop the object where you have stopped on the frame.

Another way of moving an object is to access the object's properties, change its Position properties, and type in an exact position. If you want to move an object on the frame, use the X-axis to move it left to right and use the Y-axis to move it top to bottom.

When you created this new application, MMF2 automatically created a frame of 640×480, or 640 pixels wide by 480 pixels high. This is the area of the white playfield. If you want to place an object anywhere else on the frame in the gray area, you have to use a negative number. So to move it on the X-axis to the left of the white area, you would use −Value.

Let's do this now: place and move the Pages object.

1. Single left-click on the Text Adventure Pages object. You will know when you have correctly selected an object because a number will appear on the top left-hand corner of the object, and a set of properties will appear in the Properties window on the left-hand side of the application window. You can see this object's Properties window in Figure 3.7.

Figure 3.7
The object's Properties window.

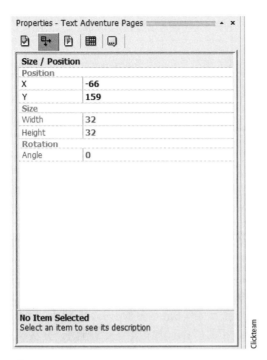

Figure 3.8
Example of the Position properties of an object.

2. There are a number of icons on the Properties window; these allow access to various tabs of information. The second tab, the Size/Position tab, contains all information regarding the object's position on-screen as well as its size. You can see this in Figure 3.8 (your current values may be different depending on where you placed the object).

3. You will see in the X and Y position areas two values. To change the object's position on-screen, type in the value −55 for the X position and **10** for the Y position. This will place the object to the top left of the playfield.

Now we need to add a counter. The count will be used to display the current topic number on-screen as a visual cue, but also it will be used in the code to keep track of the exact topic the player is currently viewing. This is the first example of an object that is visible data.

4. Double-click on the playfield and then select the Counter object from the Create New Objects list. Double-click on the counter or click on OK to return to the frame and then click anywhere on the screen to place the counter.

First let's place the counter in the correct area on the screen.

5. Click on the counter to reveal its properties.

6. As you previously accessed another object's Size/Position tab, it will be automatically selected for the counter (if not, click on it). Type in **307** for the X position and **34** for the Y position. This will place it approximately on the top middle of the playfield.

By default the counter is set to 0, which would be fine if our adventure game started from topic 0, but we've decided to start it from topic 1. So we need to change the value of the counter to begin at 1. We could do this via code, but you can also set the starting values/properties of objects via the Properties window.

7. Ensure that the counter is selected to reveal its properties sheet, and then click on the Settings tab; this is a small icon that looks like a piece of paper with a tick in it. You will now see an entry for an initial value. This will currently be set to 0, so change this to **1**. The minimum value defines what the lowest number of the counter can go to. As we will never go below 1, we should set this to **1**. You will see the changes in Figure 3.9.

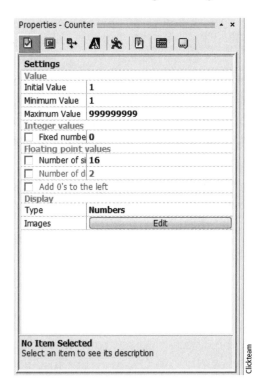

Figure 3.9
The properties of the counter.

Note

If you suddenly find that a counter isn't going above or below a particular value and your code looks correct, always look at the object properties to ensure you didn't set up a particular limit.

We now need to add the String object. This will be used to store a set of text paragraphs which will contain all of the topic text of our game.

8. Double-click on the playfield. When the Create New Object dialog box appears, select the String object by double-clicking on the object and then clicking anywhere on the playfield to place it.

You will now see the String object with the default word of Text currently displayed. We will change this Text object to contain all of our text for our topics. We will do that shortly, but for now let's just change its position and size, because in this case, as we need to display paragraphs of text, the object needs to be made larger to be able to display it.

9. Ensure that the String object is selected, and then click on the Size/Position tab in the Properties window. Change the position of X to **26** and the Y to **70**.

10. Now change the Size properties to **585** and **257**. You can see these completed settings in Figure 3.10.

Finally we need to add three buttons; these three buttons will be used to allow the player to move to a different topic. If you were reading an adventure book, these would be the jump to links that you find at the bottom of each topic. The great thing about using a button is that it can contain text, so we can place our jump to link text in them, and also they are quite easy to program for.

We are only going to have three buttons within our adventure game, but not all buttons will be shown at one time. It's quite common in adventure books to have any range of options from a single jump to topic, to three or four options per topic. These types of books do not normally have more than three or four options, just because the book would be very difficult to write with too many story branches.

So now let's add three buttons. We will add the first button and then show you a way of creating additional ones without needing to go into the Create New Object dialog box.

11. Double-click on a blank area on the playfield, and then double-click on the Button object. Place it anywhere on the playfield.

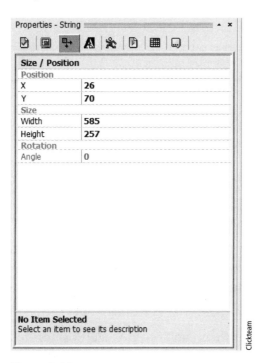

Figure 3.10
The updated properties of the String object.

Now that the object is on-screen, we need to move its position and resize it.

12. Click on the newly placed Button object to access its properties, ensure that the Size/Position tab is selected, and then put in **23** for the X position and **329** for the Y position.

13. We need to add **590** to the Width, and the Height will be the same, at **32**.

Your properties should be set as shown in Figure 3.11, and Figure 3.12 shows the end result as it would look on the frame.

We now have a button, but we need another two to complete our three buttons on-screen. We can do this manually by inserting them onto the playfield using the Create New Object dialog box, or we can use the Copy/Clone options.

The Copy and Clone options are two separate options. The first (Copy) creates an exact copy of an object, and any changes to any copies of that object will change all other copied objects. So if you create a button and then copy five more but change the size in the first, the other five will also change their size.

Copy is great to use when you have objects that look the same and will act the same. But the Copy method is not helpful if you want to change an object's particular

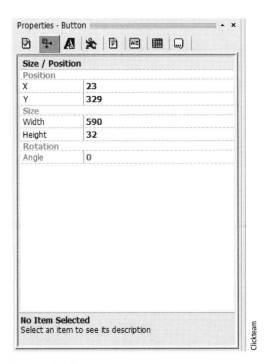

Figure 3.11
The updated properties of the Button object.

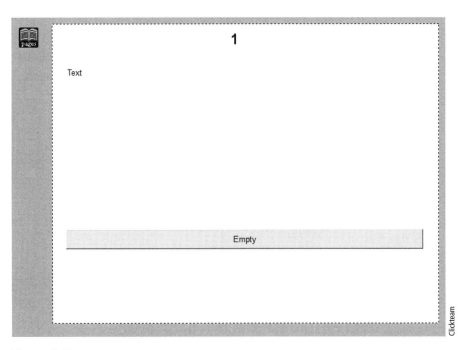

Figure 3.12
The current set-up of the frame.

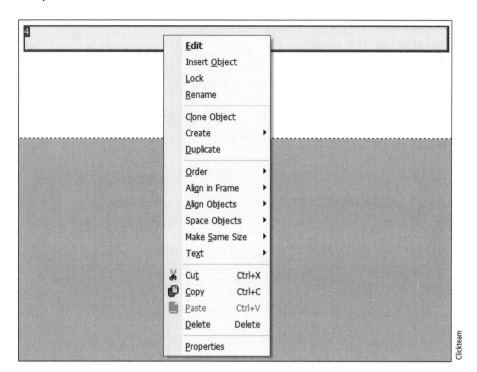

Figure 3.13
The pop-up menu when you right-click on an object.

values, such as its size. Though you can create events that affect only a particular object, it is better to use the Clone method if you want to interact with a particular object.

The Clone object will take all the current properties of an object and allow you to change the object when required without affecting any other objects.

In this following example, we need two further buttons, and we will use the Clone method to create them.

1. Select the Button object that you have placed on the frame.

2. Right-click on the object to bring up a pop-up box (see Figure 3.13).

3. Now select Clone Object. This will bring up a dialog box, which asks you how many times you wish to create this object, if you want to create rows or columns, and if you want any spaces between them. In this example, we want to create two additional buttons below the first, so we want to create rows. (Columns are used when creating additional objects to the right of the original object.) So change the Rows value to **3**, keeping all other values the same, as shown in Figure 3.14.

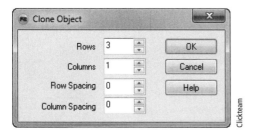

Figure 3.14
The Clone Object dialog box.

We have now added all objects we need for this example on-screen, but we still need to add our topic text to the String object.

We will now go through the process of adding some text to show you how the String object works.

1. Single-click on the String object to bring up its properties.

2. Click on the Settings tab. Here you will see some text that says Paragraph 1 and next to it in bold the word **Text**. This is the actual text that is displayed on the frame.

As we are going to start numbering our topics from 1, this helps a lot as we can match that up with a particular paragraph number.

3. Delete the word **Text** in Paragraph 1 and replace it with the following text:

The noise of the engines was terrifying, but this is what you had been trained for over the last two years. Over the comm's you can just about hear someone shouting, "3 ... 2 ... 1 ... lift off, we have a lift off!"

This is it, the moment everyone had been waiting for, you were finally off to the moon. The first manned mission since the end of the Apollo missions in the 1970s.

Your first stop on the way to the moon is the ESS (Earth Space Station) to pick up your cargo, some food, and a set of building materials to create the first moon base. Once your equipment has been packed, you will then spend two days traveling to the moon, before landing on the moon and setting up AlphaBeta Base.

The properties will now show part of the text you have typed in (see Figure 3.15), and the text will automatically populate the String object on the frame (Figure 3.16).

We are now ready to run the game to see what happens.

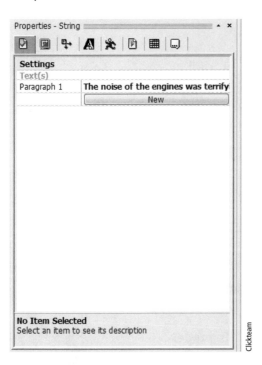

Figure 3.15
The text typed into Paragraph 1.

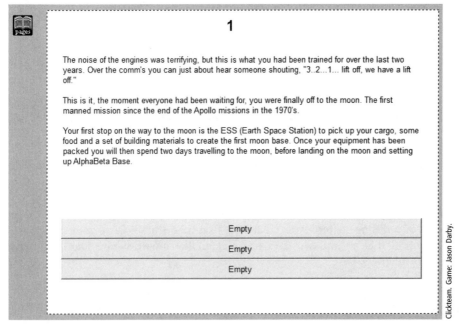

Figure 3.16
The current setup of the frame with the new text added.

Note

We are adding text to a string as a quick way of getting a game up and running, but for longer games, this process would be quite laborious and probably not the best way to handle the data. We will be looking at using other methods of storing and loading data in Chapter 5.

Note

We will go into more detail about this and the other objects in Chapter 4. This chapter will give you a better idea of all the special objects that we have created specifically to help you make your own adventure games.

Running Your Game

The great thing about MMF2 is that unlike traditional programming languages, where you might type in some code and make a typing mistake, which then prevents the game from running, MMF2 will always run the game. It may exhibit incorrect behavior if you have programmed it incorrectly, but you will visually see what the problem is in many cases.

We can run this game anytime we like. At the moment, all we have done is place the objects on-screen and in a few cases, such as the String and Counter objects, we have configured their properties. This means when we run the game, all we will see are the objects that have been configured and placed on the frame, with any default settings.

In Figure 3.17 you can see the three options to run the game. These are:

- **Run Project:** If you have created multiple applications within a project, you can run them all using this option. We will not be using this option in the book.

- **Run Application:** The current opened application will be run from the first frame. Your game can contain many frames, but in the *Moon Traveller* example, we have a single-framed game.

- **Run Game:** Run the game from the currently selected frame. In *Moon Traveller* we only have a single frame, and so the game will always run the first frame. In games that have many frames, you may not want to run through the whole program to get to a particular frame.

Figure 3.17
The Run options.

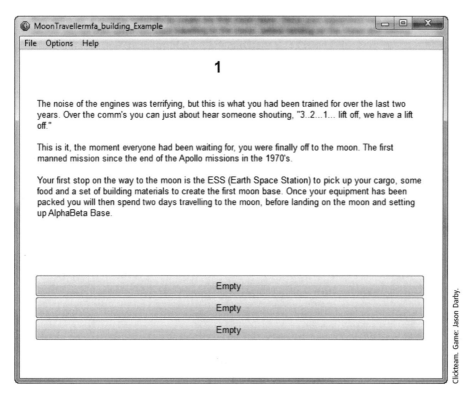

Figure 3.18
The *Moon Traveller* game running.

Run the game by clicking on the Run Application button. You will see the application appear (see Figure 3.18). We can change how this application looks by removing and adding various options. But for now, you can click on any of the buttons, although nothing will happen.

Once you are ready, you can click on the red x in the top right-hand corner of the application window to close it, or use the text menu bar and select File | Quit.

Note

The Run Game option is extremely helpful to test a frame and save you time. If you had a game that was 500 frames (screens) and you wanted to test a particular frame in the middle, it would probably take you a long time to get to it if you were running from the very beginning. Unfortunately any global values, such as score or lives, will not be carried through to this frame as it only uses the data that's available on that particular frame.

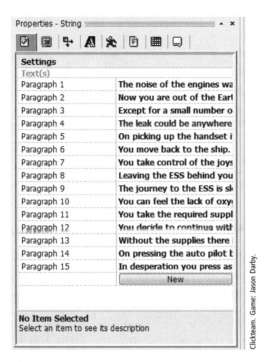

Figure 3.19
All topics added to the String object.

Adding All the Topic Text

To get all of topic text data into the game, you will need to add the other topics into the String object. To make this process easier, you can download a completed example from www.castlesoftware.co.uk in the books section (look for the Adventure Game book link and follow the instructions from there).

The file name of the file with the text already added is called: MoonTraveller_TextAdded.mfa. This will be contained in the Chapter 3 folder.

Once you have added all of the topic text, you will see that you have 15 pieces of text in the String object (see Figure 3.19).

Creating the Code

Now that we have all our objects in place and we have set up any specific object properties, we are ready to begin coding our game.

Before we do, let's look at a rundown on how the game code is going to work:

- On loading the game, it will display Topic 1 and will display any options available in the buttons at the bottom of the screen.

- If any of the three options are not available, only the number of options available will be shown.

- When the player has clicked on a button, the topic number, topic text, and topic link text will all be changed to reflect this new topic.

There are a couple of things that we can think about logically that we need to do to get our game working, and this will be reflected in our coding:

- **Initialization:** We need to set up the data for our game, which primarily involves setting up the number of links for each topic. We will then use these to check how many buttons we need to display. We also need to ensure that the topic link text is set up for each link.

- **Button Clicked:** When the player clicks on a button, we need to update the relevant topic number. This is so the game can keep track of where the player is moving to, and we can use this information to update any other data. This will then automatically enable a group of events that will handle the data update (button updates).

- **Button Updates:** When the player has clicked on a button (button clicked) and it has updated the topic number, we will then reset the number of topic buttons to show the topic text and the text for the topic links. Once this has been done, we will then disable this group of code.

You can see a simple flow of the game code in Figure 3.20. The game uses fewer than 17 lines of code to work, demonstrating that it takes very few lines of code to get something up and running. We can easily reduce that code by better managing the data that goes into our game by using editors and loading in data, but we will be looking at that later on in the book (Chapter 10).

We are now ready to start work on the code for our game, so ensure that you can currently see the frame of the game, and then click on the Event Editor button (see Figure 3.21). You can also use the quick keys of CTRL+E.

You will now be in the Event editor, with a single event line that has the text **New condition** within it. We are now ready to begin our programming.

Creating Comments

The first line in the Event editor will be a comment. Comments are great for reminding you what a particular event does in your game. This is really important as you begin to build up your game and the number of events begins to rise or if you decide to leave a game and come back to it at a later stage. A comment is a small description of what the event or group of events does.

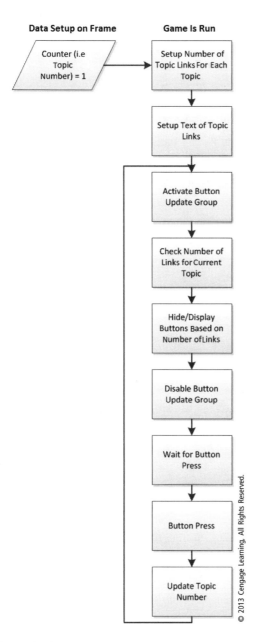

Figure 3.20
The game code flow for *Moon Traveller.*

Figure 3.21
The Event Editor button.

To create a comment:

1. Right-click on the number 1 in the Event editor. This will bring up a pop-up box, as shown in Figure 3.22

2. Select Insert | A comment.

3. The Edit Text dialog box now appears. This is where you type in the comment that you want to display. You have a number of text options, including changing the color and size as well as background color. Type in the text **Start of Program**, as shown in Figure 3.23, and then press OK to save this to the Event editor. You will now see the text in the Event editor, as shown in Figure 3.24.

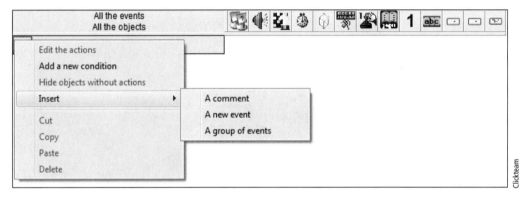

Figure 3.22
The pop-up box after right-clicking an event number.

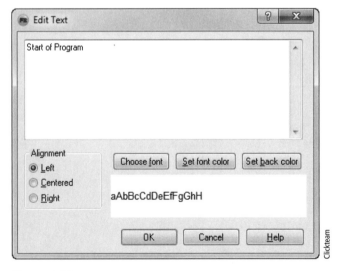

Figure 3.23
The Edit Text box.

Figure 3.24
The comment added to the Event editor.

Congratulations! You have added your first comment. We will be adding a few more for the rest of this game.

Game Initialization

Initialization is the process of setting up a game's data and values before it is run. We did a little bit of this in the object properties—for example, setting the value of a counter to 1. The counter will automatically have this value as the game is run. We need to do a little bit more initialization as the game starts, and we can do this using the Event editor.

We can create an event that will run as soon as the game is started but then will not run again. This condition is called Start of Frame.

1. Click on the New condition text and a New Condition dialog box will appear (see Figure 3.25).

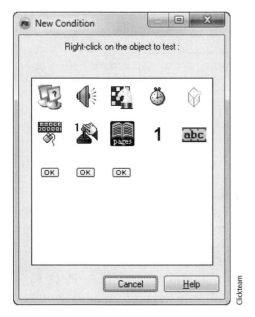

Figure 3.25
The New Condition dialog box.

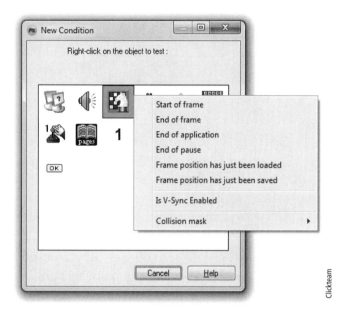

Figure 3.26
The pop-up menu for right-clicking the Storyboard Controls item.

The middle object in the first row is the Storyboard Controls (the chess board with the knight). This handles things such as moving between frames and between the start and end of a frame. Each frame has its own set of events, and so because we had Frame 1 selected and then went into the Event editor, any events we create here are for this frame only.

2. Right-click on the Storyboard Controls icon, and a pop-up menu will appear (see Figure 3.26).

3. Select Start of Frame.

This will now place the Start of Frame condition in event number 2 (see Figure 3.27), and we have our first event. This means any actions we now create to the right of this event will be run only when the game is first run.

The first actions that we need to create are for the link numbers for each topic. These are stored in the Text Adventure Pages object. So, for example, the first link for topic 1 is 2, because we have only one link (which is some additional text), while topic 2 has three links (of 10, 4, and 15).

1. Move your cursor to the right of the Start of Frame condition until you are directly under the Text Adventure Pages object. Right-click on the empty box below it to reveal a pop-up menu. Select Set Topic Links.

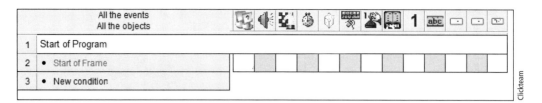

Figure 3.27
The first condition in an event line.

2. An Expression editor dialog box will appear. This will ask you which topic number you are looking at (see Figure 3.28). In this case, we want to look at topic 1, so type in the number **1** and then click on the OK button.

3. You will then be asked what topics link from this topic and also to separate multiple topics with a comma. As we only require one link from topic 1, which is topic 2, type in the number **2** between the quote marks and click on OK.

You have now added your first action, which is displayed as a tick in the action box. If you hover your mouse cursor over the box, it will show you the contents of the action (see Figure 3.29).

Now you need to add all the other links for the other topics (see Figure 3.30). Enter them using the same process as you did when you added the first; you right-click on the action box with the tick on and then select the Set Topic Links.

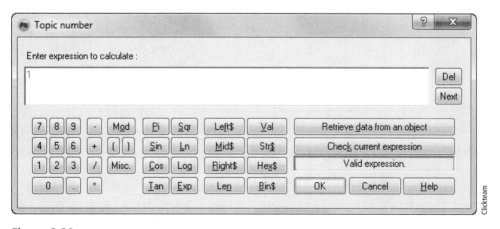

Figure 3.28
The Expression Editor asking for a topic number.

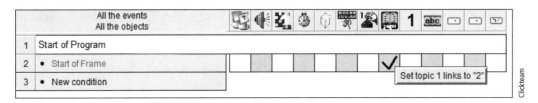

Figure 3.29
The actions in the action box for the Text Adventure Pages object.

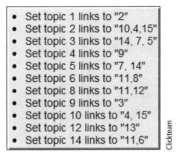

Figure 3.30
All of the topic links for *Moon Traveller*.

Note

You may notice that numbers 7, 11, 13, and 15 do not exist in the list shown in Figure 3.30. This list contains only the topic links that are available in each topic. The other four topic numbers are all game endings and so do not contain any further links to other topics.

Now that we have set up all the topic links, we need to also set up all of the topic link text. This is the text that will be displayed for any links—for example, "If you eat an apple go to 7." These bits of text will be placed in buttons when the player goes to the correct topic. But first we need to set them up. We could have placed the following actions in the same box as the first one, but as there are quite a few, sometimes it's preferable to break it up a bit to make it more readable. So in this example, we will create a new event, which will contain the set-up information.

First we will add a comment called "Data Set-up":

1. Right-click on the event number 3 and select Insert | A comment.

2. In the Edit Text dialog box, type **Data Set-up** and then click on OK.
   Now that we have a comment to describe what this event will do, we need to add a new event. We will use a timer-based event to create the trigger for adding this new data.

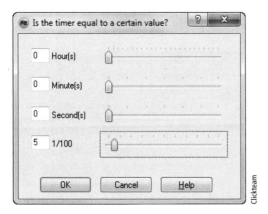

Figure 3.31
The timer setup dialog box.

3. Click on the New Condition text in event line 4.

4. Find the timer object which looks like a stop watch, then right-click on it.

5. From the pop-up box, select Is the Timer Equal to a Certain Value?

6. A timer box will appear. Set up the seconds to equal **0** and the hundredths of seconds to equal **5** (see Figure 3.31). Then click on OK.

   This now creates an event that will run very quickly after the frame has started. We now need to add all of the actions for this event, which will be to set up all of the link text. We will go through the process of adding the first, and you will need to add the rest. This will store the data in the Text Adventure Pages object so that when the game is running, you can call on that data when you require it.

   So now let's add a text link.

7. Move across from the Timer equals 00-05 line until you are directly under the Text Adventure Pages object. Right-click on the empty action box and select Set Topic Links Text. The Expression Evaluator appears, asking for the topic number. We want to add a link for the first topic, so type in the number **1** and click on OK.

8. It will now ask for the Index of Nth Link. This is the number of the link we are setting. Because there is only one link, this will be the first link. Leave this value at 0 and click on OK.

9. It will now ask for the Text associated with this link. Type in **Now turn to 2** and then click on OK. You will now be back at the Event editor. You can see the action you have added in Figure 3.32.

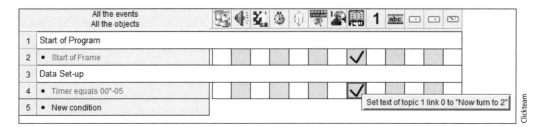

Figure 3.32
The action for adding text to a link.

Before we go any further, let's explain exactly what we had to do there and why we used 0 rather than 1 for the link number.

In our choose-your-own-path games, you can have a maximum of three links; this will be represented by three buttons. If there are no buttons (no links), then the game has finished either because you won or because you lost. If you haven't won or lost, then there will be at least one link (button) up to a maximum of three.

We were asked to enter a number and in the dialog box it stated that the number started from 0. In programming, many numbering systems can start from either 0 or 1. It is common in many programming languages to use the 0 base numbering systems, where it begins counting from 0. So when we are talking about the text for our first button, it will actually be using the contents from link 0, while button 2 will be using the text from the contents of link 1.

In some cases in MMF2, the numbering system can start from 1, or you can specify which starting number you prefer. For example, you can set it to be 1 or 0 when using the Arrays object.

Base numbering systems can be slightly confusing but hopefully will become clearer when you start to use them more.

You now need to add all of the other links in the same method. The data for these links can be found in Figure 3.33.

Button Update Group

Now that we have our data in place, we can set up a group to hold the main parts of the code, which will update various text/buttons data. Using groups is a brilliant way of ensuring your code isn't run incorrectly at the wrong time. The reason for this is that you can disable them until they are ready to be used.

MMF2 reads the conditions from top to bottom very quickly. If it finds them to be true, it will run the relevant actions before moving on to the next event. Sometimes

- Set text of topic 1 link 0 to "Now turn to 2."
- Set text of topic 2 link 0 to "You decide to pull your visor down, turn to 10"
- Set text of topic 2 link 1 to "You try to locate where the leak is coming from, turn to 4."
- Set text of topic 2 link 2 to "If you decide to press as many dials as you can in the hope it will fix the problem, turn to 15."
- Set text of topic 3 link 0 to "Do you press the auto pilot button, if so turn to 14."
- Set text of topic 3 link 1 to "Do you decide to dock the ship manually, if so go to 7."
- Set text of topic 3 link 2 to "You decide to pick up the radio handset and talk into it, go to 5."
- Set text of topic 4 link 0 to "You can now carry on with your mission. Go to 9."
- Set text of topic 5 link 0 to "Do you decide to dock the ship manually, if so go to 7."
- Set text of topic 5 link 1 to "Do you press the auto pilot button, if so turn to 14."
- Set text of topic 6 link 0 to "You decide to go back and take the supplies, go to 11."
- Set text of topic 6 link 1 to "You decide to leave for the moon, go to 8."
- Set text of topic 8 link 0 to "You go back for the supplies, go to 11."
- Set text of topic 8 link 1 to "You carry on your journey. Go to 12."
- Set text of topic 9 link 0 to "You sit patiently, go to 3."
- Set text of topic 10 link 0 to "You open a liquid food container, turn to 4."
- Set text of topic 10 link 1 to "If you decide to press as many dials as you can in the hope it will fix the problem, turn to 15."
- Set text of topic 12 link 0 to "Now turn to 13"
- Set text of topic 14 link 0 to "You take the supplies, turn to 11."
- Set text of topic 14 link 1 to "You decide that Ryan is particularly rude and go back to the ship, go to 6."

Figure 3.33
The Text Links content.

you will need to restrict conditions to prevent them from being run at the wrong time. Groups are also very good for tidying up your code, and they can be left in an enabled state, meaning they will still be run if the conditions are correct.

First we will create a comment to show what this group is about:

1. Right-click on the event number 5, and select Insert | A comment.

2. In the Edit text box, type **Button Update Group** and click on OK.

Now that we have added the comment, we need to add the group.

3. Right-click on the number 6, and select Insert | A group of events.

4. The Group Events dialog box will appear. Type in the title of the group to be **Button Update**. (You do not need to password protect it.) Ensure that Active When Frame Starts is unchecked, because we want to control when this group is enabled and the code is run. If the Group Events dialog box looks like that shown in Figure 3.34, click on the OK button.

You now have created a group in the Event editor. Notice that it is currently grayed out. This means that it is currently disabled. You may also notice that there is an indented New Condition line directly under the Button Update group. This is for any events that will be run when this group is enabled.

We now need to create our events for the Button Update group. These events will check the current topic number, which is stored in the counter, and then display up to three buttons, depending on how many topic links are available from this topic.

Figure 3.34
The Group Events dialog box.

Our first event in the Button Update group will check the number of links within the specified topic (which is stored in the counter) and if it equals 0 (no links), we will then hide all of the buttons. Zero links will mean the end of the game through bad luck or through winning. To do this we need to compare two values: the number of links within a topic, and the number we want to check, which in this case is 0.

1. Click on the New Condition text within the Button Update group. When the New Condition dialog box appears, right-click on the Special group (this, the first icon in the list, looks like two computers). Select Compare Two General Values.

2. You will now see the Expression Evaluator with two values being compared (see Figure 3.35). Both values are currently zero, and we have an operator (in the middle), which is set to Equal.

Every object can store data/information which can be retrieved and then compared against another value, such as a number or string. This is extremely useful and will be something that you will use a lot when making your own games in MMF2. In the first part of our code, we stored both the number of links and the topic link text in the Text Adventure Pages object, which can be retrieved.

3. Highlight the 0 in the first box.

4. Now click on Retrieve Data from an Object. A list of objects will appear. We need data from the Text Adventure Pages object, so right-click on the object to receive the pop-up box. From the pop-up, select Get the Number of Links in This Topic.

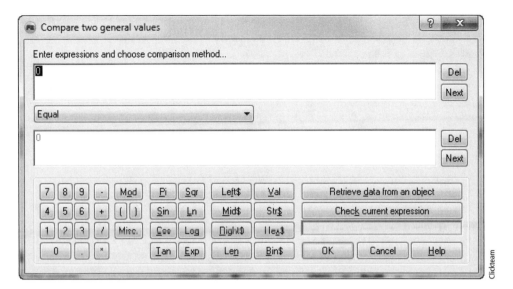

Figure 3.35
The Expression Evaluator—comparing two values.

5. The Expression Evaluator will now have a line of text in there. You will see the text >Topic< is highlighted (see Figure 3.36). This means that it needs to be replaced with the topic number.

We are using the Counter object to store which topic we are currently on. So every time you change to a different topic, update the counter to show the correct topic

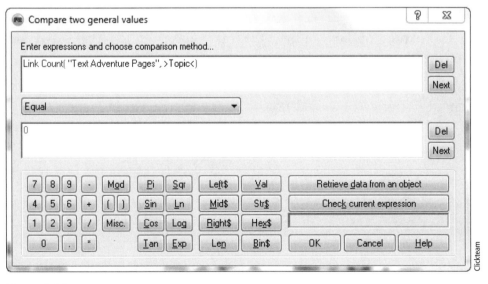

Figure 3.36
The Expression Evaluator—getting data from the Text Adventure Pages object.

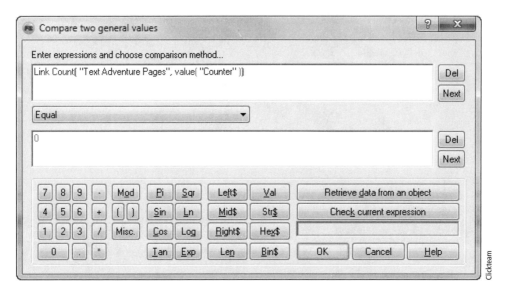

Figure 3.37
Finding the number of links in the Text Adventure Pages object of the current topic.

number. You can pull the current value from the counter and use it here to find the current line count of that topic.

6. With >Topic< currently highlighted, again click on Retrieve data from an object.

7. Right-click on the Counter object and select Current Value. You will now see the text updated in the Expression Evaluator (see Figure 3.37).

So now in the first expression box we have the link count from the Text Adventure Pages object for the current topic (stored in the counter).

8. As we want to compare when this equals 0, we can leave the second value as 0, so click on OK. Your event should now look like that shown in Figure 3.38.

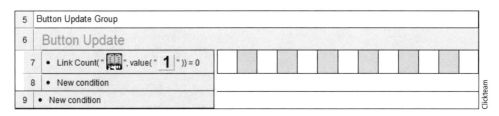

Figure 3.38
Finding the Link Count event in the Button Update group.

We now need to create a further three events with very similar information in them. The only thing that will be different is the second number that is being compared. We will want to check if there is a 1, 2, or 3 link available in each topic.

We could go through the same process again and manually create each event. But MMF2 is a drag-and-drop tool, so you can drag events, conditions, and actions to other lines.

9. Single click on the condition just created in event line 7, and while holding the left mouse button down, drag the condition to the line called new condition. Then release the left mouse button to drop it into place.

10. Do this process again from line 8 to 9 and then from 9 to 10. You should now have four events with the Link Count condition in them. But they all contain the value 0, so if you double left-click on the condition in event line 8, it will open up the Expression Evaluator for that condition.

11. Move down to the second box, where it currently says 0, and change it to **1**, and then click on the OK button to save the change.

12. Change the third event (line 9) in the same method and enter the number **2**.

13. Change the fourth event (line 10) and put in the second value as **3**.

Your Button Update events should now look like Figure 3.39. So each of these will be true only when the number of links in the current topic equals 0, 1, 2, or 3. For the actions, we need to hide/unhide the buttons when the correct number of topic links is selected.

So, for example, when the number of links is set to 0, which means there are no text jumps, we will hide all the buttons, while if the value equals 3, we will show all buttons.

Now we need to add actions for the first event in the group (event line 7) for each of the buttons. We added the buttons in order, and so they have been aptly named

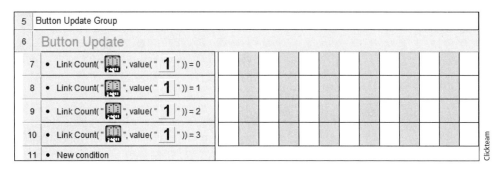

Figure 3.39
The four Link Count events.

button, button 2, button 3. In cases where you are adding many different objects of the same type, it is a good idea to rename the object so that when you are adding actions to it in the Event editor, you do not accidentally add it to the wrong item.

So let's make all the buttons invisible when there are no links.

14. Move across from event line 7 until you are in the Button action box. Right-click and select Visibility | Make Object Invisible.

15. Now do the same for button 2 and button 3 (remember you can also drag and drop actions for the same object type if you want).

You will now have set the visibility of the three buttons to be invisible when there are no links. We need to do a similar process for event line 8, but this time we need to have button visible and button 2 and 3 invisible (we are only displaying a single button because we only have a single link).

16. Move across from event line 8 until you are in the Button action box. Right-click and select Visibility | Make Object Reappear.

17. On the same event line, make button 2 and button 3 invisible by selecting Visibility | Make Object Invisible.

For event line 9, we are checking that two links exist, so we need to have the first two buttons visible and the last button invisible.

18. Move across from event line 9 until you are in the Button action box. Right-click and select Visibility | Make Object Reappear. Do the same for button 2.

19. On the same event line, make button 3 invisible by selecting Visibility | Make Object Invisible.

Finally, for event line 10 we need to make all buttons visible.

20. Move across from event line 10 until you are in the Button action box. Right-click and select Visibility | Make Object Reappear. Do the same for buttons 2 and 3.

Now that we have hidden or made visible the three topic buttons, we now need to update the buttons to display the correct topic link text.

1. Event line 7 will not require any further actions.

2. For event line 8, we will have a single button being displayed, so we need to add an action under the first button to load in the topic link text.

3. Move across from event line 8 until you are directly under the Button object.

4. Right-click on the action box and select Change text. When the Expression Evaluator appears, we will need to retrieve the link text.

5. Click on the Retrieve data from an object button.

6. Right-click on the Pages object in the New Expression dialog box and choose Get text of Nth link. You will now have some text in the Expression Evaluator, and it will be asking for a Topic and an Index.

7. For the topic we need to retrieve the current topic number from the counter, so ensure that the >Topic< text is highlighted and click on Retrieve data from an object.

8. From the New expression dialog box, right-click on the Counter object and choose Current value.

9. You will now be back at the expression and need to select >Index< and replace it with the value of 0. Remember that the Index for the Pages object uses a 0 based index.

10. Click on the OK button to save this information to the Event editor.

As the first Button object will need to display the link text when there are 1, 2, or 3 buttons being displayed, you will need to add this action to event lines 9 and 10, under the Button object. Rather than adding this individually, you could drag and drop this (and its Make Object Reappear actions) to the action boxes.

Now that you have added that action, you will need to do the same for event line 9 and 10 under button 2 for line 9 and button 2 and button 3 for line 10. You will need to also ensure that the Index in the Expression Evaluator will be "1" for the action in event line 9 and "2" for event line 10.

Finally, we need to disable this group once it has run through these options. The reason for this is that if we had this group enabled, one of these lines would be true every time MMF2 reads down the different events. This is not good for performance, as it will read all the events very quickly and will update the visibility of the buttons multiple times a second. We don't need to update it that often. Because we only want to make a change when the player has clicked on one of the buttons, we would then update once.

Even though the group is currently disabled, we will be enabling it later in the code and so need to make sure we switch it back off once it has activated one of these four events.

21. Click on the New Condition text in the Button Update group, on event line 11.

22. When the New Condition dialog box appears, right-click the Special object (the two monitors icon) and then select Always.

Figure 3.40
The Deactivate group dialog box.

The Always condition will always run every time MMF2 loops through all of the events. In this case we will be disabling the group, so it will not be run automatically. We will then enable the group later, allow the code within the group to be processed and then disable it before MMF2 can run the events again.

We now need to disable the Button Update group.

23. Move across from the Always event that you just created, until you are under the Special Conditions action group.

24. Right-click on this empty action group box and select Group of Events | Deactivate.

25. A Deactivate box will appear (see Figure 3.40). Because we only have one group, there is only one group available. Click on the OK button.

This code will now deactivate this group when it has been enabled and has gone through the four events.

Note

You can rename objects in the Frame editor by right-clicking on them and selecting Rename.

Note

You can find out the name of an object by hovering your mouse cursor over it in the Frame editor. A tooltip graphic will appear, showing you the object's name. This is also true in the Event editor. If you hover the mouse cursor over the icon, it will tell you the name.

Note

You can also rearrange the order of objects in the Event editor. Do this by dragging and dropping the objects where they belong across the top column. This is particularly helpful if you want to reorder them in proper sequence.

Button Clicked

The last events we need to create are the button presses. This is to check when the player presses any of the three (if visible) buttons to move to the next topic.

There are three events to check each individual button press, and then three actions for each event, first to update the topic number to the selected topic we jump to. We then need to update the String objects paragraph so it shows the current topic text, and finally we need to activate the Button Update group. This will ensure that the correct number of buttons of the next topic are displayed correctly.

First we will create a comment for our code:

1. Right-click on the last event line number, which should be event line 13, and then select Insert | A comment.

2. When the Edit Text box appears, type in the text **Button has been clicked** and click OK.

We will now add three conditions to check when the user has left-clicked on a button.

3. Click on the New Condition text on event line 14.

4. When the New Condition dialog box appears, find the button object (there will be three of them in the dialog box, but it's important to select the item called button), right-click on it and select Button Clicked.

You will now have an event that will be true when you click on the first button. You will notice that the condition has some red text; this means this is an immediate condition. An immediate condition means that this condition will only be tested when a particular event takes place. In the case of a button press, MMF2 will only test this event when the player presses a button. All conditions in black are constantly tested as they can be true at any time.

You will also notice that the button is in a small box. This box allows you to change the object that is being looked at. For example, if you want to change the exact object you want to test—say, for example, from Button to Button 2—you can only change this to an object of the same type. This is particularly helpful when copying events, as you will now find out as we create the two additional button clicked events.

5. Click on the condition text in event line 14, hold down the left mouse button and drag it on to the New Condition text on event line 15. This will create an additional event.

6. Drag and drop the button clicked condition from event line 15 on to line 16.

If you hover your mouse cursor over each button icon, you will notice that each one currently states it is called button. We need to change it so event line 15 is button 2 and event line 16 is button 3.

7. Double-click on the button icon in event line 15. This will bring up a dialog box displaying two buttons as shown in Figure 3.41. It is displaying two because one of the three buttons is currently selected and cannot be chosen.

8. If you hover your mouse over the first button in the dialog box, you will notice it is called button 2. Select this object and click on OK.

9. We now need to do the same process for the button in event line 16, so double click on the button icon, and when the dialog box appears, select the second button which should be button 3.

We now have all three of our conditions in place; we now need to create the actions.

Our first action will be to set the Counter object (which is used to display the topic text and the button links/button text) to the correct topic number that we have

Figure 3.41
A dialog box to select a different object.

decided to move to. So if we see three buttons, in the first it tells us to go to 7, second says 9 and third says 4, and we click on the second button, it should change the current topic number to 9. We can then use this number to set up the correct story text (String object) and set up all of the correct button jumps (link numbers) for topic 9.

So we need to place the topic number of the clicked button into the counter. If you recall we set up all of the links for each topic in the Start of Frame condition. By retrieving the link for the current topic, we can then move to that new topic and reset all of the screen data.

10. From event line 14 move across to the right until you are directly under the Counter object, right-click on the action box and select Set Counter.

11. The Set Counter dialog box appears. Click on the Retrieve data from object button, and the New expression dialog box then appears.

12. Select the Text Adventure Pages Object and choose Get Nth Link.

The Get Nth Link allows us to get the links in each topic for a particular numbered slot. For example, in topic 1 there is only one Link Number, and this is in slot 0, and the link number is 2. So when clicking on the first button from topic 1, you would be telling the game you want to move to topic 2.

Once you have selected Get Nth Link, it will fill out the Expression Evaluator with an expression as shown in Figure 3.42. It is now missing a topic number and an index.

13. Ensure that >Topic< is highlighted, and then click on Retrieve Data from an Object. Select the Counter object and then Current Value.

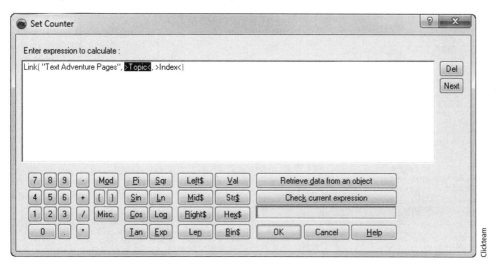

Figure 3.42
Expression Evaluator for setting the counter to the link of the current topic.

Now that we have the current topic number, we need to specify the current slot for the link. Because this is the first button, we need to specify the value to be 0 (as this is the first slot in the links, and if you remember, it uses a 0 based index).

14. Replace >Index< with the number 0.

What this has done is take the link number in a particular slot and then updated the current topic number in the counter. This means that the code that we placed in Button Update, when run, will be able to check the number of links for this new topic number when it's been enabled.

Now that we have created that action to update the topic number, we need to display the correct text in the String object. The text will be the latest topic that the player has moved to. As we are using the String object, we just need to specify the paragraph of the text that we are currently on, which is the current topic number—which again is stored in the counter.

15. From event line 14, move to the right until you are directly under the String object. Right-click the action box and select Set Paragraph. The Set Paragraph dialog box appears and displays a list of all of the content we added at the start of the program, as shown in Figure 3.43.

We could specify a particular text, but as we are changing this based on the current topic rather than forcing it to a particular item, we need to use a calculation.

16. Click on the Use a calculation button.

17. An Expression Evaluator dialog box will appear, as we need to get the current topic number. Click on Retrieve data from an object.

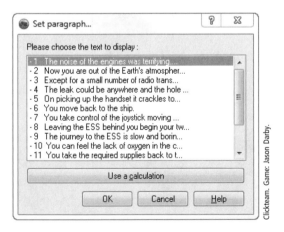

Figure 3.43
A list of paragraphs with data in.

18. Select the Counter object and select current value, then click on OK to close the dialog box.

It is important that we updated the Counter value to the link we were jumping to before setting the paragraph. Otherwise we would be showing incorrect data for the old link rather than the new one we were moving to.

Note

> The order of events and actions is very important to the correct running of your game. You should always consider what might happen if you put any of them in the wrong order. For example, it may prevent other code from running correctly or display incorrect information.

Now that we have updated the data, we have one action left to do, and this is to enable the Button Update group. This will find out the number of links in this new topic and display the correct number of buttons, as well as change the links within the buttons. As we have already created this code, all we need to do is enable the group. Remember it will be disabled again once it has read that code, and so will only be activated again on another button click.

1. On event line 14, move across until you are directly under the Special Conditions object. Then right-click and select Group of Events | Activate.

2. The Button Update group will already be selected, so click on OK.

If you run the game now, you will see that the topic starts at 1, but the buttons still have the word **Empty** in them. If you click on the top button, you will see the topic number change. The topic text and the buttons will also contain the correct link jump text.

This is because we have set up our program to react to a button press, but we have not set up any code to sort out the very first time the player plays the game. This is easily solved, as in event line 4 we use a timer to set the topic link text. We can also enable the Button Update group, as this event will only run once near to the start of the game running and will populate the buttons, disabling the Button Update group, which can then only be enabled by pressing a button.

3. Move to event line 4. Next move to the right until you are under the Special Conditions action box. Then right-click and select Group of Events | Activate.

4. The Button Update group will be selected, so click on OK.

If you run the game now, hopefully you should see the topic number of 1, some text, and only a single button, advising the player to go to 2 (see Figure 3.44). Play the game and enjoy your space adventure.

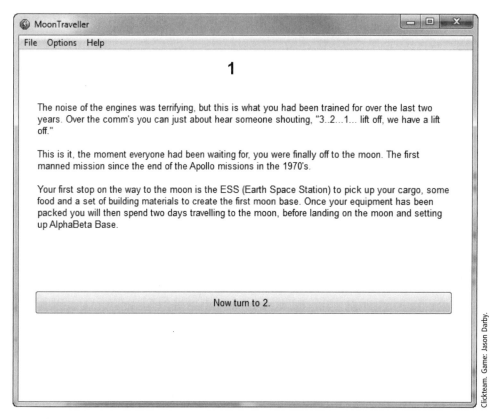

Figure 3.44
The first topic of the *Moon Traveller* game.

Congratulations! You have completed your first game with MMF2. If you have any problems with your game, you can compare it to the completed version, which you can download from www.castlesoftware.co.uk.

Download the content from the relevant book page, and within the folder called Chapter 3, you will find a completed version called MoonTraveller_Complete.mfa.

FURTHER FEATURES

If you enjoyed making this type of game and want to expand it further, here are some ideas that you can explore:

- **Background graphics and figures:** You could add graphics to your choose-your-own-path adventure story. Adding graphics would provide an extra level of detail and quality to the reader/player. This could be in the form of a background graphic, which is placed behind all other objects and covers most if not all of the game window. You could add small images to break up text or you could replace the Windows buttons with graphical elements to make it more interesting.

■ **Battle systems:** One aspect of the adventure books was battles with other people, trolls, giants, giant crabs, and so on. You will need to consider what types of battles are available: Will it be just sword play? Or will you have magic or laser guns? You will need to decide how battles will take place and whether you will have a health system. How will the player decide if he has made a hit or has been hit? Will there be potions to improve a player's stats or food to recover health? Most adventure books keep the number of items involved in a battle system quite simple, such as only a basic hit/miss system and two or three player stats, such as health, stamina, and luck.

■ **Sound:** Sound can add a lot to a game, and in a book-based computer adventure game, it could really add a level of atmosphere. For example, perhaps you explain in a chapter that the player reaches a door and opens it—wouldn't it be great to activate the sound of a door creaking as the player is shown this topic? Sound will help players visualize a game world better, particularly if that game world is only displayed in text.

Throughout the rest of this book, we will be exploring further some of these features in other types of adventure games.

CHAPTER SUMMARY

In this chapter, you learned about choose-your-own-adventure books and how to make one into a computer game. This has hopefully shown you the basics of creating your game's content and programming it in the Event editor. You have taken a big step on your journey to making adventure games, but if you are feeling a little lost, remember that you can go back and reread the instructions or look at the full code to see how everything works. Practice makes perfect, and hopefully as you try and add your own code, you will learn lots more about how MMF2 and adventure game creation works. In the next chapter, we will be taking a closer look at the objects that will help you make your adventure games.

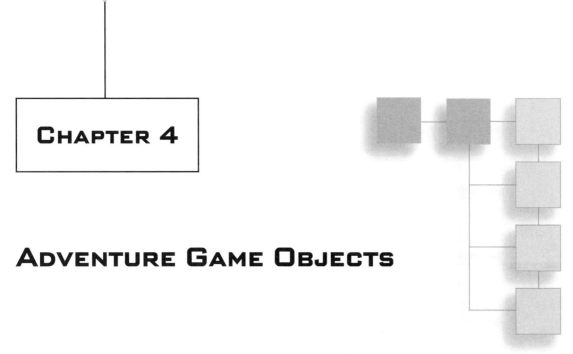

Chapter 4

Adventure Game Objects

We have created five new objects for MMF specifically for this book. These new objects allow you to concentrate on writing and creating your adventure games rather than worrying too much about how you are going to write the various adventure systems needed to run your game.

In this chapter, we will discuss the various options available in these objects, to give you a better idea of all the features available and how you might use them within your games.

Note

We won't be using all the features available in these objects for this book, so make sure you explore them fully to see if there is anything you can use in your own games.

You can see the graphic icons for the objects in MMF in Figure 4.1. These objects are as follows:

- **Text Adventure Map:** Can be used to create virtual maps of your game world. Useful for text/graphic adventures and could also be used for RPG and other story-based games.

- **Text Adventure Markup:** Is similar to the string object shown in Chapter 3 but works using markup text, much like Internet forums. It allows you to change the style of the text in your adventure game by providing wrappers to a piece of text.

- **Text Adventure Messages:** Allows you to display messages based on user input, such as, **You've eaten an apple** when you have typed in **Eat apple**.

Figure 4.1
The icons for the five Adventure Game objects.

- **Text Adventure Pages:** Allows you to create a storybook adventure game, as shown in Chapter 3.
- **Text Adventure Words:** Allows you to create words and common phrases in your adventure games.

Note

This chapter details specific information about the core Adventure Game objects written to go with this book. You can carry on to Chapter 5 without reading this section and use this chapter for reference when you want to find out what a particular menu item does, or you can read through it, get familiar with each object, and then carry on.

THE TEXT ADVENTURE MAP OBJECT

The Text Adventure Map object is the key system for mapping out your game world but also for applying logic to where the player can and cannot go within this world. The Text Adventure Map object also contains inventory and object-based management; for example, if you have a particular object in your inventory, you may be able to proceed past a magic door.

Note

The Text Adventure Map object is extremely useful and can be used to create maps for both text adventure games as well as grid-based role-playing games.

Properties

When the object is selected in the Frame editor, its properties will appear in the Properties window (see Figure 4.2).

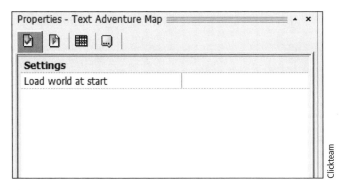

Figure 4.2
The Text Adventure Map properties.

■ **Load world at start:** You can specify a filename if you wish the application/game you are making to automatically load an adventure file. This allows you to be able to create an editor to quickly create your game data and then load it into the game.

Conditions

To access the conditions for the Adventure Game object, you will need to be in the Event editor. Click on the New Condition text, and the New Condition dialog box appears. Then right-click on the object to access its properties. You can see a list of conditions in Figure 4.3.

■ **Player travels to new location:** The player has moved to a location not previously visited.

■ **Can move in a certain direction?** What directions can a player move in? (For example, can the player move north?)

■ **Player previously visited this location:** Has the player already visited this map location?

■ **Player previously visited a particular location:** Has the player visited a particular location on the map (not necessarily the player's current position)? You could use this to trigger a particular event only if the player has been elsewhere. You may want to trigger different events if the player has been elsewhere.

■ **Object is in current location:** Is an object in the player's current location?

■ **Object is in a particular location:** Is an object in a particular location elsewhere? For example, is the golden key still in the northeast room of the castle? If so, the player cannot open the door in the current location.

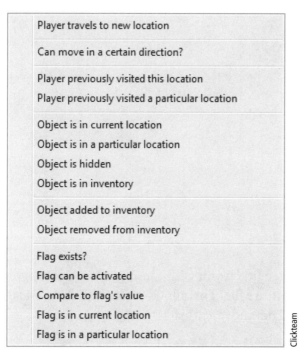

Figure 4.3
The top-level conditions for the Text Adventure Map object.

- **Object is hidden:** An object may not be automatically visible to the player. This condition will check if the object is currently hidden.

- **Object is in inventory:** Is an object currently within your inventory? This is useful if you wish to prevent certain situations from occurring unless the player has an item in inventory. You could also set up a situation where the player attempts to light a fire, has matches in his inventory, but doesn't say "Use matches." You could display a message to the player such as "Perhaps you have an item in your inventory that will help."

- **Object added to inventory:** Has the player just added an item to the inventory?

- **Object removed from inventory:** Has an object been removed from the inventory?

- **Flag exists?** Does a flag exist? A flag allows you to check the state of a particular event, such as light is on or off, door is locked or open, and so on.

- **Flag can be activated:** Can the specified flag be activated? It may already have been activated—for example, a switch.

- **Compare to flag's value:** Compare a flag's value; for example, is it 0 or 1?

- **Flag is in current location:** Is a particular flag in the player's current location?
- **Flag is in a particular location:** Is a flag in a specified location?

Expressions

Expressions are values that you can use in other objects. So if you were setting an object to the current position of the mouse cursor, you could use an expression to get its X and Y coordinates and place an object at that exact position. Expressions are extremely useful for doing calculations and comparisons.

You can see the top-level expressions available in the Text Adventure Map object in Figure 4.4.

Available in the menu selections are a number of options, which we will now look at in detail.

Maps

The Maps section allows you to do calculations and value checks on the maps you have created. You can see the available options in Figure 4.5.

Figure 4.4
The top-level expressions available in the Text Adventure Map object.

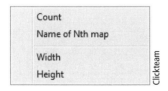

Figure 4.5
The options available in the Maps menu.

- **Count:** The number of maps currently being used. As you can create multiple maps, you may want to find out how many you are currently using.

- **Name of Nth map:** The name of a particular numbered map. Having the name of a particular map can be useful when you want to push the map name into another object.

- **Width:** The width of the map (X-axis, or left to right).

- **Height:** The height of the map (Y-axis, or top to bottom).

Map Tiles

The Map Tiles section allows you to check particular tiles within a map. You can see the available options in Figure 4.6.

- **Number of directions:** The value for the number of different directions available on a particular area on a particular map. So if you have a location that can move north, east, and west, it will return the value of 3.

- **Name of Nth direction:** The name of a particular direction.

- **Direction target map name:** The direction a tile can go.

- **Direction target X:** The direction of a particular X tile.

- **Direction target Y:** The direction of a particular Y tile.

- **Long description:** A long text description of the specified location.

- **Short description:** A short text description of the specified location.

- **Graphic filename:** The graphic associated with a particular map and tile. Before you can use this expression, you must already have set an appropriate graphic file to a particular map and tile.

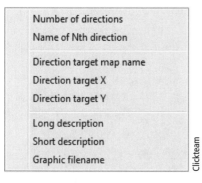

Figure 4.6
The options available in the Map Tiles menu.

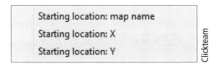

Figure 4.7
The options available in the World menu.

World

The World section contains information pertaining to a world. You can see the available options in Figure 4.7.

- **Starting location map name.** The map name where the player is starting from.

- **Starting location X:** The X grid location for the map's starting location.

- **Starting location Y:** The Y grid location for the map's starting location.

Current Location

The Current Location section returns data for the player's current location. You can see the available options in Figure 4.8.

- **Map name:** The name of the map at the player's current location. As a game can consist of many maps, you may want to retrieve the current map name.

- **X:** The current X location of the player.

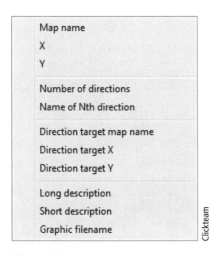

Figure 4.8
The options available in the Current Location menu.

- **Y:** The current Y location of the player.

- **Number of directions:** The current number of directions from the player's current location.

- **Name of Nth direction:** The name of a particular numbered direction from the player's current location.

- **Direction target map name:** The name of the map the player will be moving to from the current location.

- **Direction target X:** The X location of the target map. If the player is currently on one map and that location has a jump to another map, what is the X position on this new map that the current location is linked to?

- **Direction target Y:** The Y location of the target map. Returns the Y position of the connecting location on another map.

- **Long description:** Long description of current location.

- **Short description:** Short description of current location.

- **Graphic filename:** The graphic filename assigned to the current location.

Objects

The Objects section allows you to retrieve data from any objects you have created for your game. You can see the available options in Figure 4.9.

Figure 4.9
The options available in the Objects menu.

- **Number of objects:** The number of objects that have been created.
- **Name of Nth object:** The name of a particular object, specified using its slot number.
- **Map name:** The map name of a particular object.
- **X:** The X location of a particular object.
- **Y:** The Y location of a particular object.
- **Description:** The description of a particular object.
- **Weight:** The weight of a particular object.
- **Size:** The size of a particular object.
- **Cost:** How much a particular object costs.
- **Custom string:** A custom string for an object.
- **Custom value:** A custom value for an object.
- **Number of aliases:** The number of aliases a particular object has.
- **Nth alias:** The alias of an object using an index (number).

Inventory

The Inventory section allows you to get data for objects in your inventory (that you are currently carrying). You can see the available options in Figure 4.10.

- **Number of objects in inventory:** The number of objects currently stored in the inventory.
- **Name of Nth object in inventory:** The name of a particular inventory item, based on the given index name.

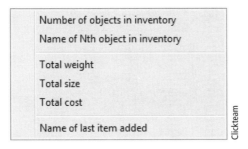

Figure 4.10
The options available in the Inventory menu.

- **Total weight:** The total weight of all the objects in the inventory.
- **Total size:** The total size of all the objects in the inventory.
- **Total cost:** The total cost of all the items in the inventory.
- **Name of last item added:** The name of the object that was last added to the inventory.

Flags

The Flags section deals with retrieving data from the flags and checking how they are set. You can see the available options in Figure 4.11.

- **Number of flag:** The number of flags available.
- **ID of Nth flag:** The ID name of a particular flag in a particular index position.
- **Number of names:** The number of names assigned to a particular flag ID.
- **Nth name:** The name of a flag assigned to a flag ID in a numbered slot. You can have multiple flags in a single ID name.
- **Map name:** The map name where a particular flag ID has been assigned.
- **X:** The X location of a particular flag ID.
- **Y:** The Y location of a particular flag ID.
- **Category:** The category a particular flag is assigned to.
- **Value:** The value of a particular flag ID.

Figure 4.11
The options available in the Flags menu.

Clickteam

Figure 4.12
The option available in the Count menu.

- **Activation policy:** The activation policy you have set for a particular flag, such as on/off, increment.
- **Activation policy limit:** The policy limit for a particular flag ID.

Count

The Count section allows you to count how many objects of a particular type have been added onto a frame. You can see the available option in Figure 4.12.

- **Number of objects:** The number of objects you have on the frame. This is a standard option in objects but is not relevant for this object. In most cases, the number of objects would be one. This option is more useful when you are dealing with active objects, such as enemy characters, and you wish to count how many remain in play.

Retrieve Fixed Value

Retrieve Fixed Value is a common menu option that you will see on most objects.

- **Retrieve fixed value:** A value that has been previously placed into the object. This is a standard option in all objects, where you can place a value in the object for later retrieval.

Actions

Actions are what you want to happen when a particular event or condition is true. Many of these actions will affect what data the Text Adventure Map object will store.

You can see the top-level actions for the Text Adventure Map object in Figure 4.13.

Available in the menu selections are a number of options, which we will now look at in detail.

Maps

You can see actions relating to maps in Figure 4.14.

- **Add:** Create a new map by specifying its name and its height and width.

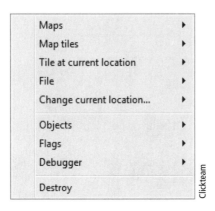

Figure 4.13
The top-level actions for the Text Adventure Map object.

Figure 4.14
The Maps actions available in the Text Adventure Map object.

- ■ **Delete:** Delete a map by name from memory.
- ■ **Set size:** Set the X and Y size of a map.

Map Tiles

You can see actions relating to particular map tiles in Figure 4.15.

- ■ **Set directions:** Set the directions that are allowed on a particular tile. You would type in the actual directions possible, such as **north, east, south,** and **west.**
- ■ **Add link to another tile:** Link one tile to another tile. This could be a tunnel, or perhaps you are creating a transporter of some kind. You can create a link between two points on the same map or a link between two maps. So you could create a link between two different worlds; for example, the player is told he has stepped into a spaceship, and the other map link is a space base in another city.
- ■ **Add link (different name on each side):** This will allow you to create a link between two named points.

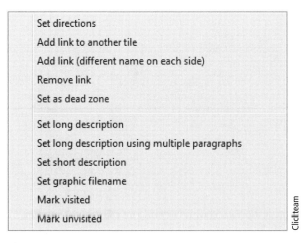

Figure 4.15
Map tiles actions.

- **Remove link:** Remove any links that are currently in place. You will need to specify the name of the link.

- **Set as dead zone:** Set a particular area as dead. This is useful if you want the player to move to a particular tile, but an event happens that keeps them from going back. For example, a rock fall prevents the player walking back in the same direction they came.

- **Set long description:** Set the long description for a tile.

- **Set long description using multiple paragraphs:** Break your long descriptions into multiple paragraphs.

- **Set short description:** Set the short description for a tile.

- **Set graphic filename:** Set the graphic filename associated with a tile.

- **Mark visited:** Mark a tile visited, so the system knows the player has been to a particular location.

- **Mark unvisited:** Set a tile to unvisited. This could just be the setting up of your map, or while in the game you could change a once-visited tile to be unvisited, especially if you decide to push the player back to a particular part of the story (such as in a time travel game, where the player repeats certain steps).

Tile at Current Location

This option will affect any tiles at your current location. You can see the available features in Figure 4.16.

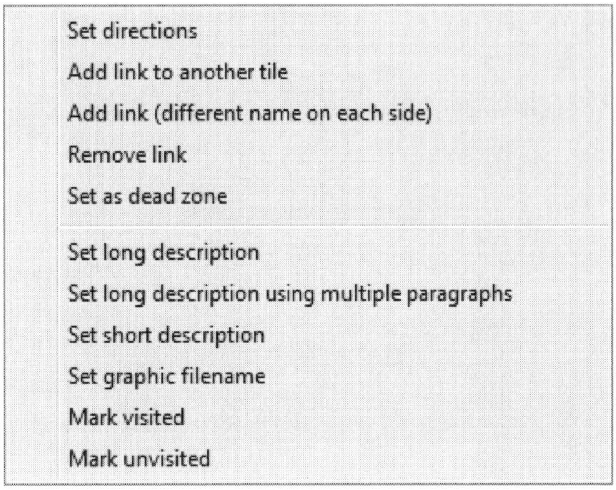

Figure 4.16
The tile at current location options.

- **Set directions:** Set the directions that are allowed from the current tile. You would type in the actual directions possible, such as **north, east, south,** and **west.**

- **Add link to another tile:** Link one tile to another tile from the player's current position.

- **Add line (different name on each side):** This will create a link between two points, where the starting position is the current tile.

- **Remove link:** Remove any links that are in the current location.

- **Set as dead zone:** Set current location as a dead zone.

- **Set long description:** Set the long description for the current tile. This is useful if when leaving the tile you want to create a new description when it is revisited.

- **Set long description using multiple paragraphs:** Break your long descriptions into multiple paragraphs.

- **Set short description:** Set the short description for the current tile.

- **Set graphic filename:** Set the graphic filename associated with the current tile.

- **Mark visited:** Mark the current tile visited, so the system knows the player has been to a particular location.

- **Mark unvisited:** Set the current tile to unvisited.

File

The file option allows you to save any created data into a file or load it into your game. You can see the available options in Figure 4.17.

Figure 4.17
The File options.

- **Save world:** Save the current settings of the world into a file.
- **Load world:** Load the current settings of the world into the application/game.

Change Current Location

The Change current location options allow you to make changes to the player's tile location. You can see the available options in Figure 4.18.

- **Travel in specified direction:** Travel in a particular direction or to a named link location. This will immediately transport a player to a new location.
- **... to a location in the same map:** Transport the player from current location to another on the same map.
- **... to another map:** Transport the player from current location to another location on another map.

Objects

Objects are the items that a player can collect (such as a backpack) and place in their inventory. You can see actions relating to objects in Figure 4.19.

- **Add object:** Add an object to the world.
- **Remove object:** Remove an object from the world. An example might be when an item has been destroyed (in battle perhaps) or used (a potion that has been drunk).
- **Set location:** Set the starting location of an object.
- **Set hidden:** Set whether an object is initially hidden.
- **Set in inventory:** Place the object into the player's inventory.

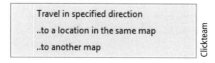

Figure 4.18
The Change current location options.

Figure 4.19
The Objects options.

- **Set description:** Create a description for an object.

- **Set weight:** Set the weight of the object.

- **Set size:** Set the inventory size.

- **Set cost:** Set the cost of the item.

- **Set custom string:** Set an additional string for an object. This is particularly useful for an object that is changing, such as a sword that is beginning to gain power.

- **Set custom value:** Set an additional value to the object. This allows you to create values that you might think are useful for an object, such as damage, wear, and number of times used.

- **Add alias:** Create an alias (name) for the object that can be referenced elsewhere in the game.

- **Clear aliases:** Clear all aliases from an object.

Flags

Flags are used to keep track of values throughout your games. The most common flag is an on/off flag, where 0 represents off and 1 means that the flag is on. You can use these flags to keep track of particular items picked up, puzzles solved, or doors locked/unlocked.

- **Add flag:** Add a new flag.
- **Remove flag:** Remove an already created flag.
- **Set location:** Set the room location for the flag.
- **Clear location:** Clear any location information from a flag.
- **Add name for flag:** Give a flag a text name which can be referenced in your code.
- **Clear names for flag:** Clear any text names given to a flag.
- **Set category:** Create a category for a particular flag.
- **Set value:** Give a particular flag a value.
- **Activate flag:** Enable a flag.
- **Activation policy:** Set the flag's activation policy. A common policy is true or false, where the value of 0 is false and the value of 1 is true.

Debugger

The Debugger is a dialog box that appears when you run any application. You can use the Debugger for testing your game by checking the game's values and current settings. You can add an object to the Debugger via code rather than via the Debugger dialog box. You can see the Debugger option in Figure 4.20.

- **Add object to debugger:** This will automatically add the object to the Debugger. The Debugger allows you to view data about the object, such as its position and values.

Destroy

Destroy, a common option in MMF2, allows you to remove an object from memory. When an object is no longer needed in your game, you can remove it, thereby freeing

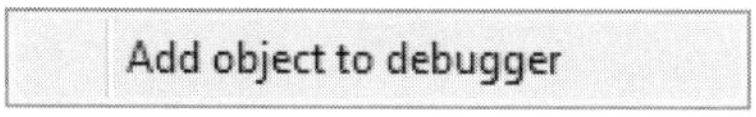

Figure 4.20
The add object to Debugger option.

up any memory that was assigned to it. This is particularly useful with memory hogs like graphic objects; freeing up that extra memory can improve the performance of your game.

■ **Destroy:** The destroy option removes an object from memory.

THE TEXT ADVENTURE MARKUP OBJECT

The Text Adventure Markup object is a text-based object, which is similar in use to the RTF and String objects. It is used for displaying text, but its main feature is that it supports markup commands; these are common in website forum systems where you can apply formatting using <letter> and ending with </letter>.

An example of this could be using the following:

Hello

This would display the text when shown on-screen as **Hello**, with the text appearing in bold.

Some common commands you can use in the Text Adventure Markup object are:

<u>text</u>
text
text

These allow you to create underlined, bolded, and italicized text, respectively.

Properties

Every application, frame, and object has a set of properties; these could be its size, position, or in the case of objects, a value to configure them. For the Text Adventure Markup object, these properties also include the text that appears on screen when you run your game.

You can type text directly into the Properties window as shown in Figure 4.21. When you click on the text edit area in the properties, an edit button will appear; if you click on this edit button you will see Figure 4.22. You can see its output onto the frame in Figure 4.23.

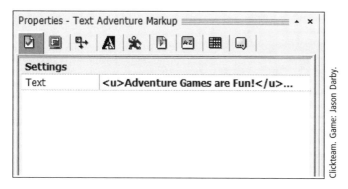

Figure 4.21
The Settings tab for the Text Adventure Markup object properties.

Figure 4.22
The data within the Edit Text box.

Figure 4.23
The formatted text displayed on the frame.

Conditions

Conditions allow you to check if something is true; when it is, MMF will then run any actions that have been entered. The Text Adventure Markup object contains standard position and size conditions as well as those to check for a particular text formatting.

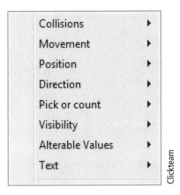

Figure 4.24
The top-level conditions for the Text Adventure Markup object.

You can see the top-level conditions for the Text Adventure Markup object in Figure 4.24.

Collisions

Collisions conditions check when the object collides with (hits) or overlaps another object. You can see all available Collisions conditions in Figure 4.25.

- **Another object:** Is the Text Adventure Markup object colliding with another object? If so, you will be asked which object.

- **Overlapping another object:** Is the Text Adventure Markup object overlapping another object? If so, you will be asked which object.

- **Backdrop:** Is the Text Adventure Markup object colliding with a backdrop object? A backdrop object is a particular type of object used for displaying the backgrounds to a game.

- **Overlapping a backdrop:** Is the Text Adventure Markup object overlapping a backdrop object?

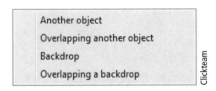

Figure 4.25
The Collisions options in the Text Adventure Markup object.

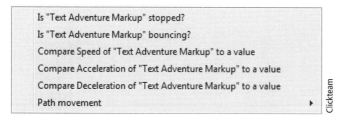

Figure 4.26
The Movement options in the Text Adventure Markup object.

Movement

Movement conditions handle any events dealing with the object moving on the screen. You can see all the available options in Figure 4.26.

- **Is "Text Adventure Markup" stopped?** If you assign a movement to the object, is it currently stopped?

- **Is "Text Adventure Markup" bouncing?** Is the object bouncing?

- **Compare Speed of "Text Adventure Markup" to a value:** Do a comparison of the speed of the Text Adventure Markup object and another value.

- **Compare Acceleration of "Text Adventure Markup" to a value:** Get the current acceleration value of the object.

- **Compare Deceleration of "Text Adventure Markup" to a value:** Retrieve the current deceleration value of the object.

- **Path movement:** Check the object movement against the path movement, to see whether it has reached the end of a node, for example.

Position

Position conditions check the position of the object on the screen. You can see the available options in Figure 4.27.

- **Test position of "Text Adventure Markup":** Check the position of the object. Is it moving out of the frame, currently in the frame, or moving into the frame?

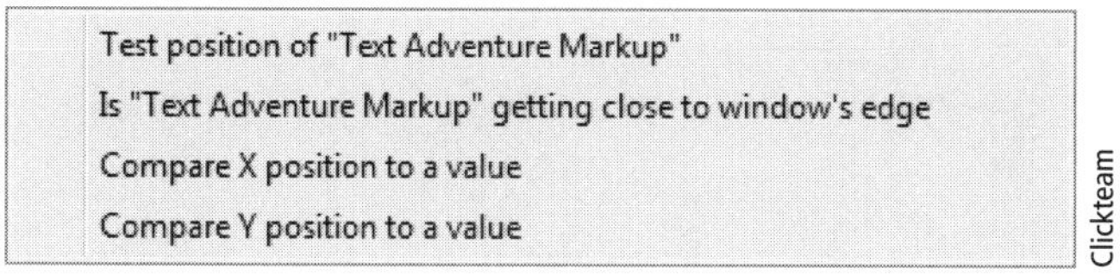

Test position of "Text Adventure Markup"
Is "Text Adventure Markup" getting close to window's edge
Compare X position to a value
Compare Y position to a value

Figure 4.27
The Position options for the Text Adventure Markup object.

Figure 4.28
The Direction option of the Text Adventure Markup object.

- **Is "Text Adventure Markup" getting close to window's edge:** Check to see if the object is moving close to the window's edge (the edge of the frame).

- **Compare X position to a value:** Compare the current X position of the markup object with a value.

- **Compare Y position to a value:** Compare the current Y position of the markup object with a value.

Direction

Direction conditions check the current direction of an object. You can see the available option in Figure 4.28.

- **Compare direction of "Text Adventure Markup":** Compare the current direction of the object with a particular direction.

Pick or Count

Pick or Count conditions allow you to perform calculations to see how many of these objects you have placed in the game world. These are common to objects that can have movement, and you will find them in other objects as well. You can see the available options in Figure 4.29.

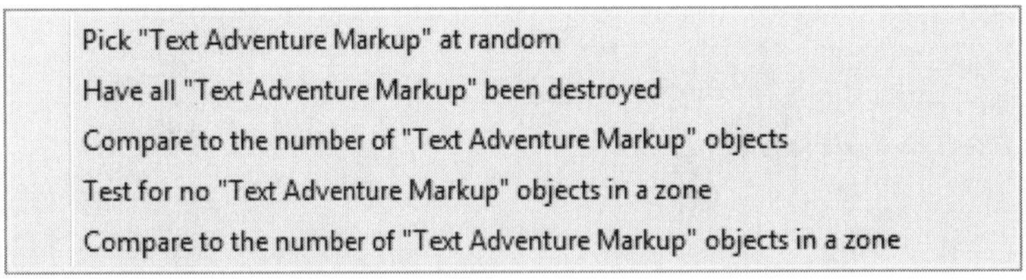

- **Pick "Text Adventure Markup" at random:** If you have multiple Text Adventure Markup objects on-screen, pick one at random. You can then apply any actions to that picked object.

Figure 4.29
The Pick or Count options in the Text Adventure Markup object.

- **Have all "Text Adventure Markup" been destroyed:** Have you destroyed all of the Text Adventure Markup objects?

- **Compare to the number of "Text Adventure Markup" objects:** Do a number comparison on the number of Text Adventure Markup objects.

- **Test for no "Text Adventure Markup" objects in a zone:** Check to see if there are any Text Adventure Markup objects with a specified area on the screen. You will be asked to pick the area that you want to check.

- **Compare to the number of "Text Adventure Markup" objects in a zone:** Do a number comparison on the number of Text Adventure Markup objects within a specified area on the screen.

Visibility

Visibility conditions allow you to check whether the object is visible or invisible on the screen. This is not about whether you can physically see it, as it may be off-frame, but rather, would it actually be visible if you were to move the game to that area of the screen. You can see the available options in Figure 4.30.

- **Is "Text Adventure Markup" visible:** Has the object been set as visible?

- **Is "Text Adventure Markup" invisible:** Has the object been set to invisible?

Alterable Values

Alterable values are values (text or number) that can be altered (changed). Alterable values can be set on objects, storing any numbers you might wish to retrieve at a later date. You can see the available options in Figure 4.31.

- **Compare to one of the alterable values:** Compare one of the object's alterable values with another value.

- **Compare to one of the alterable strings:** Compare one of the object's alterable strings with another value.

- **Compare to fixed value:** Compare a fixed value (a value that is not changeable) with another value.

- **Flags:** Two flag options: Is the flag for this object on or off?

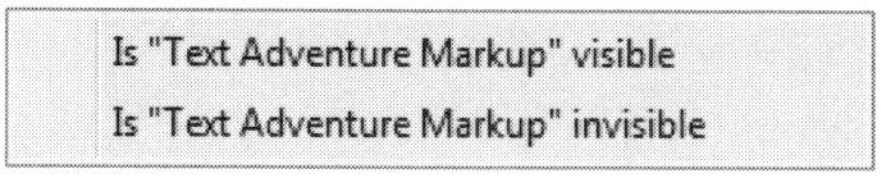

Figure 4.30
The Visibility options in the Text Adventure Markup object.

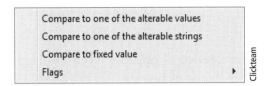

Figure 4.31
The Alterable Values option in the Text Adventure Markup object.

Note

You can access the object's alterable values and strings by clicking on the object in the Frame editor. Then in the Properties window, click on the Values tab.

Text

The Text options allow you to check if the text has been set to a particular value. You can see the available options in Figure 4.32.

- **Is font bold?** Has the font property been set to bold?

- **Is font italic?** Has the font property been set to italic?

- **Is font underlined?** Has the font property been set to underlined?

- **Is font strikeout?** Has the font property been set to strikeout?

Note

The options in the Text conditions only work if you have set the object's font property in the Properties window.

Expressions

The expressions for the Text Adventure Markup object are a lot like many other text-based objects. You can see the majority of the Text Adventure Markup expressions in Figure 4.33.

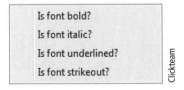

Figure 4.32
The Text options for the Text Adventure Markup object.

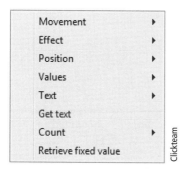

Figure 4.33
The top-level expressions for the Text Adventure Markup object.

The following gives you an overview of what each group contains:

- **Movement:** Check the object's speed, acceleration, and deceleration.
- **Effect:** Check for any graphical effects currently being used on the object.
- **Position:** Check the position of the object on the screen.
- **Values:** Compare/retrieve values that have been assigned to the object.
- **Text:** Get text details, such as font size, name, and color.
- **Get text:** Get the text currently displayed in the object.
- **Count:** Determine how many objects of this type there are.
- **Retrieve fixed value:** Retrieve a fixed value that has been assigned to the object.

Actions

The actions for the Text Adventure Markup object contain common actions in objects such as string and RTF. You can see an example of the actions in Figure 4.34.

- **Movement:** Change the assigned movement on the object; make it bounce, for example. If you had an earthquake in your game, you could make the text box shake.
- **Position:** Change the position of the object on-screen.
- **Direction:** Change the direction of the object. Not really something that you will likely use.
- **Visibility:** Change the visibility of the object (make it visible or invisible).
- **Order:** Change the order of the object on the frame, this means putting it in front of or behind other objects.

Clickteam

Figure 4.34
Some of the top-level actions for the Text Adventure Markup object.

- **Effect:** Change the graphical effect of the object.

- **Launch an Object:** Launch another object from a specified point on the Text Adventure Markup object.

- **Alterable Values:** Set/change the alterable values of the object.

- **Alterable Strings:** Set/change the alterable strings of the object.

- **Flags:** Change flag settings.

- **Text:** Change the font settings, such as size and color.

- **Set text:** Change the current text in the object.

- **Append text:** This will append text to any text already in the object.

- **Debugger:** Add the object automatically to the Debugger.

- **Destroy:** Destroy the object, after which it will no longer be shown on-screen and no conditions or actions for this object will work.

THE TEXT ADVENTURE MESSAGES OBJECT

The Text Adventure Messages object is a key object in making text adventure games. It can take the input that the player types and create a tailored response. For example, if you type **Pick up apple,** you can get a response saying, "You pick up the

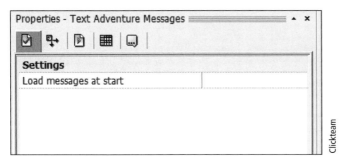

Figure 4.35
The Text Adventure Messages properties.

apple." Because you can have multiple objects, you would need to use **pick up** as a keyword and confirm that there is an apple.

Properties

When the object is selected in the Frame editor, its properties will appear in the Properties window (see Figure 4.35).

- **Load messages at start:** Allows you to create a text file that can be loaded at the start of the frame. This feature is very useful for making your own game editors.

Conditions

There is only a single condition for the Text Adventure Messages object (see Figure 4.36).

- **Specified message exists:** Specify a message ID to confirm it exists.

Expressions

The Text Adventure Messages object stores lots of data about text strings and various arguments, so there are quite a few options available in the expressions (see Figure 4.37).

Figure 4.36
The specified message exist condition.

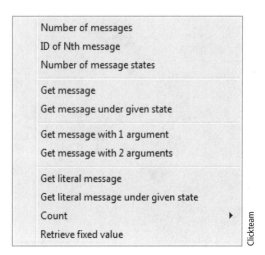

Figure 4.37
The top-level expressions for the Text Adventure Messages object.

Note

An argument allows you to tell MMF that you want to replace a specified tag with a value. Perhaps you want a message to say "You pick up the.." and you want to specify an object that the user has picked up. To do this you would need some text that can change, so we can specify an argument that will be replaced by text. In the case of the Text Adventure Messages object, you can use an argument by using %number. So you could write **You pick up the %1.** This will then replace the %1 argument with a value that you have specified.

- **Number of messages:** How many messages are there.
- **ID of Nth message:** What is the ID name of a particular numbered message.
- **Number of message states:** You can specify a numeric value for a message, such as 0 or 1, and then retrieve what the current state of the message is.
- **Get message:** Get the text for the current message.
- **Get message under given state:** Get the message for the current state. Perhaps you have a message for **on** or **off.**
- **Get message with 1 argument:** Get the message and one argument value.
- **Get message with 2 arguments:** Get the message and two argument values.
- **Get literal message:** Get the message using its ID.
- **Get literal message under given state:** Get the message using its ID and its state.

Figure 4.38
The top-level actions for the Text Adventure Messages object.

- **Count:** Determine the number of Text Adventure Message objects currently being used.
- **Retrieve fixed value:** Retrieve the fixed value that has been set.

Actions

The actions for the Text Adventure Messages object can be seen in Figure 4.38.

- **Set message:** Set the message using an ID and specifying arguments (if any).
- **Set message under a given state:** Set the message when it is in a particular numeric state.
- **Unset message:** Unset the message state.
- **Set message argument:** Set an argument for a message. You can use up to 99 arguments.
- **File:** You can load and save settings for the Text Adventure Messages object.
- **Debugger:** Add to the Debugger.
- **Destroy:** Destroy the object, but use this only if you no longer need the object in the game you have created (in real time).

THE TEXT ADVENTURE PAGES OBJECT

The Text Adventure Pages object was used in Chapter 3 of this book to create a simple game called *Moon Traveller*. You should have a good idea of some of the available options, but we will cover the rest of the features here for completeness.

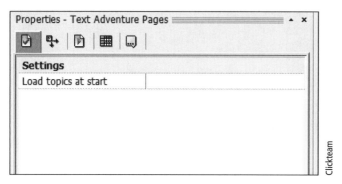

Figure 4.39
The properties for the Text Adventure Pages object.

Properties

When the object is selected in the Frame editor, its properties will appear in the Properties window (see Figure 4.39).

Conditions

There is only a single condition for the Text Adventure Pages object (see Figure 4.40).

■ **Topic is blank:** There is no content for a specified topic.

Expressions

The expressions that are available for the Text Adventure Pages object are shown in Figure 4.41.

■ **Number of topics:** Get the current number of topics created.

■ **Get topic content:** Get the text of a topic from a particular topic number.

■ **Get topic image filename:** Get the image filename from a particular topic.

■ **Get number of links in topic:** Get the number of links within a topic.

Figure 4.40
The conditions for the Text Adventure Pages object.

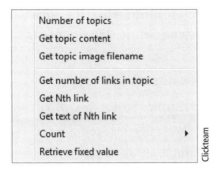

Figure 4.41
Expressions available in the Text Adventure Pages object.

- **Get Nth link:** Get the link that is assigned to a particular topic link. Say, for example, in the first topic you have three links, which have links to other pages. You will retrieve the number that is assigned in one of those links.

- **Get text of Nth link:** Get the link text of a particular link number.

- **Count:** Determine the number of Text Adventure Page objects.

- **Retrieve fixed value:** Retrieve the fixed value assigned to this object.

Actions

The actions that are available for the Text Adventure Pages object are shown in Figure 4.42.

- **Set topic content:** Set the text content of a particular topic number.

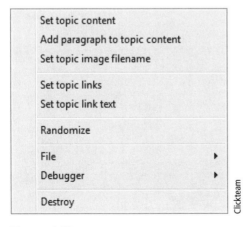

Figure 4.42
The actions available for the Text Adventure Pages object.

- **Add paragraph to topic content:** To add a large amount of text into a topic, you can use the Add Paragraph to split up your content, but it will all appear in the same topic.

- **Set topic image filename:** Set the image filename for a particular topic.

- **Set topic links:** Set the link numbers for a particular topic. So topic 1 might have three links, to topics 5, 8, and 15.

- **Set topic link text:** Set the link text for each of the links in a topic.

- **Randomize:** Randomize the topic numbers. This will mix up the text groups, allowing the topic numbers to be randomly assigned. If you write your story in order, then using the Randomize will mix it up for you. Some people may find writing it in numerical order easier, so this option will help you if you do.

- **File:** Load and save information for the Pages object.

- **Debugger:** Add information to the Debugger.

- **Destroy:** Destroy the Text Adventure Pages object.

THE TEXT ADVENTURE WORDS OBJECT

The Text Adventure Words object is the key system for managing text within the game, and in particular, text entry comparison from the player. You can create phrasebooks and dictionaries of common words that the player can use.

Properties

When the Text Adventure Words object is selected in the Frame editor, its properties will appear in the Properties window (see Figure 4.43).

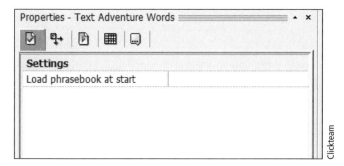

Figure 4.43
The Text Adventure Words properties.

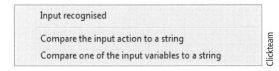

Figure 4.44
The Conditions for the Text Adventure Words object.

- **Load phrasebook at start:** You can specify a filename if you wish the application/game you are making to automatically load a phrasebook file.

Conditions

The conditions for the Text Adventure Words object can be seen in Figure 4.44.

- **Input recognised:** The input that the player has entered has been recognized when compared to the phrasebook.

- **Compare the input action to a string:** Compare the action to a string.

- **Compare one of the input variables to a string:** Compare one of the variables to a string.

Expressions

All of the expressions for the Text Adventure Words object are stored under menus, so we shall detail each group. There are four groups broken down into the following:

- Input
- Phrases
- Dictionary
- Count

We also have a single item for Retrieve Fixed Value, which we have covered in previous objects.

We will now look at each of the four groups in detail.

Input

Input expression options deal with text input from the user (see Figure 4.45).

- **Action name:** An action is something that the player might do, such as examine an object, drink, throw etc. So the expression will retrieve the action name.

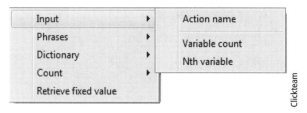

Figure 4.45
Input options for the Text Adventure Words object.

■ **Variable count:** Returns the number of variables that have been matched in the current phrase.

■ **Nth variable:** Returns a particular numbered variable.

Phrases

Phrases are collections of words that can all be typed by the user, such as **Eat an apple.** You can see the available expression options in Figure 4.46.

■ **Number of phrases:** Get the number of phrases in the phrasebook.

■ **Text of Nth phrase:** Get the text of a particular phrase in the phrasebook.

■ **Action of Nth phrase:** Get the associated action of a particular numbered phrase in the phrasebook.

Dictionary

In the Dictionary section, you can create groups of words. You can see the available expression options in Figure 4.47.

■ **Number of categories:** Retrieve the number of categories that you have created.

■ **Name of Nth category:** What is the name of a particular created category?

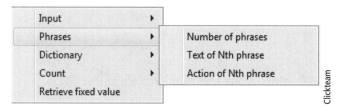

Figure 4.46
The expression options for Phrases.

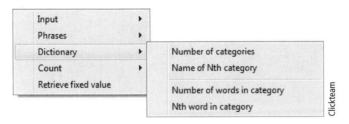

Figure 4.47
The Dictionary expressions.

- **Number of words in category:** How many words are in a specified category?
- **Nth word in category:** What is a particular numbered word in a category? So if you have six words in a category called directions, you can determine the word in a particular number.

Count

The count expression allows you to do a numeric comparison with the number of Text Adventure Words objects that have been added to the frame.

You can see the only available expression option in the Count menu in Figure 4.48.

- **Number of objects:** The number of Text Adventure Words objects used within your game.

Actions

You can see the available actions for the Text Adventure Words object in Figure 4.49.

The actions at the top level are as follows:

- **Set TA Map object:** Set the name of the TA Map object. This is so the object can identify and communicate with it. You must have the Text Adventure Map object also placed on the frame to use the Text Adventure Words object.

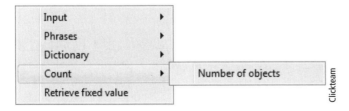

Figure 4.48
The Count option.

Figure 4.49
The actions of the Text Adventure Words object.

- **Parse input:** Take the input and parse it (read it). This can then be used to check against available words/variables.

- **File:** You are able to load or save a phrasebook. You must have previously created a phrasebook if you intend to load one into MMF.

- **Phrases:** Add, remove, and clear the phrasebook.

- **Dictionary:** Add and remove a word to a category, delete a category, and clear the dictionary.

- **Debugger:** Add object to the Debugger.

- **Destroy:** Destroy the object is a standard option in MMF, and it is unlikely you would destroy the Text Adventure Words object.

CHAPTER SUMMARY

In this chapter, you have learned all about the various objects that have been written to help you create your adventure games. It may be a lot to take in, but remember that if you need to remind yourself about a particular option, you can always try it out in a game or return to this chapter and take another look.

We won't be using every single option in this book, so make sure you investigate what each feature can do and consider how you might use each within your own games.

In Chapter 5, you will create your very first text adventure game called *Dungeon of Text*.

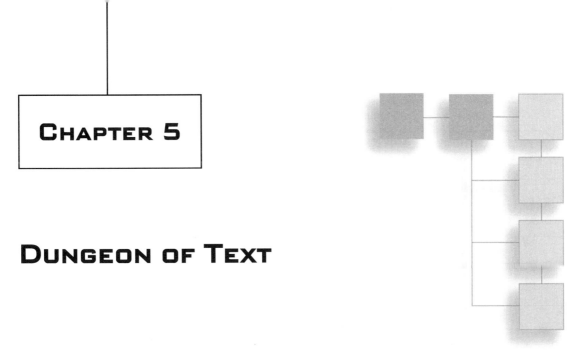

CHAPTER 5

DUNGEON OF TEXT

In this chapter, we will create a very simple text adventure called *Dungeon of Text*, but rather than enter text to move around the game world, we will be using some buttons with directions, such as north, east, south and west, to simplify the game. The goal of this chapter is to introduce you to the Text Adventure Map object. This object is extremely important for setting up and moving around your game worlds.

Once you have learned the basics of the Text Adventure Map object, we will then use what we have learned in this chapter as the basis for a more complex text adventure in Chapters 6 and 7.

GAME CONCEPT

In *Dungeon of Text*, you have been captured by a group of brigands (highway thieves/robbers) and in the struggle to get away, you have been knocked out. When you awake, you find yourself in a dark, damp room. You are in a dungeon.

The aim of the game is to escape from the dungeon and back to the nearest town where you can seek refuge.

We will be keeping things quite simple in this game so that you can learn more about how the Text Adventure Map object works. You won't have any puzzles to solve, but you will need to navigate around the world using buttons. We will take a look at more complex design features in Chapter 6.

Note

In traditional text adventures, you will navigate around the world using text entry, but because we are introducing the Text Adventure Map object in this chapter, we will concentrate on moving around the world. In Chapter 6, we will introduce text entry.

In Figure 5.1, you can see the map of our game. It's a relatively simple map, but remember the player cannot see this map while playing. This means it will take him longer to figure the way out as he will need to explore each direction to understand where he can go. In larger games, you will have traps and puzzles, and certain road-blocks that will prevent the player from proceeding, taking him even longer to finish the game. For this example, though, we are keeping it simple.

In Figure 5.1, we have identified each area with a number. You will also see a number of crosses; these crosses signify that moving in that direction will trigger a "game over" message. To identify each room, we have also placed a small amount of text into each box.

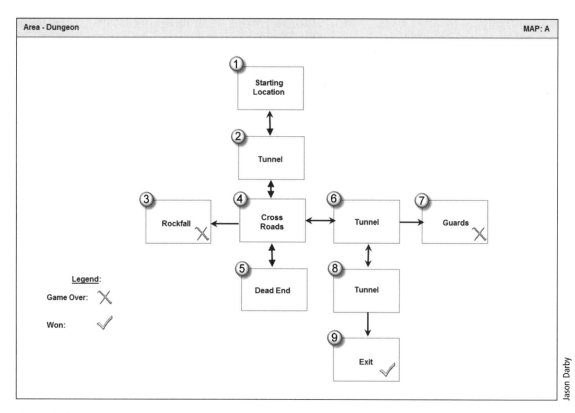

Figure 5.1
Map and legend of *Dungeon of Text*.

Note

You can put whatever you want on your own map to make it easy for you to design and to remember the location of each room in the event you return to it after a few days, weeks, or months.

MAPS

In Figure 5.1, you can see the basic structure of our map, which details all of the key locations. A single box in *Dungeon of Text* represents a single room, but you can have multiple boxes represent various parts of a room, or even towns and counties. You can initially draw your map using a more traditional method as you can see in the crudely drawn image in Figure 5.2.

In the Text Adventure Map object, a map is created using a number of squares; you could think of it as a grid of boxes. These squares have a height and a width, and we will tell MMF2 which of those squares are locations. You can see a basic grid in Figure 5.3. These grids are very simple to use and are common in role-playing games to draw out dungeons and areas that players will visit.

You do not need to use every square, and not every square needs to be linked to another square. Using MMF2, you can virtually link a location to another square, so

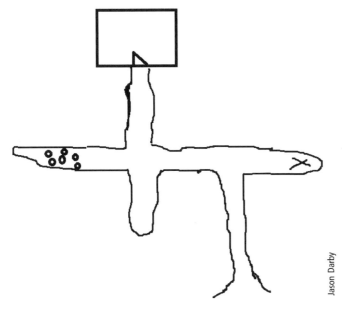

Figure 5.2
A rough map of our dungeon.

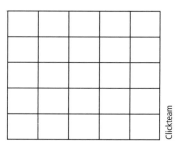

Figure 5.3
A starting map that is five squares by five squares.

when completing a particular task, you can be teleported to another world or location.

MMF uses a system called zero-based indexing to identify each room or location. For example, think of a hidden treasure map game, perhaps at a school fete, where you have a big map split into squares and you have to guess where the treasure is buried. You would give coordinates for the location of the treasure. This is similar to how MMF works with maps.

We use two coordinates—X and Y axes—in MMF to find a particular square. The X axis is from left to right, while the Y axis is from top to bottom. If we were to draw our *Dungeon of Text* map in a grid, it may appear similar to Figure 5.4.

In Figure 5.4, I have created a grid of four squares in width and five squares in height. The black squares are ones that I have colored in to show that no room exists. Not all squares are linked together. For example, the number 5 in X1, Y3 is not a room that can move across to the number 8 in X2, Y3. This is why you need to create two maps when making your game, a room layout map in Figure 5.1 and then where this information is stored in the Map object as shown in Figure 5.4.

Figure 5.4
Our *Dungeon of Text* game converted to a grid map.

Game Features

Now that we have an idea of our game area, we should consider how we are going to present this information to the player. We can do that in a simple paragraph explaining how the system will work. For more complex games, you will need to break this down further into a detailed design, but as this game is quite simple, we can keep the text relatively short.

- **Basic Usage**: The user will see a text box on-screen and read the instructions. Once the player has read the instructions, she will then decide which direction to move in. The directions—north, east, etc.—she can move in will be displayed on buttons that have text on them. If she cannot move in a certain direction, then the button will be disabled. There will be certain times when a player has finished the game by being recaptured, by an event, or by escaping. When such an event happens, the player is informed that the game is over. In these cases, all the buttons will be disabled.

Using the basic usage description, we can work out what we need:

- **Text Box**: We need a Rich Edit text box to display all of our room descriptions.
- **Buttons**: We need to have some buttons that the player will press to move around the game world.
- **Room Descriptions**: In the Rich Edit text box, we will need to display room descriptions. If the player has already been to the room, they will receive a shorter text description.
- **Game Over**: If the player can no longer continue, she will receive a "game over" message at the end of any story text that is displayed.

We will add two counters to this example for testing purposes (but you can add in your own games to help the player). The two counters will display the player's current X and Y locations within the game world.

Setting Up the MMF2 File

Now that we have our location and grid maps, we are ready to start putting our MMF2 file together. So create a new MMF2 file and then start placing the following in their associated positions onto the frame as shown in Table 5.1. If you want to skip this part, you can download the relevant file called Dungeon_Text_Chp5_no_code.mfa.

Table 5.1 Objects Needed to Create the Scene for Your Game

Object Type	Object Name	X Location	Y Location	Size X	Size Y
Text Adventure Map	–	5	-38	–	–
Text Adventure Messages	–	53	-38	–	–
Rich Edit	–	11	13	475	415
Edit Box	–	23	437	599	23
Button	Btn_North	531	72	64	32
Button	Btn_East	566	106	64	32
Button	Btn_South	530	142	64	32
Button	Btn_West	495	106	64	32
Counter	CounterX	539	231	–	–
Counter	CounterY	539	264	–	–

We also need to set the text for each of the buttons, so Btn_North will display the word North; Btn_East will display East, etc. To do this, double left-click on each of the four buttons and a text entry dialog box will appear; type in the text *North, East, South* or *West* on the appropriate button.

Note

If any objects should be left at their default settings for a particular property, they will be shown as a dash in the table.

Now that you have set the scene, we can turn our focus to what code we will need to add to our game by listing its key features and how it will be used. For larger games, you will do this as part of a set of design and story documents.

CODING DUNGEON OF TEXT

In this part of the chapter, we will code our game *Dungeon of Text*. The code for this game is approximately 72 lines, including blank and comment lines. A lot of the code is very simple and duplicated between objects. Seventy-two lines may seem like a lot, but much of the code you use here can easily be put into your own games, so as you begin to build your adventure games, think about how you can re-use the code for your next game. For example, perhaps you will write some code to manage text descriptions for when you have visited a room and then display a short description when you have previously visited the room. If your next game is going to do the same, why not re-use the code?

Note

Re-using code is one way to speed up the process of creating your next game. This is something that is common in the gaming industry, taking the code you already have, making improvements to it, adding new features, and then releasing the next game. Of course this is on a bigger scale, with a lot more people, resources, and assets (graphics and music), but the method can also be used for a team of one making games in MMF2. You can make a new game with improved code and features with less effort than starting from scratch.

So what does our code need to do to meet the requirements listed in the "Game Features" section of this chapter? We need to do the following:

- **Start of Frame**: We need to set up our text and any initialization (for example, setting up starting values and configuration).

- **Timer**: After a very short period of time, we need to set our starting location and its long description. The timer is there to allow the rest of the code to be read and the room setup descriptions to be loaded into the game.

- **Room Description Setups**: We need to set the text descriptions for each room. This is both the long description when first entering the room and a short description when returning to the room. Within this part of the code, all we are doing is setting the descriptions into the Text Adventure Map object. This code will be contained within a group to keep it clean and easy to read.

- **Can Move in Direction**: If a player can move in a particular direction, we will enable a button. In a normal text adventure, we might tell the user within the descriptions that he can move in a particular direction.

- **Cannot Move in Direction**: If a player cannot move in a particular direction, we will disable the buttons.

- **Move Direction**: If a player can move in a particular direction, we want to tell the Text Adventure Map object that the player has moved in a direction, allowing the object to update the player's current location. This code will activate a group called New Location, which will decide if it should put in the short description or long description into the Rich Edit box.

- **Always**: We will always set the counter objects to the current X and Y player location for testing purposes only and can be removed if required. It's important when testing your game to know your exact location so you can compare the contents of the game (such as room descriptions) with the current location to confirm that all is correct.

- **New Location Group**: This code is used to send the long or short description text into the Rich Edit box.

- **Location Dead Zones**: When you move in particular places within *Dungeon of Text*, you cannot move out of that zone, because you have been captured, blocked, or have escaped and the game is over. At this point, we want to set the zone to a dead zone, which means there will no longer be any direction the player can move.

Now we have covered the main aspects of the game, it's time to start explaining the code.

Setting Up the Start of Frame Code

Our first task is to set up the Start of Frame code, which will configure our basic map details within the Text Adventure Map object, set two messages, and disable all four direction buttons.

1. First go into the Event Editor and click on the New condition text on event line 1.

2. Right-click on the Storyboard Controls object and select Start of Frame.

Now that we have our event, we need to set up the Text Adventure Map grid size and the directions the player can move in. When setting the directions, you only need to specify the key directions. For example, if you had two rooms, you only specify the directions from the first to the second room; you do not need to specify the direction from the second room to the first, because setting up the first link has by definition created the opposite direction.

Our first task is to set the grid size:

1. Move across from the Start of Frame condition until you are directly under the Text Adventure Map object.

2. Right-click on the blank action box and select Maps Add.

An Expression Evaluator appears asking for the map name, which should be a unique name that will define all of the locations within this map/game. It can be any name you want to make it easier for you to remember what area you are setting up. In this example, we are creating a single set of rooms that are all connected within a dungeon.

3. In the Expression Evaluator, type **"Dungeon"** and click on OK.

4. You will now be asked for the map width. Type **4** and click OK.

5. You will now be asked for the map height. Type **5** and click OK.

Note

When entering text within the Expression Evaluator, you must always ensure that it is enclosed in quote marks; otherwise, MMF will return an error.

Now that we have set the grid size, we need to set the available directions that the player can move. Again, we do this in the Text Adventure Map object. In this example, we will set the first, you will then need to follow the process to add the rest as per Figure 5.5.

6. Move across from the Start of Frame event and right-click on the Text Adventure Map object.

7. Select Map Tiles and set the direction.

You will now be asked to enter the compass directions from a particular map and tile.

8. Type **"North, South"** and then click on OK.

9. When asked for the Map name, type **"Dungeon"** and click on OK.

10. When asked for the X location, type **1**.

11. When asked for the Y location, type **1**.

See Figure 5.5 for the other room directions.

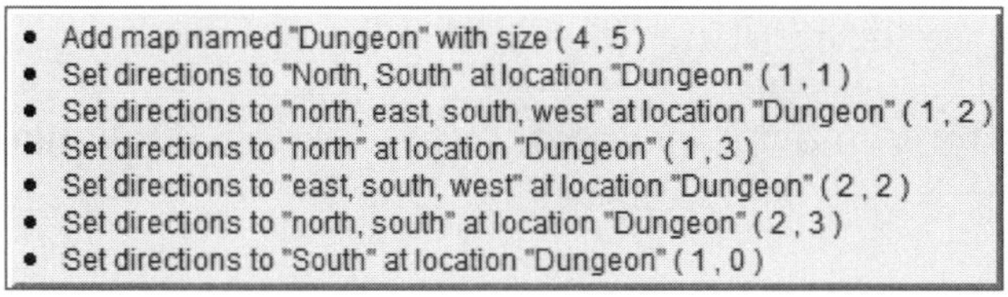

- Add map named "Dungeon" with size (4 , 5)
- Set directions to "North, South" at location "Dungeon" (1 , 1)
- Set directions to "north, east, south, west" at location "Dungeon" (1 , 2)
- Set directions to "north" at location "Dungeon" (1 , 3)
- Set directions to "east, south, west" at location "Dungeon" (2 , 2)
- Set directions to "north, south" at location "Dungeon" (2 , 3)
- Set directions to "South" at location "Dungeon" (1 , 0)

Clickteam

Figure 5.5
The actions to set up all of the directions.

Next, we need to set up two messages in the Text Adventure Messages object. These messages will display "Game Over" and "Well done, you have escaped" in the edit box when we need them. Setting them up in the object allows us to call these messages any time.

1. Move across from the Start of Frame event until you are directly under the Text Adventure Messages object. Right-click the action box and select Set Message.

2. When asked for the Unique ID of the message, type **"GameOver"**, then click on OK.

3. When asked for the text of the message, type **Game Over**, then click on OK.

We need to add the second message:

4. Move across from event line 1 until you are directly under the Text Adventure Messages object. Right-click and select Set Message.

5. For the ID type Won, type **"Well done, you have escaped"** as the message.

Another thing we need to do in the initialization stage of our game is to turn the focus of the Rich Edit box to Off. This will prevent any initial flashing cursor to appear in the edit box to indicate that the Rich Edit box isn't currently selected by the user.

6. Move across from event line 1, until you are directly under the Rich Edit object.

7. Right-click the action box and select Control | Auto Focus | Off.

Finally, we want to initially set all buttons to be disabled. We will enable them once we have moved into the first room and know the directions the player will move in. If we leave them enabled, buttons may be incorrectly set to available when, in fact, that direction is not actually available.

8. Move across from event line 1 until you are under the Btn_North object, right-click the action box and select Disable.

9. Drag and drop the disable action from Btn_North and drop it onto the Btn_East object, and do the same for Btn_South and Btn_West.

You will now have disabled all buttons and your Event List code will look like Figure 5.6.

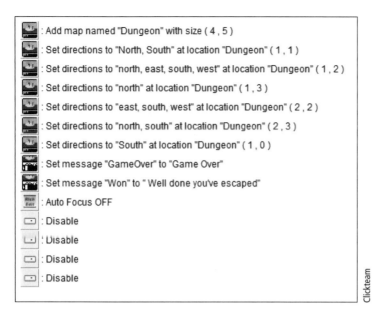

Figure 5.6
The Event List editor for event line 1.

Note

You can click on the Event List Editor button in the MMF2 toolbar to show all actions available on a single event line. Remember this option is very useful for changing the order of the actions in an event line, but we are also using it to confirm you have followed the code portions of this book correctly.

Timer Setup

The next event we need is a condition that runs at half a second to set the player's current location, set the current room description, and then finally tell the Text Adventure Map object that the location has been visited, so if the player returns to this room, he will see a different room description.

Note

We could have placed this code in the Start of Frame event, but setting the room description is not done until after the start of frame, so half a second is enough for it to load this data in later. You have to remember to set up your data as early as possible; otherwise, you might run into issues where data is not displayed.

First, we need to create the event for half a second has passed:

1. Click on the New condition text on event line 2.

2. Right-click on the Timer object (Stopwatch icon) and select Is the Timer Equal to a Certain Value.

3. Remove the one second item, type **50** in the 1/100 box, then click on OK.

Now we have the event we need to create our actions. First, we will set the long description for the starting location. Type **1,0** into the Rich Text object so that the first bit of text the player sees will be the starting location description, which will let them know where he is.

4. Move across from the Timer equals 00"-50 condition until you are directly under the Rich Text object. Right-click on the action box and select Control | Set Text.

5. The Expression Evaluator will now appear, asking for the text from the Text Adventure Map object. Click on the Retrieve Data from an Object button.

6. Right-click on the Text Adventure Map object and choose Map Tiles | Long Description.

7. In the Expression Evaluator, we need to fill in three items of data. Type the text **"Dungeon"** (including quotes) to replace the >MapName< placeholder, then type **1** for >MapX<, and **0** for >MapY<. You should see the following text: Long Desc$("Text Adventure Map", "Dungeon", 1, 0)

8. Click on the OK button to save the expression.

Now that we have displayed the room description, we need to update our Text Adventure Map object so that it knows that starting location:

9. Move across from event line 2 until you are directly under the Text Adventure Map object, right-click the action box and select Change Current Location | to another map.

10. Type the name **"Dungeon"** (in quotes) for the map, then click on OK.

11. For the X location, type **1** and then click on OK.

12. For the Y location, type **0** and then click on OK.

Now we need to add another action on the same action box to tell MMF2 that the room has now been visited.

13. Move across from event line 2 and right-click on the Text Adventure Map object action box. Select Tile at Current Location | Mark Visited.

You have now finished the code for event line 2, the Event List editor code should look like Figure 5.7.

Figure 5.7
The three actions for event line 2.

Room Setup

In the next bit of code, we need to set up all of the room's descriptions both long and short. In reality we should have done this before the Timer and in the Start of Frame event, but as this is more readable, we have changed the location of the code.

There is a lot of room data to write about. Therefore, we have provided a file with all of the content for the rooms already written so that you can continue making the game without adding all of the text required for it.

The file is called:

Dungeon_Text_Chp5_RoomText.mfa

You can see the basic structure of the events in Figure 5.8.

First we have to set up a group to contain all of our room descriptions. The group will be called Room-Setup. This group is used to hold the data only and is enabled as soon as the frame starts. We've placed the code for this in a group to keep our code tidy. Once we have written our code for this part, we can hide it by collapsing the group.

You can also see we have split long descriptions and short descriptions to the top and bottom half of the group. Again, this is for readability; we could have placed each of the actions for each description into a single event line.

Finally, you will notice that we have used a Run This Event Once condition to ensure this code is only ever run on the first reading of the events by MMF2. Even though the group is always enabled, all of these events are ignored after they have been run once, so there is no performance hit for having this code in an always-enabled group.

Note

In Chapters 10 and 11, we will show you how to load and store data to help speed up the process of game creation by using editors and loading data in at the start of the frame.

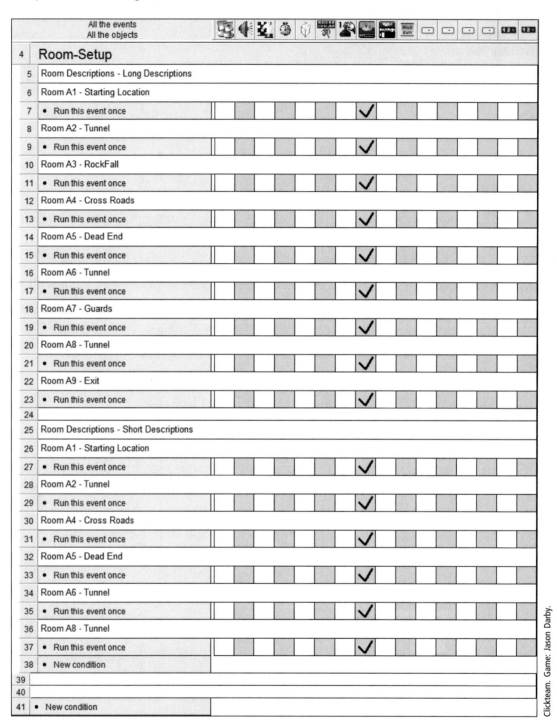

Figure 5.8
Room description code.

The actions are all under the Text Adventure Map object, and we have used three possible actions:

- **Set Long Description**: This creates a long room description as a single paragraph of text.

- **Set Long Description Using Multiple Paragraphs**: MMF2 can load in long amounts of text, but the Evaluation Editor can only accept a limited number of characters. This allows you to string together multiple paragraphs to enter more content at runtime.

- **Set Short Description**: This allows you to set a short room description.

Note

In most cases, you would store all room descriptions in an array file (or other data object that can load content) and load this data into the game at runtime. This is a better option than trying to enter all the text directly into the Text Adventure Map object that can only accept a limited number of characters typed directly into the Evaluation Editor.

Adding New Line Spacing to Text

When adding text to the Text Adventure Map object using the Set Long Description Using Multiple Paragraphs, it will place all text directly below each other, creating one big paragraph without any spacing. From a formatting perspective, this doesn't look very good, so to fix this we can use the Newline option, which gives you the ability to create a new line between bits of data and is very useful when dealing with any objects that use text.

In this example, we are going to show how we created a newline for event line 7, which is the starting location's long description.

1. Right-click on the Text Adventure Map Object Action box and select Set Long Description Using Multiple Paragraphs.

2. Enter the first paragraph of text:

"As you open your eyes you notice that you are in a dark damp dungeon. There is a small window just behind you which is throwing a small amount of light into the room. Your head hurts, probably due to being hit on the head."

3. If we click on OK, we would be asked to enter another paragraph that would appear directly under the first paragraph. So we need to add a newline in the

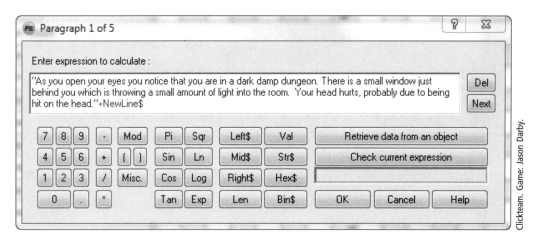

Figure 5.9
The first paragraph of text with a newline added.

Expression Evaluator by adding a + (plus) sign directly after the quote mark and then clicking on the Retrieve Data from an Object button.

4. Right-click on the Special object and use the Strings item, and select Newline.

The entry would look like Figure 5.9.

We then entered additional paragraphs. For those with no text, we left them blank with quotation marks, entered the map name, and its location in the X and Y axis.

Moving in Directions

The next bit of code for this example is to check whether the player will be able to move in a particular direction (or not) and if so (or not), enable/disable the direction buttons.

You should currently see the Room-Setup group from the previous example. Double-click on it to collapse it so that we can tidy up the code a little before continuing.

Line 39 will contain a blank comment line; these are useful for creating spaces between code. At event line 40, we need a comment to advise what the next bit of code is going to do. The text for the comment at line 40 will be "Can Move in Direction." Remember, to create a comment, right-click on the condition number where you want to insert a comment and then use Insert | A Comment.

Now we are ready to add four event lines that will check what directions a player can move:

1. Click on the New condition text on event line 41, and then right-click on the Text Adventure Map object. Select Can Move in a Certain Direction.

2. You will now be asked to enter the direction you want to check. In this case, we want to check north, so type **North** between the quotation marks and click on OK.

3. Repeat for the other three directions.

You should now have four events that check if you can move north, east, south, or west.

Now we need to do this again, so we can set up four directions that the player cannot move in.

4. Create a comment line on event line 45, and type the text **Can't Move in Direction**.

5. You can drag and drop each of the directions into each condition line or click on the New condition text to create them that way. You should now have another set of Can Move (direction) events. The second set now needs to be changed so that it checks if the player cannot move in a particular direction. So on event lines 46 to 49, right-click on each one and select the Negate option.

You should now have a set of events that look like Figure 5.10.

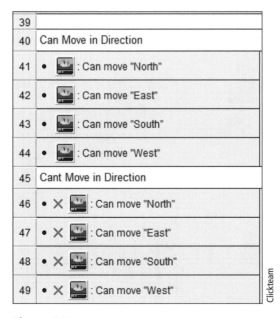

Figure 5.10
The events for moving and not moving in a particular direction.

Note

The Negate feature means that whatever condition is set, it will be opposite. In this case, the player is not able to move in a particular direction.

Now we need to enable the four direction buttons, depending on if we can or cannot move in a particular direction. For each direction the player will be allowed to move in, we need to set the associated button to Enabled; if the player cannot move in that direction, we need to set the button to Disabled.

6. For event line 41 where it specifies that we can move north, we need to set Btn_North. So from event line 41, move across until you are directly under the Btn_North object. Right-click the action box and select Enable.

7. For event lines 42 to 44, we need to follow the same process for enabling just those buttons, so right-click on the relevant action box and select Enable.

Now we need to follow the same process but disable the relevant buttons:

8. For event line 46, move across until you are directly under the Btn_North object and right-click the action box and select Disable.

9. For event lines 46 to 49, follow the same process for disabling the relevant buttons.

You should now have some events and actions that look like Figure 5.11.

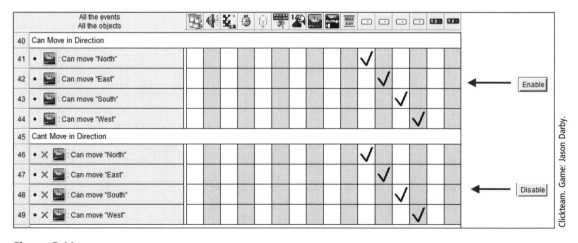

Figure 5.11
Enabling and disabling the direction buttons.

Direction Not Visited 1

For the next bit of code, we need to move in the direction based on the button being clicked. We will then replace the text within the Rich Edit object with blank text. Doing this allows us to reset the contents. We would then activate a group, but because we haven't created the group yet (later on in this chapter), we will have to create some of the events and code and then come back to this code group later.

1. First let's set up our initial items:
   - Event line 50 should be a blank comment line.
   - Event line 51 should be a comment with the text "Direction and Not Visited."
   - Event line 52 should be a comment with the words "North."

Now that we have our comments set up, we will add our first condition for this event to check when the Btn_North button has been clicked.

2. Click on the New condition text and then right-click on the Btn_North object and select Button Clicked.

We now need to add a second condition to this event that will check if the button is enabled. This is a check to prevent the player from pressing the button when the button is disabled. Sometimes it's sensible to add a second condition to ensure that your code is correct and prevent it from running when you don't require it to.

3. Right-click on the condition you have just added in event line 53 and click Insert. Right-click on Btn_North and then select Is Enabled.

You will now have the event with two conditions, so now we are ready to add the actions.

4. Move across from event line 53 until you are directly under the Text Adventure Map object. Right-click on the action box and select Change Current Direction, and then Travel in a Specified direction.

5. You will be asked for a direction, so type **"North"** and click on the OK button.

Now we need to reset the contents of the Rich Edit object:

6. Move across from event line 53 until you are under the Rich Edit object. Right-click on the action box and select Block | Select All.

Now that we have selected all of the text in the Rich Edit object, we now need to replace it.

7. Right-click the action box and select Block | Replace Selection.

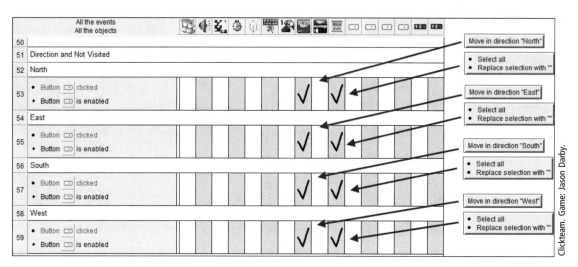

Figure 5.12
Moving the player in the right direction.

8. The Evaluation Editor appears. We want to set no text, which is effectively blanking out the current text, so leave the entry as two quotation marks and click on the OK button.

Now we need to repeat the process for east, south, and west, telling the Text Adventure object to move in the particular direction and then selecting the text and blanking it out.

Once you have done this, you should have the Event editor looking like Figure 5.12.

We have now completed the code for this section. We will come back to this code again to activate a group called New Location once it has been created.

Updating Debug Counters

In the Frame editor we added two counters that will keep track of where the player has moved in the world using one counter to store/display the X axis and the other to display the Y axis. We will use the Always event to ensure that these counters are updated with the correct location.

1. For event line 60, create a blank comment line.

We now need to create an Always condition.

2. Click on the New condition text.

3. Right-click on the Special object and select Always.

You now have an Always condition. We now need to update the counters CounterX and CounterY with the latest player position from the Text Adventure Map object:

4. Move across to the right until you are directly under the CounterX object.

5. Right-click the CounterX action box and select Set Counter.

6. Click on the Retrieve Data from Object button, right-click on the Text Adventure Map object, and then Current Location | X.

7. Click on the OK button.

We now need to do the same for CounterY.

8. Move across from the Always condition until you are directly under the CounterY object.

9. Right-click on the CounterY action box and select Set Counter.

10. Click on the Retrieve Data from Object button, right-click on the Text Adventure Map object, and then Current Location | Y.

For spacing purposes, create another blank comment line on event line 61 after the Always condition.

You can see the event and actions in Figure 5.13.

New Location Group

The purpose of the New Location Group is to set up the room descriptions; if the room hasn't been visited before, set the long description; if it has been visited before, then set the text to the Rich Edit object to be the short description.

First we need to create a group and ensure that it is disabled at start, as we will call this from the code when we need it to run.

1. Right-click on the New condition number on event line 63.

2. Select Insert | A group of events.

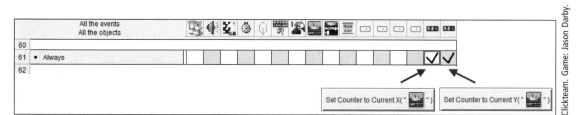

Figure 5.13
The Always condition and its actions.

3. In the Group Events dialog box, type the title of the group: **"New Location"**. Ensure the Active When Frame Starts check box is unchecked, and then click on the OK button.

Now we will create an event that will check if the player has previously visited the location.

4. Click on the New condition text in the event in the New location group.

5. Right-click on the Text Adventure Map object and select Player Previously Visited This Location.

Now we will set the short description to the Rich Edit object:

6. Move across from this event line, until you are directly under the Rich Edit object. Right-click the action box and then select Control | Set Text.

7. The Expression Evaluator now appears. To display the short description from the Text Adventure object, click on Retrieve Data from an Object.

8. Right-click on the Text Adventure Map object and then Current Location | Short description.

9. Click on OK in the Expression Evaluator to save the information to the action box.

For the next event, we need to create the same condition as before but negate it.

10. Click on the New condition text in the event in the New Location group, which should be event line 65.

11. Right-click on the Text Adventure Map object and select Player Previously Visited This Location.

12. Now you have the condition in event line 65, right-click on it and select Negate.

We can now create the two actions that are to set the long description to the Rich Text object and then tell the Text Adventure Map object that we have now visited this location:

13. Move across from event line 65 until you are directly under the Rich Text object then select Control | Set Text.

14. Click on the Retrieve Data from an Object button and then right-click on the Text Adventure Map object and choose Current Location | Long description.

15. Click on the OK button in the Expression Evaluator to save the data to the Event editor.

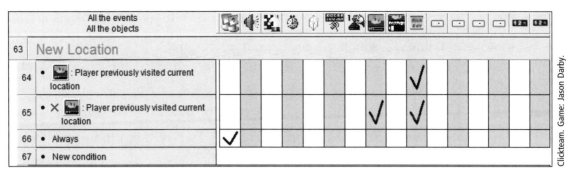

Figure 5.14
The New Location group events.

Now the second action:

16. Move across from event line 65 until you are directly under the Text Adventure Map object.

17. Right-click the action box and select Tile at Current Location | Mark Visited.

Finally, we need an event, which will always run when this group is enabled, to disable the group.

18. Click on the New condition text in event line 66.

19. Select the Special object and choose Always.

Now we need to disable the group:

20. Move across from the Always condition on event line 66 until you are directly under the Storyboard Controls object, right-click the action box, and select Group of Events | Deactivate.

21. When the dialog box appears, choose (2)–New Location and then click on the OK button.

To complete this code, ensure there is a blank comment line on event line 68.

You will see the conditions as shown in Figure 5.14.

Direction Not Visited 2

Earlier in this chapter we created some code, but we couldn't complete the code because we needed to activate a group called New Location. As we hadn't created the group at that time, we couldn't put in the required code.

Now that we have created our New Location group, we can go back and activate it.

1. Go to event line 53 which should be an event that checks if Btn_North is clicked. Move across to the right of it until you are directly under the Special Conditions object.

2. Right-click on the action box and select Group of Events | Activate.

3. When the Activate dialog box appears, choose (2)–New Location and click on the OK button.

4. We need to do the same for the other directions, so drag and drop the action to enable the group into event lines 55, 57, and 59.

Game Over

Our final bit of code is to check when the player has moved into a location that is a game-ending location. This can be the final area that the player has escaped, an area where the player dies, or an area where the player loses and cannot go any farther.

For the next three events, we need to check a particular location that the player has entered. Each location is a place where the player ends the game. First, we will create the events and then look at the actions. We will then need to compare two general values: the player's current location and a particular map location that we know will end the game.

1. Click on the New condition text in event line 69.

2. Right-click on the Special object and select Compare Two General Values.

3. The Expression Evaluator appears. The number 0 will be selected in the first box. Click on the Retrieve Data from an Object button.

4. Right-click on the Text Adventure Map object and select Current Location | X.

5. The second box contains a 0, which is fine, so click on the OK button.

Now we need to add a second condition on the same event line:

6. Right-click on the condition you just added in event line 69, then select Insert.

7. Right-click on the Special object and select Compare Two General Values.

8. The Expression Evaluator appears. The number 0 will be selected in the first box. Click on the Retrieve Data from an Object button.

9. Right-click on the Text Adventure Map object and select Current Location | Y.

10. The second box contains a 0. Replace it with a **2** and click the OK button.

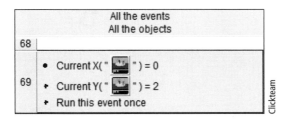

Figure 5.15
Checking the player's current location.

Finally we need to add a condition to the event to ensure this only runs once when this is true:

11. Right-click on the condition you have just added in event line 69, then select Insert.

12. Select the Special object and then Limit conditions | Run This Event Once.

You will now see the event as shown in 5.15.

We now need to copy and paste this condition twice so that we can set up two other location checks:

1. Click once on the event line number 69 to highlight it.

2. Press Ctrl+C to copy it to the clipboard.

3. Press Ctrl+V twice to paste it twice into the Event editor.

Now we need to edit the numbers in event lines 70 and 71 to represent the correct locations we want to check.

4. If you double-click the conditions for the numbers in event lines 70 and 71, it will bring up the Expression Evaluator, allowing you to edit the numbers.

5. For event line 70, X should equal 3, Y should equal 2; for event line 71, X should equal 2 and Y should equal 4.

You will know if you have this right if your conditions look like Figure 5.16.

6. Now we need to create the actions for these conditions. First we need to tell the game that the area the player has moved into is a dead zone, which means the player is unable to move in any direction.

7. From event line 69, move across until you are directly under the Text Adventure Map object. Right-click on the action box and choose Tile at Current Location | Set Dead Zone.

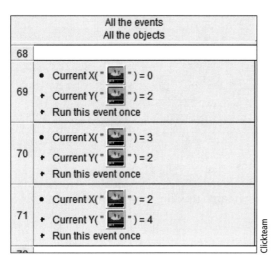

Figure 5.16
The conditions to check locations.

8. You can drag and drop this to the action box on event lines 70 and 71 under the Text Adventure Map object.

Now we need to update the text in the Rich Edit box.

9. Move across from event line 69 until you are directly under the Rich Edit Text object, and right-click the action box and choose Control | Set text.

10. When the Expression Evaluator appears, click on the Retrieve Data from Object button and then right-click on the Text Adventure Messages object. Select Get Message.

11. A piece of text will appear in the Expression Evaluator, and you will see >ID< is highlighted. Replace this with **"GameOver"** (include the quotation marks). Click on the OK button.

12. You can drag and drop this action to event line 70.

Event lines 69 and 70 represent a rockfall and being re-captured, so the GameOver message is the most appropriate message for this event. Event line 71 and its location represents when the player has escaped. At the start of the game, we set up two messages; we need to specify the second message that tells the player he has won and the game is over.

1. Move across from event line 71 until you are directly under the Rich Edit Text object. Right-click the action box and select Control | Set text.

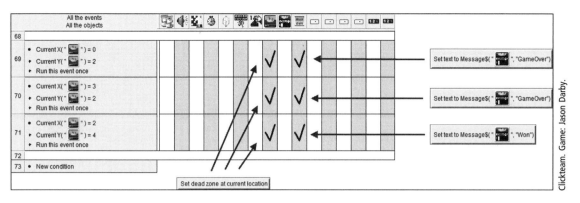

Figure 5.17
The final events to check for the end of the game.

2. When the Expression Evaluator appears, click on the Retrieve Data from Object button and then right-click on the Text Adventure Messages object and select Get Message.

3. Select the >ID< part of the text and replace it with **"Won"**.

4. Click on OK to save to the Event editor.

Your final events and actions should look like Figure 5.17.

CHAPTER SUMMARY

In this chapter, we learned the basics of the Text Adventure Map object and how to create our game worlds using a grid. We showed how you can navigate around the world and how to provide messages to the player.

We also showed how to display different messages depending on the room that the player had entered and how to end the game.

In the next chapter, we will be looking at some more complex concepts and how to improve your text adventure games.

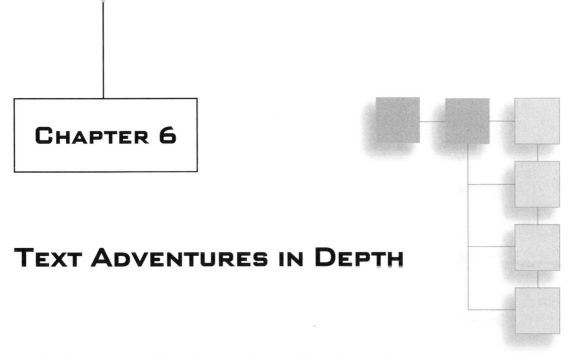

CHAPTER 6

TEXT ADVENTURES IN DEPTH

In this chapter, we will be taking a closer look at the text features that you can add in to your own text adventure games. We will be using a number of simple example files to show you how to create some of the features that you would see in any text-based adventure game.

Note

In Chapter 16, we'll cover a number of example files and editors that can be used to save and load data.

SIMPLE TEXT-ENTRY DIRECTIONS

In the *Dungeon of Text* game in Chapter 5, players were able to move in different directions using directional buttons, but to be a true text adventure game, we need to create a game that allows a player to move in a particular direction if he types "Go North" or "Go N" into an edit box.

In this example, we will show you how to read basic text and make the player move in that particular direction. In *Dungeon of Text*, players used buttons to move in the selected direction. We will use this code as a starting point. At this stage, our goal is to add a new method of movement. We have created an example file called Chp6_Directions.mfa that has all of the code ready for you to use.

We have added a simple edit box that will provide the area where the player can enter text, and we have added a String object to hold the string that the player enters. This allows us to clear the original edit box of text and then compare the text within

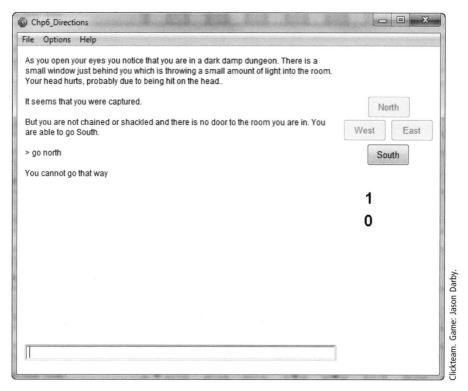

Figure 6.1
Text displayed when you type in a direction using "go north."

the String object with a particular direction such as "Go North". Sometimes it is a good idea to use multiple objects to move data around, as the edit box in this case is our user's view and so we don't want the text to stay in the edit box after he has pressed the Enter key.

Run the application so you can understand how it works:

1. Type in the words **go north**.

2. You should see the text as shown in Figure 6.1.

3. Now type in **go south**. Since this is a direction the player can move in, you will see the text as shown in Figure 6.2.

You will notice that when you have typed in a command, it starts with the character ">", which means that it is a player-entered command. This allows you to show the user what he has entered and allows you to break up the text. We have also added a few newlines to space out the text.

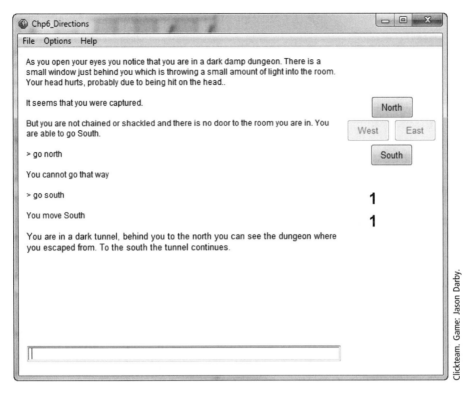

Figure 6.2
Text displayed when you type in the direction using "go south."

Note

It is very important that you break up your text so that the player can tell the difference between the game text and the text that is entered. In this example we used line breaks and a ">", but you could also use colored text, or even a separate window for each set of text.

Note

The directions that you type in are case sensitive.

Simple Direction Code

We have modified our original example file from Chapter 5 with the following new features:

- **Set messages:** Sets up a number of messages to advise users when they have moved in a particular direction and when they cannot.

- **Press Enter:** Checks for when the player has modified an edit box and has pressed the Enter key.

- **Text-entry directions:** Presents a player with either success or failure messages when he types a particular direction using the edit box (for example, he types a word and then presses Enter). The success message will be followed by the room description of the new location, while the failure message will await the next player's input.

- **Scrolling Rich Edit box:** Reduces issues with too much text on-screen. (We added a simple event that scrolls the text.)

Now that you have an overview of what is involved in the code in this updated file, let's take a closer look.

Set Messages

In the Text Adventure Messages object, you can set up a number of messages (replies) to an input. To create a message you need to specify a unique ID, which will be referenced in your code, and a state. This state is a numeric value, allowing you to create on/off states of a message. You will also need to enter the text of the message for that state.

On event line 2 under the Text Adventure Messages object, you can see a number of message actions have been created as shown in Figure 6.3. You can see that we have created four message IDs: one for each direction and two message states for each ID, one of which says you cannot move in a particular direction and another that lets you know that you have moved. We can reduce the number of actions by creating a single "You cannot move in that direction" message rather than having a message for each invalid direction.

- Set message "GONORTH" under state 0 to "You cannot go that way"
- Set message "GOEAST" under state 0 to "You cannot go that way"
- Set message "GOSOUTH" under state 0 to "You cannot go that way"
- Set message "GOWEST" under state 0 to "You cannot go that way"
- Set message "GONORTH" under state 1 to "You move North"
- Set message "GOEAST" under state 1 to "You move East"
- Set message "GOSOUTH" under state 1 to "You move South"
- Set message "GOWEST" under state 1 to "You move West"

Clickteam

Figure 6.3
The different messages used to reply to the user.

Note

You can also use message states and arguments to help reduce the amount of text messages that you need to enter, allowing you to specify "Error" messages. We will cover this shortly.

Pressing Enter

On event line 73, we have created two conditions: the first checks if the edit box where the player types in instructions has been modified, and secondly if he has pressed the Enter key. If both of these conditions are met, then the following actions will be run:

- **Set text to the Rich Edit box:** In the Rich Edit object (the contents area), create two newlines, which will create a line space between the old text and the new text. It will then add a ">" sign on the line to signify to the player that this text was something he has typed in, followed by the text from the edit box. So if I type "hello" in the edit box and then press Return, the text will then appear as ">Hello" in the content area of the screen.

- **Set entered text to String object:** You will use a String object to temporarily store the text that was entered by the player in the edit box so that when you delete the text (which you will delete after the player has pressed Enter), you can still check what the player has entered.

- **Reset the Edit box:** Now that you have copied away what the player has entered, you can reset the edit entry box by entering two quotation marks, which is effectively blanking the current contents.

You can see the actions for this event in Figure 6.4.

Text-Entry Directions

There are two events for each direction: one that checks for the player entering text for a direction that is currently available and another event that checks if the player is unable to move in that direction.

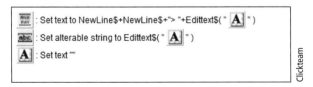

Figure 6.4
The actions to set the entered text to the content area.

Let's take a look at the first of these events (lines 77, 80, 83, 86). In this example, we will be looking at event line 77.

- **Check entered string:** The first thing you do is check the text that was entered into the edit box and compare it to the text "go north".

- **Can move north:** Selecting the Text Adventure Map object enables you to check if the player can move north from the current map location.

The actions for this event can be classified as follows:

- **Go north text:** You want to tell the player that when he is able to move in a particular direction, he will see the message "You Move North." Surround this text with newlines so that space will be added between the entered text and any room description text.

- **Set string to "":** The string was checked if it matched the words "go north" since you are in the actions for this event, which would mean that the conditions were successful. Therefore, this is a good time to reset the string object to ""; otherwise, the condition will loop and continue to run while the string has the text stored in it.

- **Activate group:** Activate the New Location group, which is old legacy code that tells the game when the player has visited a location.

- **Move in direction:** This action tells the Text Adventure Map object that the player has moved north.

You can see these actions in Figure 6.5.

Note

The events mentioned will be the same for event lines 80, 83, and 86 but will have the other locations mentioned.

Figure 6.5
The actions for event line 77.

Figure 6.6
The actions that do not allow a player to move in a particular direction.

The second event that details if the player cannot move in a direction has two conditions:

- **Check Entered String:** Does a check to see if the player entered "go north".
- **Cannot Move North:** From the current player's location, checking the Text Adventure Map object, the player is not able to move north.

There are only two actions for this event: to set the String object to "" and set the Rich Edit object to the message text indicating when the player cannot go in that particular direction. You can see the two actions in Figure 6.6.

Scrolling

Our final bit of code is used to scroll the Rich Text object when a particular amount of text has been entered. This will ensure that you always have the text on-screen for the user to read without him having to scroll down.

We use the Always condition to always run the action to obtain the line count of the Rich Edit object and then scroll to that line plus two lines. You can see this action in Figure 6.7.

Simple Direction Issues

The biggest issue with the implementation of this system is that you will need to think of all the different terms the player might enter and then code them, which could end up being very time-consuming in terms of coding.

For example, the player types:

go north

Figure 6.7
The scrolling action.

This would work fine as your text comparison checks the term "go north," but if the player were to type Go North or go n, then it would fail to work. You would have to add an OR condition that would check all possible combinations within the code.

Note

This example shows you that it is possible to create your own system using the objects for handling text entry, but you can also see that, even though the code is pretty straightforward to create, it can get unwieldy quickly. Ultimately trying to handle all of the different responses from users could require a lot of work.

Using States and Arguments

You can reduce the code you have written for specifying multiple directions at the start of the game by using message states and arguments. We used eight messages: four to let the player know that he has moved in a direction and another four to advise the player that he cannot move in a particular direction.

You can use another method for setting a message by combining states and arguments. If you consider for a moment the messages that you want to relay to the player when he types in go north, go east, go south, or go west.

- You cannot go north.
- You go north.

So if the player were to enter "go north," he will receive one of these messages: "You cannot go north" or "You go north."

Using the code earlier in this chapter, you would have to set up a message for each direction and each possible type of message (for example, you can or cannot move in that direction). If you look at both messages, they have one common set of text:

- go north

The player will be entering the direction into the edit box, and so we can create two messages containing the text:

- You cannot
- You

You can then use message arguments to fill in the gaps, which will be the "go north" or other direction. This means you can reduce the number of messages to just two.

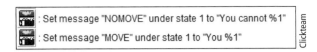

Figure 6.8
The two actions for setting a message with an argument.

We have created a file called Chp6_Directions2.mfa that contains the new code, so let's look at the first, which is a set of actions to create these two messages as shown in Figure 6.8.

The actions are set under the second event, under the Messages object. We use the set message under a given state. We are asked the following information:

- **Unique ID of the message:** This must be a unique identifier for our message; you use two actions as seen in Figure 6.8.

- **Numeric state:** You can specify a message based on a number, which means you can create common messages and specify each one to a number under the same message ID.

- **Text of message:** You then enter the text of the message and enter an argument. To specify an argument, use the %number (i.e., %1, %2).

Note

You can think of an argument as a stored variable that will be replaced at a later stage.

The other major change we have made to our code is for the movement directions: these are event lines 77 to 87. You can see an example of the actions in event line 77, which checks if the player can or cannot move north in Figures 6.9 and 6.10, respectively.

In Figure 6.9, you can see the first action we create is to set a message argument 1 to "go north". In the second action, you create two newlines in the Rich Edit object and

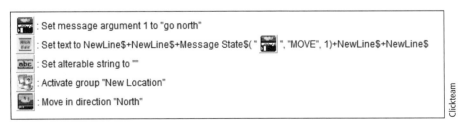

Figure 6.9
Actions for moving north.

Figure 6.10
Actions when the player cannot move north.

then place the contents of message MOVE with a state of 1 (which you created in event line 2). You then create two additional newlines to insert a space after the text that will appear in the content window.

In Figure 6.10, you can see that the second action is setting the messages object argument 1 to "go north". The third action is creating two newlines in the Rich Text object window and then placing the text from the Message object with an ID of NOMOVE with a state of 1.

Remember that we set up the original IDs and states in event line 2, and then we are forcing an argument into that message.

Using the Words Object

In the previous examples, we have been using text comparisons to check if the word that has been entered matches what the user has inputted. Though this is a perfectly good way of seeing what the user has entered, it is not very scalable and certainly cannot cope with the different types of words that could be entered by the user.

Think of the following entries the player could type for moving within the game world:

■ Go north

■ Go n

■ Move north

■ Move n

■ Walk north

■ Walk n

■ Run north

■ Run n

The problem is further compounded when using objects:

- Look at apple
- View apple
- Eat apple
- Destroy apple
- Throw apple
- Clean apple
- Wash apple

As you can imagine, the events could start to become quite complicated as you will need to work out every single combination of wording that the player could use, but using the Text Adventure Words object can make this process far less overwhelming.

We have a number of core components that we will be looking at in the next example file:

- **Categories:** Containers for sets of words. You could create a container for movement, looking, eating, and drinking.
- **Words:** Keywords that describe an object or nouns.
- **Phrases:** Phrases are sets of words that describe an event in the game (Eat apple, Go north, and so on).
- **Actions:** The word (verb) that is used to describe the player's action, such as go, eat, drink, and so on.

Note

A phrase contains both words and actions.

Note

Verbs are words that tell MMF2 what your character is currently doing in the game and are typically common words such as eat, run, sleep, walk, and talk. In the Text Adventure Words object, these are part of a phrase, and we use the term *actions*.

Note

Nouns are the items/objects and things in your adventure, so we could be describing a place, animal, a person, direction, or an object such as an apple. These are called *words* in the Text Adventure Words object.

In the following example called Chp6_test.mfa, we have created a simple example that shows the message that displays when the player types the words "look north" (or any other direction).

Let's look at the different things the player could type if he wanted to look in a particular direction:

- Look n
- Look north
- Look e
- Look east
- Look south
- Look s
- Look west
- Look w

The first word in this group is the action "look." You could have multiple actions that achieve the same aim; in this case, you could have also used "peer" or "stare."

The second bit of text is the word, and in this case they are all directions. So we can create a single category called DIRECTIONS, which will contain all of these words.

Finally, the combination of the action and the word creates the phrase.

Load the example file Chp6_test.mfa in the Frame editor to see the current objects on-screen as shown in Figure 6.11:

- **Text Adventure Map object:** This object is used to create the world in which the player will move around. In this example, we have created a blank 5/5 world.

- **Text Adventure Words object:** This object connects to the Text Adventure Map object and provides us with the ability to add phrases, words, and actions.

- **Edit boxes:** We have two edit boxes: one to contain the user entry and the other to contain the last user entry, which is because once the player presses the Enter key, the first text entry disappears. In a real game, the second entry would be hidden from the player's view.

- **String object:** This contains some text that explains what is currently happening and is a great way of testing that your code is working correctly by having something on-screen update. You can always remove this string from the screen or hide it when you release the game.

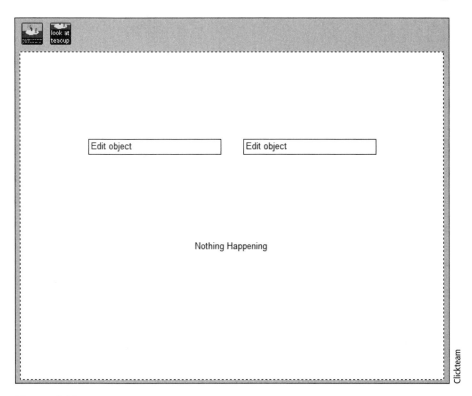

Figure 6.11
The Frame editor of our example.

You can see the code in the Event editor in Figure 6.12.

The code is split into three key tasks:

- **Initialization:** As with any game, we need to set up any variables and values.
- **Text input check/parsing:** This part of the code will check that the player has modified the text box and then has pressed the Enter key.
- **Input comparison:** Here we will compare the text that the player has entered against our database of words/phrases and actions.

We will now take a closer look at the code, starting with the Start of Frame event in event line 1. You can see the actions in Figure 6.13.

The first action is creating a phrase and action. We have created a phrase called:

Look $DIRECTION

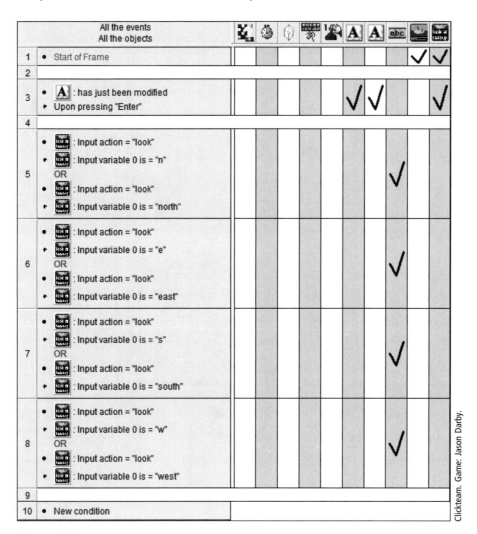

Figure 6.12
The code events.

The phrase is made up of two parts: the first is the word that describes the action part of the phrase and the second is a category called DIRECTION. Anything that begins with a $ sign is a category. So, in this case, if the player types in "look" and then a word that is contained in the DIRECTION group, this will be true.

We decided to use "look" as the action ID name. We could have called it anything we wanted, but you should try to give it a name that is easy to remember. You can see from the actions that we have created many words in the category DIRECTION for all possible combinations the player might use when entering direction information.

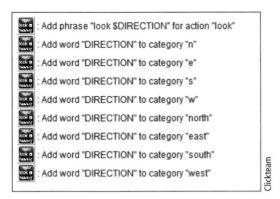

Figure 6.13
The Start of Frame actions

- To add a phrase, right-click under the Text Adventure Words object and select Phrases | Add Phrase for Action.
- To add a word to a category, you need to right-click under the Text Adventure Words object and then select Dictionary | Add Word to Category.

Note

There is a small display bug in the Text Adventure Words object that states in the Event editor that the action is Add word "DIRECTION" to category "n" for example, but it should display this as Add word "n" to category "DIRECTION".

Event line 3 checks for when the player has made a change to the edit box and has pressed the Enter key. There is a new action within this event that is really important for the Words object. See Figure 6.14 for the actions.

The first two actions you may recall from previous examples. We are copying the text entered by the player into a second edit box, which will be used by us to check what the player has entered, and we then delete the contents in the original edit object.

The third action is new and is used in the Text Adventure Words object to tell the program when to check the text that has been entered by reading (parsing) the text.

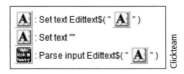

Figure 6.14
The actions for the Enter Text event.

We parse the second edit box to see if the text entered matches any of the text entered in the first event.

The final set of conditions checks if any action is found to be true (parsed from the edit box) and if any input variables are found to match. An input variable is a noun, and the value is the word found in the phrase. You can check for multiple variables in the phrase to see if they match. So in event line 5, you can see we have an input action of "look" and we are checking if the letter "n" or "north" has been entered. The only action for the event is setting the String object to advise you what text has been matched.

1. Run the application and then type in **look at apple**. You will notice nothing happens.

2. Type in "**look n**", and some text appears.

3. Type in **"look south"**, and the string text changes.

Using this code, we can quickly build up actions that use the same variables in $DIRECTIONS. For example, the file Chp6_test2.mfa contains an example file that also uses the action "go" and uses the same $DIRECTIONS variables. All we have had to do is add a phrase at the start of frame and copy and slightly amend the code.

OBJECTS

Objects are a key part of and are a requirement for any good adventure game. Objects can range from those that you would expect to see in the real world such as food, cutlery, keys, books, electronic devices, to the more strange and bizarre, such as wooden cubes and paper circles. The objects in your world do not have to be real objects, but if they are not, then you must ensure that the objects' descriptions are sufficient enough to provide the player with some idea of what they are.

Objects allow you to create puzzles, such as having to find a key to enter the wizards' spell room or to cast a spell. You may use objects to eat and drink food items, which can improve your health and increase any character attributes such as skill or speed.

You should always place objects around your game world; some should be visible and some invisible. Having characters and situations reveal additional objects to players will help your game be more entertaining to those who like to search every corner of the game world and replay it multiple times.

Remember to place essential and non-essential objects around the game world. Doing this will ensure that the player will not know which objects are important to his

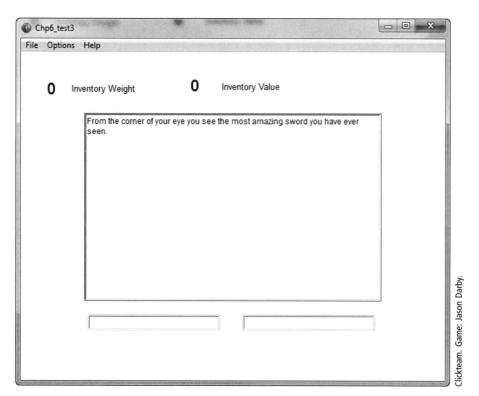

Figure 6.15
An example program using objects.

quest. The weight of the objects can also limit the number of objects a player can carry, which will force the player to think about what items he really needs rather than picking up every object he can find.

In the following example, we will show you a simple example for how to pick up an object that is available in the game world, as well as show you how you can use an object's properties such as weight and cost values.

You can see a screenshot of our example file in Figure 6.15. In this image, you can see the following objects and their uses:

- **Weight counter:** A counter that will be used to store the total amount of objects in the player's inventory.

- **Value counter:** A counter that will be used to store the total value of the objects in the player's inventory.

- **Rich Edit object:** The output window used to display messages about the world, objects, and events taking place in the example file.

- **Edit box:** The edit box on the left is for the player's input; type the commands in this edit box.

- **Edit box 2:** This edit box is used to contain the last inputted text entry. We will then do text comparisons on the text here. We have done the same process throughout this chapter so that you can remove any text from the player's entry box as soon as he has pressed the Return key.

We are also using two objects in this example that cannot be seen in Figure 6.15: the Text Adventure Map object that is used for detailing our objects and the Text Adventure Words object that allows us to check for user input.

Note

The Text Adventure Map object is case sensitive.

Objects Code

We have created an example file for you to explore that is called Chp6_test3.mfa. Load this file and take a look at the code in the Event editor.

The code for this example is relatively simple. You may recognize some of it from other example files in this chapter.

You can see the full code in Figure 6.16. We will now explore the code and point out the important bits that you will need to understand before implementing objects in your own games. Before we break down each bit of code, you can see a simple flow of what the code is doing in Figure 6.17.

- **Initialization:** Setting up all of the basic objects' configuration and properties.

- **Is text modified?:** The example file will wait for the player to enter some text and will only work once the player has pressed the Enter key.

- **Check entry and react:** Once we are sure that the player has pressed Enter, we activate a selection of code to read and identify what the user has typed and then take the appropriate actions.

As with many MMF2 programs, we start off with a Start of Frame event that contains all of our initialization code. You can see the actions for this event in Figure 6.18.

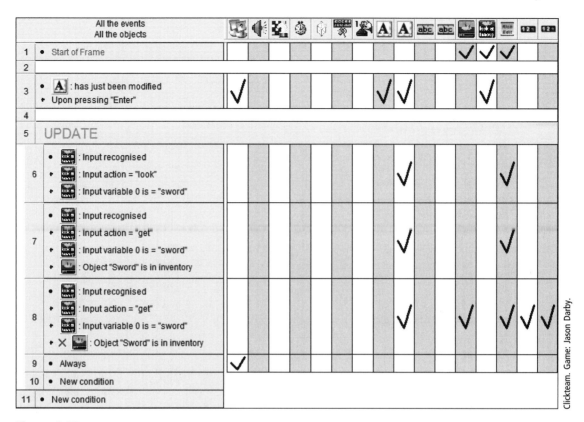

The following table represents the code shown in Figure 6.16:

	All the events / All the objects																	
1	• Start of Frame												✓	✓	✓			
2																		
3	• A : has just been modified ◆ Upon pressing "Enter"	✓						✓	✓			✓						
4																		
5	UPDATE																	
6	• : Input recognised ◆ : Input action = "look" ◆ : Input variable 0 is = "sword"								✓					✓				
7	• : Input recognised ◆ : Input action = "get" ◆ : Input variable 0 is = "sword" ◆ : Object "Sword" is in inventory								✓					✓				
8	• : Input recognised ◆ : Input action = "get" ◆ : Input variable 0 is = "sword" ◆ ✕ : Object "Sword" is in inventory								✓		✓		✓	✓	✓			
9	• Always	✓																
10	• New condition																	
11	• New condition																	

Clickteam. Game: Jason Darby.

Figure 6.16
Code for our object's example.

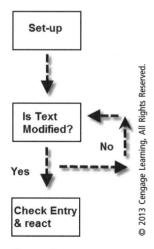

© 2013 Cengage Learning, All Rights Reserved.

Figure 6.17
The flow of the example file.

Figure 6.18
The actions for the Start of Frame event.

Let's explore what we are doing in this initialization:

- **Words object connection:** When using the Text Adventure Words object and the Text Adventure Map objects together, we must first link the two together. To do this, right-click on the Words object action box and select Set TA Map object. In the Expression Evaluator, click the Retrieve Data from an Object button, right-click the TA Map object, and select Get Fixed Value.

- **Create world:** We have created a simple game area called "World," which is 20 by 20 in size.

- **Create object:** In action three, we create an object using the Text Adventure Map object action box and selecting Objects | Add Object. We then enter the object name in the Expression Evaluator.

- **Place object:** Now that we have created the object, we can place it in the world.

Event line 3 contains code to check when the player has just typed text into the edit box and has pressed the Enter key. We have four actions for this event, which can be seen in Figure 6.19.

- **Set text to edit box:** As we have with the other example files in this chapter, we take the user inputted text and place in its own Edit object, which we will then use to check against our phrases and actions.

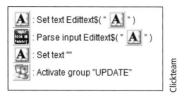

Figure 6.19
Four actions to check for input.

- **Parse input:** We use the Text Adventure Words Object Parse action to prepare it to check the contents of the edit box (this is the second edit box where we have copied the contents of the user entry).

- **Remove text:** We blank out the text entered in the first edit box, so the user can enter a new string if he wishes to.

- **Activate group:** We are now ready to enable a special group that will be used to handle the text comparisons and phrases. Once this is complete, we can disable the group and wait for the user's input again.

We now move onto the group called UPDATE. This group was created to ensure our code runs properly. As MMF2 reads the events really quickly, it is possible for multiple events to be true at the same time and run, causing issues with your code. One of the best ways to prevent this from happening is to restrict when and how your code is run. Using the Update group, we will only check the user's input when he has pressed the Enter key. Once the three events in the group have been checked, it will then disable the group, meaning that the player will need to enter a new string in the edit box and press Enter to allow this code to run.

We have three events:

- **Event line 6:** We need to check that the input is recognized, which means the phrase that the player has entered has been understood by the Text Adventure Words object. We then check if the player has entered any phrases for the action "look." We then check any words that have been typed to see if they match the word "sword."

- **Event line 7:** The second event of the three is checking if the player has typed in the action "get" and the word "sword." It also does a check to see if the object is already in the player's inventory. If this event is true, we will post a message telling the user that he already has the object.

- **Event line 8:** The third event checks if the user has typed "get" and "sword," as well as confirming that the object isn't in the inventory. It will then add the object to the inventory and calculate the inventories' total weight and cost.

■ **Event line 9:** We will always disable this group when the code gets to event line 9, which means that the code in the Update group will only run once when the group is activated.

Note

The order of events is very important. If event lines 7 and 8 were transposed, both would be true and the code would be run, meaning that you would get two messages, one telling you that you have added the object to your inventory and the other telling you that you already have the object. As we have this code in a group that is disabled by its last event, we know that each line is only run once. We also know that once an object is in the inventory, the event in line 7 will not be true the next time the player types "get."

The actions for each of these events can be seen in Figures 6.20, 6.21, and 6.22. You will be familiar with the actions in Figures 6.20 and 6.21, but in Figure 6.22, there are a few new actions we haven't used yet. The actions in Figure 6.22 are as follows:

■ **Set text:** An action to set the text of the Rich Edit object.

■ **Blank text:** We blank the original edit box where the user typed her commands.

Figure 6.20
The actions for event line 6.

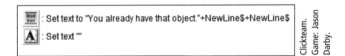

Figure 6.21
The actions for event line 7.

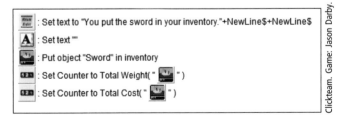

Figure 6.22
The actions for event line 8.

- **Inventory:** We place the object that is in the game world into the player's inventory.

- **Set counter 1:** We set our first counter to the total weight of the inventory objects. This action is available under the Text Adventure Map object.

- **Set counter 2:** We set the total cost of the inventory items into the counter.

CHAPTER SUMMARY

In this chapter, we looked at some ways of improving our code to make more complex text adventure games, including using improved text entry, phrases and actions, and inventory objects.

Even though we have used these concepts to introduce you to how you can program these in to your game, these methods require lots of code to be written if used for a large and complex game. We will be looking at the saving and loading of data in Chapters 9 and 16, which will help drastically reduce the amount of code needed to write your games.

In the next chapter, we will be making a game that will enable you to be a character from the Wild West. This will be a more complex game that will use some of the ideas talked about in this chapter. You will also see how you can add graphics.

CHAPTER 7

GRAPHIC TEXT ADVENTURES

In this chapter, we will look at how you can add graphics to your text adventures, and in fact how you can add graphics to any of the games that you create within MMF2. The type of game you decide to make will determine the method you will use to store and display the graphics.

GRAPHICS OBJECTS

There are a number of graphical objects in MMF2, but we are going to cover the most common ones that you may use on a regular basis. We have already covered objects briefly in Chapter 2. Here we describe particular objects and why you might want to use one over another:

- **Active:** If you have a graphic that you want to animate, move, or change direction on-screen, such as a game sprite or animated image, then an Active object is a good choice. The Active is a game-based graphic object, so you would most commonly use it as a player character, or enemy spaceship, or special effect. The Active object will look out for collisions, which can be a processor-intensive process when running many of them on-screen at once. (It still requires a condition to trigger any code, but it still needs to do a lot of math processing to see if it is happening.) You can use Active objects for backgrounds and general graphics, such as animated buttons. If you were going to create a simple image on-screen for your text or graphic adventures, perhaps with some animation, then this would be a good choice. If you want to create objects within a point-and-click game or hidden object game, then you would also use an Active object.

- **Active Backdrop:** The Active Backdrop is a background image that can be animated. For example, you could have a scene, such as a castle as a background, with a window, and in that window a character could appear walking past. The most important aspect of the Active Backdrop is that it doesn't generate any collision information (when an object hits another object). This means that it uses less processing power than an Active object at the same size. A Backdrop object always appears at the back of the frame, and so any Active objects will be placed on top of it.

- **Backdrop:** If you have a graphic that you want to sit in the background of your game and not be animated, then the Backdrop object is a possible option. It does not generate any collision information, and if you place any other objects with it, the Backdrop object will always appear at the back.

- **Picture:** The Picture object is useful for loading images off a hard drive. The image will not be animated and is commonly used for displaying single images, or images that are displayed one at a time.

- **Quick Backdrop:** Quick Backdrop objects are useful if you want to place a tiled or gradient image or color, which may be useful for backgrounds and creating sunsets and sky effects. While you may not use it much in adventure games, you might find it useful for creating simple sky/nighttime effects.

Internal and External Images

Determining how you will make and distribute your games will be extremely important when deciding which of the objects you will use for displaying an image in your adventures.

A Graphics object can be internal or external to MMF, which means that the actual graphic image data can be stored within MMF2 or stored externally within a folder.

What does this mean? Well, if you have the full version of MMF2 and the graphics are stored externally, when you compile your game and give someone the executable file, you will also need to give them any external graphics that have been linked to within MMF2. The benefit of external graphics is that if you have a lot of graphics, placing them within MMF2 will increase the size of the executable. Depending on where all your graphics are within MMF2 may mean longer load times.

Having the files externally means that you have to remember to ship the files with the game, but it will mean that the executable for the final application is much smaller and the game will load much quicker.

Deciding whether to have your graphics stored internally or externally actually depends on the size of your graphics and the number of them. There is no problem in using both systems if you need to. You should try different systems and see how long it takes to load and display the data. You can also try alternative methods; the great thing with MMF2 is that there are usually multiple methods for accomplishing the same task, allowing you to choose the best method for your game.

Note

An executable is a term for a file that can be run without additional files installed on your PC. It's a term commonly used in Windows operating systems. When you buy a game or application, it will include an executable, which is the main program that runs the code.

ADDING GRAPHICS

In this section, we will show you how to add images to the different objects. There are many options available to these objects, so make sure you take some time to familiarize yourself with the different conditions, expressions, and actions.

Active Objects

We will start with an Active object, probably the most commonly used graphical object within MMF2.

First let's add it to a blank MMF2 frame:

1. Open MMF2 and check that you are in the Frame editor.

2. Double left-click anywhere in the frame to bring up the Create New Object dialog box. Find the Active object, which can be seen in Figure 7.1, click on it and then click on the OK button.

3. Left-click somewhere on the frame to insert the Active object to add it to the frame (Figure 7.2).

Figure 7.1
The Active object icon.

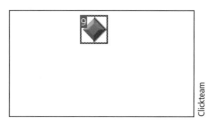

Figure 7.2
The Active object icon inserted into a frame.

You will notice some things immediately about the Active object. First, it's a green diamond. The green diamond is just a default image used as a placeholder for all Active objects. This can be replaced, which we will do shortly. You may also notice that there is a box around the object and a number 9 in the top left-hand corner. The box shows that the object is currently selected, and it will be displaying its properties in the Properties window, while the number represents the object's layer value.

Every time you add an object, it will get a number that indicates the order in which it was added to the frame, but it also signifies if an object should appear in front of or behind another object. An object with a higher number will always appear in front of an object with a lower number.

Note

The object in this example has a number 9 because eight other objects have already been added to the frame.

Active Object Properties

There are some properties that are useful to know about in the Active object. The first set is within the Display Options tab in the Properties window shown in Figure 7.3.

Some of the properties are as follows:

- **Visible at Start:** This will determine if the object will be visible when you first start the frame, which is useful if you want to initially hide the graphic item and only reveal it when the player has completed an action.

- **Save Background:** When an object moves around the screen, the computer has to take a copy of the contents of what the object is moving over, and once the object has moved away, put that content back. When playing a game, this is all seamless and you don't see this happen, but if you uncheck this box, the Active

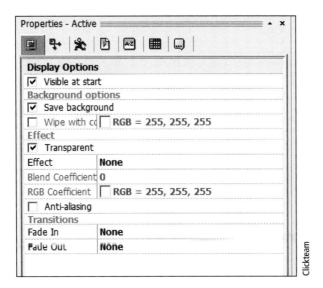

Figure 7.3
The Display Options tab in the Properties window for the Active object.

object will paint itself over the background. In most cases you should leave this as is, but it can be used if you want to create some weird graphical effects.

■ **Transparent:** Transparency is how much you can see through an object. The area around the diamond is transparent because you can see the white background.

■ **Fade In/Fade Out:** If you've ever used Microsoft PowerPoint or video editing software, you are probably already used to adding fades to your creations. A fade is an effect that makes the current object disappear or appear on-screen. There are a number of effects that you can use on objects such as Stretch, Fade, Open, etc.

You can see the properties for the Runtime Options tab in Figure 7.4, and they are described as follows:

■ **Create at Start:** If you want an object to appear at the start of the game, check this box. If you uncheck the box, you will need to remember to create the object through events. If you won't be using this feature in the short term, you might choose to uncheck it to save memory.

■ **Destroy Object If Too Far from Frame:** The white area on the Frame editor is the visible area, though if an object moves too far from this area, you can elect to destroy it. If you do, then you will no longer be able to run any conditions or

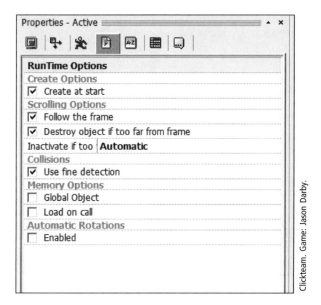

Figure 7.4
The runtime options for the active object.

actions that contain this object while the game is running because it will no longer be available. If you are finished with a graphical object, it is a good idea to destroy it because you will save memory.

- **Use Fine Detection:** An option common to Active objects, Use Fine Detection will define whether MMF2 uses pixel precision to work out collisions with another object or a hidden box. Fine detection is more accurate for collisions, but it also takes up more time for MMF2 to verify if it is true or not. If you are having issues with performance, uncheck this property on objects that don't require pixel precision.

Loading an Image

We will now load a single image into the Active object:

1. Double-click on the green diamond to load the Picture editor.

2. Click on the white piece of paper in the top left-hand corner of the Picture editor to clear out the green diamond.

3. Click on the Import button, which is the second icon along on the top row of the Picture editor. From the Open dialog box that will appear, find a graphic image on your hard drive, such as BMP or PNG, single-click on it, and then click on the Open button.

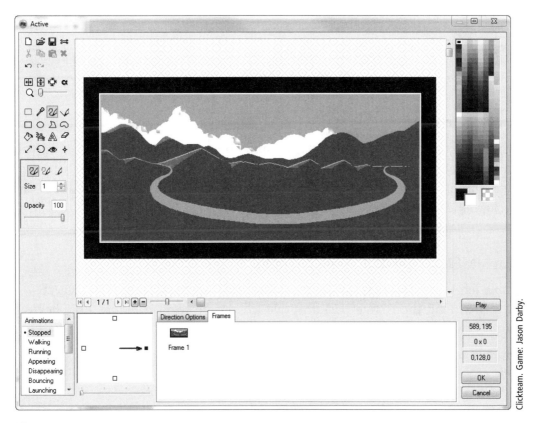

Clickteam. Game: Jason Darby.

Figure 7.5
An image imported into the Active object.

4. You will see an Import Options box. Because we are only importing a single image, click on OK.

5. You can now see the image loaded into the Picture editor as shown in Figure 7.5.

6. Click on the OK button to save it to the Frame editor.

You have now imported a single image into an active object.

Note

While you are in the Picture editor, you must click on the OK button to save your changes. Clicking on the Cancel button will cause any changes you made to be lost.

Note

There are many options available for the Active object, so it's well worth the time to check them out in the Event editor.

Active Backdrop

We will now create a simple active backdrop and animation. In this example, we will display a background and then within a window have a small object move across it. It's quite a simplistic effect, but it should show you what you need to do to create an active background.

First, let's add it to a blank MMF2 frame:

1. Open MMF2 and check that you are in the Frame editor.

2. Double left-click anywhere in the frame to bring up the Create New Object dialog box. Find the Active Backdrop, which can be seen in Figure 7.6, click on it, and then click on the OK button.

3. Left-click somewhere on the frame to insert the Active object. You can see the result of adding it to the frame in Figure 7.7.

You can see the Settings Properties in Figure 7.8. This Active Backdrop uses internal graphics and stores the graphics within the object.

Figure 7.6
The Active Backdrop object icon.

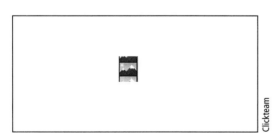

Figure 7.7
The Active Backdrop object placed on the Frame editor.

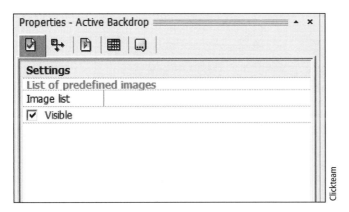

Clickteam

Figure 7.8
The Active Backdrop property sheet.

In Figure 7.8, you can see an image list option, which is where you will load your images in.

4. Click on the white box opposite the text Image List in the Properties window for the Active Backdrop. A small button with three dots appears. Click on it to load a special version of the Picture editor.

The Picture editor has many of the features of the normal picture editor for Active objects, except that it doesn't have any Animation editor, and so you must call any animation frames via the Event editor.

Let's now load up a number of images into the Picture editor with subtle differences and then create an animation.

1. The Active Backdrop Picture editor will currently be open and it will show a checkerboard with a single frame. Click on the Import button to import a graphic image. This will bring up the Open dialog box.

If you have downloaded the support files for this book, then you will be able to locate these files through the dialog box.

2. You will need to select ActiveBackdrop1.png and then click on Open.

3. You will now see the image in the Import Options dialog box. Because we've given these files similar names with only a single number being different, we can import as an animation, thus saving us from having to do this process for every single file.

4. Click on Import as Animation and the Animation Mode Options will become enabled as shown in Figure 7.9.

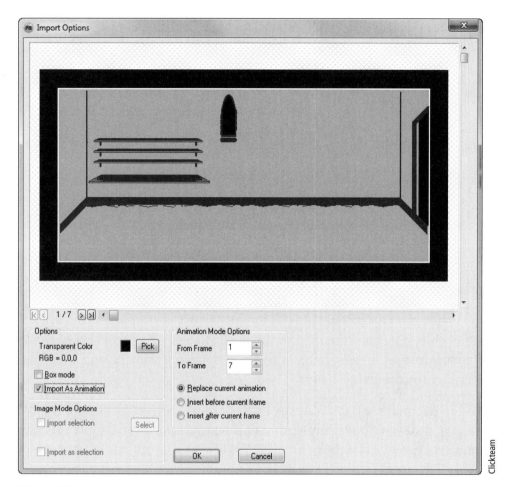

Figure 7.9
The Import Options dialog box.

5. Click on OK to import the images.

6. You will now be back at the Active Backdrop Picture editor screen. If you click on each individual frame, you will see a white object move across the window that represents a simple moon moving across the sky (but it could have been stars, etc.). Click on OK to save to the Frame editor.

Now we need to create the code for the Active Backdrop:

7. Click on the Event Editor button and you will see a blank Event editor.

8. Click on the New condition text, and then right-click on the Timer object.

9. Click on Every.

10. A Timer dialog box appears, with one second already configured to mean that this condition will be true every second. For the purposes of this example this is fine, so click on the OK button.

Now it's time to create the action:

11. Move across from the Every condition until you are directly under the Active Backdrop object.

12. Right-click the Action box and select Set Image.

You are now required to specify an image slot from the image frames that you added in the Active Backdrop. As we want to show each image one at a time, we can retrieve data from an object and get the current image number and add 1 to it. This will allow us to increment the image frame every second.

13. The Expression Evaluator currently has the value of 0, which is the starting number. Delete the 0 and then click on Retrieve Data from an Object.

14. In the New Expression dialog box, right-click on the Active Backdrop object and select Get Image Number. An expression will now appear at the end of it. Type **+1** after the ")" and then click on the OK button.

15. Run the frame and you will see that the background is animated.

Note

If you don't have access to any images, you can quickly create some basic images using Microsoft Paint, as long as each one is subtly different to provide an animated effect.

Active Picture and Picture Objects

The Active Picture and Picture objects work in the same way; they both load external files into the object, which can be loaded as the application is loading or at a specified time when the game is already running. The Picture object is used if you just want to display an external image without doing anything special to the original image.

You can see the object icons for the Active Picture and Picture objects in Figure 7.10.

Active Picture   Picture

Figure 7.10
The Active Picture and Picture objects icons.

The Active Picture is a newer version of the Picture object and contains some important extra functionality:

- **Resize:** The ability to resize the image. When resizing an object, you can specify whether you wish to use maximum speed or maximum quality as the primary resizing method. This is particularly useful if you want to save memory and/or improve the speed of your game.

- **Visible at Start:** Allows the picture to be visible or invisible when the frame starts.

- **Save Background:** Any background behind the picture will be saved, so if the image is moved, the previous background image will be restored.

- **Movement:** The ability to make the graphic move around the screen using one of the many inbuilt movement systems provided with MMF2.

- **Runtime Options:** Such as destroying the picture if it's too far away from the frame and making the image follow the frame (it will move with the frame).

- **Rotation:** The ability to rotate the image.

- **Image Loading:** The ability to use Active Picture to display a dialog box to the user asking him to select an image to load when running an MMF2-made executable. This would be useful when creating an editor, and the user needs to select an image.

Backdrop

The Backdrop object is commonly used as a background image to a game. The objects always appear in the back of the screen in terms of layering. Though it does not have as many features as the Active Backdrop, it can still be used to display simple and scrolling backgrounds.

The icon for the Backdrop object can be seen in Figure 7.11.

You can also make a Backdrop object an obstacle type, which means that it can interact with Active objects. You can configure them to be an obstacle, platform or ladder type, and it will take on the predefined requirements for that type of property. For example, if you configure a Backdrop as a ladder, the player character will be able to walk up it (once the player has been configured with the correct movement).

Figure 7.11
The Backdrop object image.

When using the Backdrop object, it is important to note that this object can only appear at the back of the screen, and any other objects will always appear in front of it.

Finally, the Backdrop object does not appear in the Event editor and, therefore, cannot be programmed, so it is very important to only use this object when necessary as you may find yourself replacing it with another object halfway through a project due to these limitations.

Quick Backdrop Object

In this example we are going to create a simple effect—using a gradient for the background—which was used in many old computer games:

1. Create a new application.

2. Double left-click on the "Frame 1" text in the Workspace editor to open the Frame editor.

3. In the Frame editor, right-click on the white area that is the frame and select Insert | Object from the pop-up menu.

4. Pick the Quick Backdrop object as shown in Figure 7.12 and place the object on the play area.

We now need to change the size of the object so it fills the whole window, which in this case is 640 × 480:

5. Single left-click on the object to display the object properties in the Properties window.

6. Click on the Size and Position tab, then enter the width to be **640**, and the height to be **480**.

7. Right-click on the Quick backdrop object on the frame and select Align in Frame | Horz Center from the pop-up menu. Right-click again and choose Align in Frame | Vert Center. The item will now be perfectly placed.

Quick
Backdrop   Clickteam

Figure 7.12
The Quick Backdrop object icon.

Currently all we have on-screen is a gray-filled rectangle, so we need to access the object properties once again and configure it to be a gradient:

8. Ensure the object properties are currently displayed. If not, single left-click on the object.

9. Click on the Settings tab. You will see a heading called Fill and an item called Type, which is currently set to Solid Color. Click on this and select Gradient.

You will notice that an extra color item has appeared, so let's now change both of these color values to something a little brighter:

10. Click on the gray box that is opposite of the Color option, then select a dark blue from the color picker. Click on the box next to Color 2 and select a lighter blue.

You will notice that the quick Backdrop object has now automatically created a gradient between the two colors.

11. At the moment the gradient is moving from left to right, but for this example, we want it going from top to bottom, so click on the Vertical Gradient option.

STORING AND RETRIEVING GRAPHICS

We discussed internal and external images earlier in this chapter. How you store this information within MMF2 depends on which method you chose.

Internal images are always there within the MMF2 executable file and are generally displayed using a frame number of an animation direction. In these cases you are storing a number for a particular image. We showed you how to do this when using the Active Background, where you use the Event editor to call a frame every one second. You don't have to use a timer; you can use a particular event to change the frame, so it would only display the required image when required.

For external images, you have to use a filename and know its location to load it into the required objects at runtime (when the game is running).

The Text Adventure Pages object and the Map object can store graphic filenames; this means they are perfect for external loading of graphics.

The storing of a filename allows you to create editors as you can assign a graphic to a particular scene and to re-load it, using the filename and file location. You will learn more about editors in Chapter 10 and Chapter 11.

Note

It is always recommended that you store any external game images in the same location as the game file/executable. This ensures that when you change the location of your files, the images will still load as long as they are all located in the same folder.

Storing and Loading an Image

For this example, we are going to store an image name and its path in the Text Adventure Pages object. We will then load this filename into the Active Picture object. Before you start, locate an image file (such as bmp or png) that you will load into the game file. Wherever this file is stored is where we will need to save the application file (mfa).

1. Create a new MMF2 application.

2. Ensure you are in the Frame editor, and then insert the Text Adventure Pages object and the Active Picture object.

3. When you are asked to open a file for the Active Picture object, click on Cancel to load a blank image.

4. Place the Text Adventure Pages object at X -1 and Y -37.

5. Place the Active Picture object at X 118 and Y 99.

We are now ready to load a file into the Text Adventure Pages object and then load it into the Active Picture:

6. Click on the Event editor.

We will create a Start of Frame event to load our picture filename into the Text Adventure Pages object:

7. Click on the New condition text and when the New condition box appears, right-click on the Storyboard Controls icon (the chessboard and piece icon) and select Start of Frame.

8. Move across from this new event until you are directly under the Text Adventure Pages object. Right-click on the action box and select Set Topic Image Filename.

9. It will now ask for the topic number. In your games, you would specify different images to different topics, but in this example we will store it in topic 0. Because it already shows 0 in the Expression Evaluator, click on the OK button.

Now it is asking for the filename. The filename that I will be using is called cover.png, but you will need to change this to whatever your file is called. So first I need to set the path to where this object is so that MMF2 can find it. I will then add the filename to the end of the expression:

10. To retrieve the file location, click on Retrieve Data from an Object, right-click on the Special object, and select Filenames | Application directory.

This will now place Appdir$ in the Expression Evaluator, but this is only giving us the location of the application. We will now need to add our cover.png file on the end.

11. To do this after the $, add a +"**cover.png**" (where cover.png is the filename of your graphic). You can see an example of the expression in Figure 7.13.

12. Click on the OK button in the Expression Evaluator to save this to the Event editor.

Note

The application directory will return the folder location of the MFA/executable. This is because in this example we are storing the graphic we want to load in the same location as the MMF2 application file.

Now that we have stored the location of the image in the Text Adventure Pages object, we now need an event that will load the image into the Active Picture object. In this example, the event will be started by pressing the space bar on the keyboard; however, in a game an event might be when the player has done some kind of action, like drinking a potion or moving to a particular room.

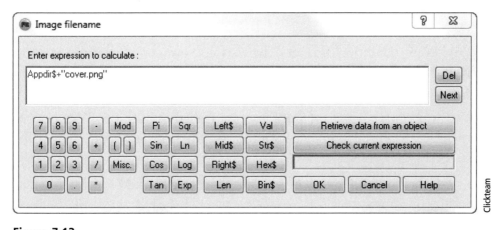

Figure 7.13
The image location and filename.

1. Click on event line 2 on the New condition text.

2. In the New condition box, right-click on the Mouse Pointer and Keyboard object, then Keyboard | Upon Pressing a Key.

3. A dialog box appears asking you to press a key, so press the spacebar. This will save this condition into the Event editor.

Now we will load the image from topic 0 into the Active Picture object:

4. Move across from event line 2 until you are directly under the Active Picture object. Right-click on the action box and select New Picture.

5. When the Open dialog box appears, click on the Expression button and the Expression Evaluator will appear.

6. Click on the Retrieve Data from an Object button in the New Expression dialog box. Choose the Text Adventure Pages object and then Get Topic Image Filename.

7. In the >Topic< area, type the number **0** and then click on OK.

You have now created all of the code required to save an image location and load it into the Active Picture object. Before going any further, you must save your work to ensure the application works. Once you have run the application, then press the space bar to load the image.

If you have downloaded the resource files that are used with this book from the website, you will find the file called imageLoad.mfa, showing you the code that you have just typed in.

Note

When dealing with any code that looks for the application path, you must have saved the application first, otherwise the path will not exist and it will not be able to find the image stored in the same directory.

CHAPTER SUMMARY

In this chapter, we discussed the different graphical objects that you can use within your games, how to display them, and how to save them for recalling later within a game.

You will now use some of this knowledge in creating your next game—a graphic adventure game called *Wild West*.

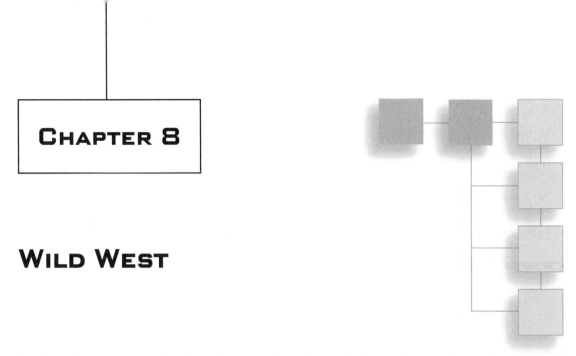

CHAPTER 8

WILD WEST

In this chapter, we will take what we have learned from the previous chapters and create a simple text/graphic adventure game that is set in the Wild West. It will contain both text and images to give the player a real sense of being in a small Western town.

The game has 18 locations, and we have also added an extra feature that was common in many early adventure games—a movement timer. This will allow you to end the game if the player has exceeded a set number of turns or moves.

GAME INTRODUCTION

In this game, you play the part of a treasure hunter who is looking for the lost town of Tombwood. After years of searching, you finally believe that you have found it, so you set out across the desert in your vehicle.

As you get nearer to the final few miles of your journey, a sandstorm arises, blocking your view and making further travel nearly impossible. Unfortunately, the sand has clogged up the engine, and your vehicle comes to a sudden stop. You now have no choice but to walk the rest of the way.

In this game, I have decided there is no "winning." The player will be unable to escape the ghost town, and if he tries, the game will end. This is a game where the player doesn't win or lose, but instead it's about the score he achieves in completing various tasks. The aim of this game is to focus mainly on adding graphics to the code we had already developed.

Hopefully this game will provide you with some inspiration for your own games or, in fact, allow you to build on it and increase the size of the game. These are the additions you could consider making to your game:

- **Sound:** Adding sound effects can really increase the quality of a game. How about adding a wind noise as you stand outside of town, or when you are in the graveyard, adding the sound of crickets?

- **Animations:** We have used simple line drawings in this game, but it wouldn't be too much additional work to add animations to the images to make them more interesting, perhaps adding a tumbleweed or dust effect, or a shadowy figure appearing in one of the windows, for example.

- **Additional scenes:** There is a big potential to add more scenes to this game. How about adding a mine with tunnels or an abandoned train station? You could also add a snake that attacks if the player goes to a particular location.

- **Puzzles:** You should consider adding puzzles into the game so that players have problems to solve as they play. You could add rooms that they need to solve a puzzle to get access to or have them try and find hidden locations throughout the game.

- **Objects:** We've not placed any objects in this game, as its main aim is to focus on implementing images into the flow of your game, but you should add objects that the player can interact with, such as a key that will allow the player to escape a jail cell or food or water that can increase the player's chances to survive in the world.

- **Story elements:** You could include the initial story elements of the game as a text or as graphics and voice-over before you start moving around the game world. You could also insert these story elements throughout your game at certain points. This is common in all story-based games, usually using a cut-scene, but in our case, it could be using text or a graphic.

- **Characters:** Even though the game is situated in a ghost town, there is no reason why—as you add further scenes or locations—you couldn't add people that the player could meet. As it is a ghost town, the "people" could be ghosts or shadowy figures that appear in the distance.

- **Menus:** At the moment, the game starts immediately, but you could create a menu to the game that includes an introduction and credits.

- **Default location graphics:** It can be very difficult to create many different location graphics, and in some cases, there isn't always something interesting to draw the player's attention. You could create a default graphic that shows when there isn't a place of interest. This was a common technique in early adventure games: the game would either not show any graphic or would replace the location image with a shaded/logo graphic.

Note

Think about how you might include a backstory of the game into your adventure: Will it be a description on a webpage, in a help document, or perhaps you will present the story to the user before he starts playing the game? It is important to provide a backstory, as this is your chance to provide some important information to the player that he may not have understood or noticed while playing the game.

Game Map

I came up with the idea of an adventure game in the Wild West and then began thinking of all of the different places the player could visit. Having come up with a basic set of locations, I then started to map out the locations as shown in Figure 8.1. The arrows in Figure 8.1 do not show all of the available directions, but rather the connectivity between the different locations. For example, you cannot travel between

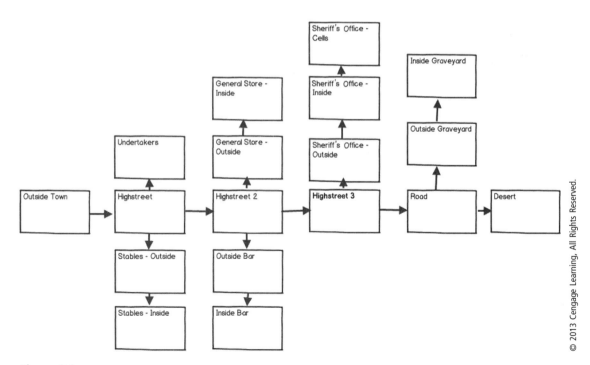

Figure 8.1
The basic map of our *Wild West* adventure.

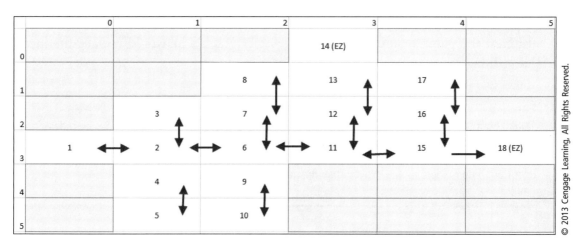

Figure 8.2
The grid map for *Wild West*.

the outside of the general stores to the undertakers as they are not linked. The game map is just the starting point of making your adventure game and is used as a reference for building more information on your game.

Grid Map

Now that we have our basic map as shown in Figure 8.1, we can start to put this into a treasure map-style grid so that we can add it to the Text Adventure Map grid when making the game. You can see this grid in Figure 8.2. In this example, we used Microsoft Excel to map out the basic structure, but we initially did everything on paper. As you can see, we have given each location a number; this number will be used to display any image for that location. You can also see in Figure 8.2 how each of the zones are connected and that both rooms 14 and 18 are "end zones" where the game ends.

Note

You will also notice that for the grid, we have created a 6x6 map but have begun numbering it at 0, because the Text Adventure Map object uses a 0-based index and so our starting location is 0,3 on a 6x6 grid.

Game Layout and Setup

The game has been slightly modified from the previous text adventure game, mainly to incorporate the graphics for each area. You can see the frame configuration in Figure 8.3. You can see these objects in the completed example file called Wildwest.mfa.

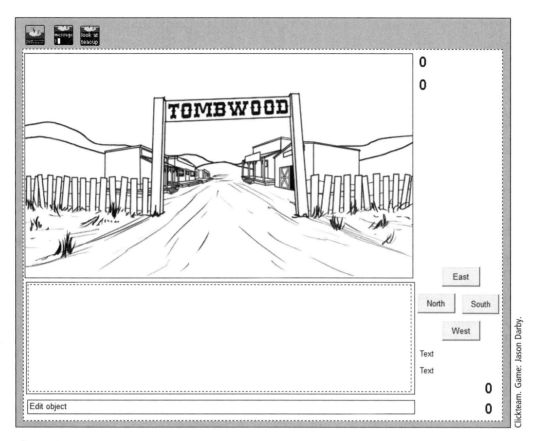

Figure 8.3
The Frame editor with the objects already in place.

You can see the following:

- **Adventure objects:** The three text adventure objects for handling various parts of the game, including maps and messages.

- **Scene images:** The different images for our locations; we have 18 animation frames and will change to a frame based on the player's current location.

- **Message window:** A rich edit box that displays all the messages in the game.

- **Edit box:** An edit box that allows player text entry.

- **Counters:** We still have two counters in the bottom right that displays the player's current location. These are not for the gamer's benefit and are for development purposes so that we can be sure that the images/text that are being displayed are the correct ones. If this game were released, we would hide these from view. We also have two new counters at the top right: the first is the

Image_Counter that indicates the number of the current room. We will use this number to set the correct frame number of the image. The second counter is called Turn_Counter and this increments each time the player moves to a new location.

■ **Direction buttons:** We still have the ability for the player to move using the buttons, but we have changed the directions around, so north is now on the left button.

Scene Images

If you load the example file called Wildwest.mfa and then open the Frame editor, you will see all of the objects in use on this frame. If you then double left-click on the Active object (the image that shows Tombwood), you will access the Picture editor that displays all of the images used by this Active object. You can see these frames in Figure 8.4. It contains 18 frames, and each frame number is associated with the number in Figure 8.2.

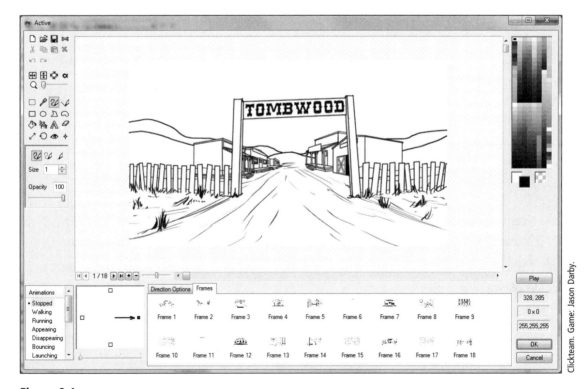

Figure 8.4
The Active object contains all 18 scenes.

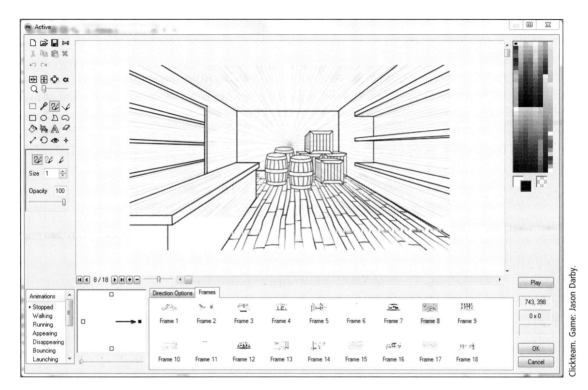

Figure 8.5
A work-in-progress image placeholder.

We have used a single active object to store all of our graphic locations. If we decide to add further locations, it is quite easy to move around the order of the animation frames. We can also add in frames for scenes that have not been completed or are currently being drawn. This allows you to get on with the game while you might be waiting for artwork from your friends. Due to the number of scenes in this example game, this is precisely what we have done. You will see frames 6 and 11 contain blank images with their location names for reference, while some of the other images are incomplete or are placeholder art such as frames 5 and 8. You can see an example of frame 8 in progress in Figure 8.5.

Note

You could also have used placeholder images, which is extremely common in computer game creation. This is where you use lower resolution or unfinished art to fill the space while the game is being made. This allows the game to be worked on without waiting for someone else to finish their work. Placeholder images could also be photos for reference and may not necessarily be drawings.

Note

You should never put copyrighted material into your game as a placeholder because you could accidentally forget to remove the image and risk the possibility of releasing your game with the content still in the program. If you are unsure, it is better to use a very poorly drawn image (perhaps drawn and scanned in) rather than using photos or content from other sources. If you do release a game with a copyrighted image without permission, you may be sued or you may have to recall it, both which may cost you time and money.

APPLICATION PROPERTIES

If you run the game, you will notice that the game has no Windows text menu as shown in Figure 8.6. This feature was removed as the game looks better without it, and in this case, very few of the default text menu options are applicable to this game.

If you want to remove this feature from your games (or indeed in this case add it back on), you can do this through the Application properties. To access the Application properties, click on the application filename in the Workspace toolbar. This will then display the properties for the whole application in the Properties window.

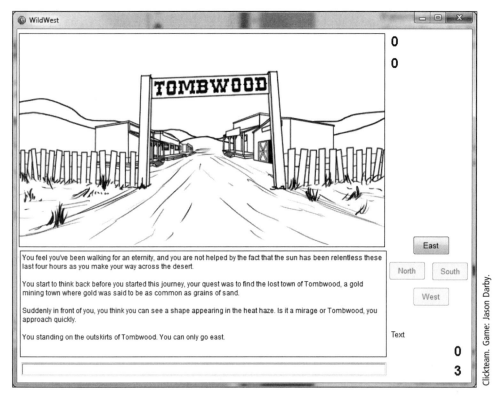

Figure 8.6
The game running without a text menu.

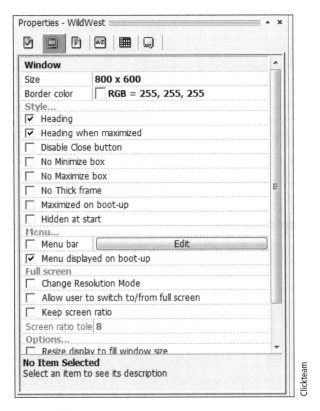

Figure 8.7
The Menu Bar property unchecked in the Application properties window.

Ensure you are on the Window tab and uncheck the Menu Bar option (or if you want to add the feature back in, make sure it's checked). You can see this property feature in Figure 8.7.

GAME CODE

We have used most of this game code before, so we will only be highlighting the most important and new parts of the code in this section of the book:

- **Start of Frame:** We replaced our *Dungeon of Text* map details with our new *Wild West* map details, which included setting up a 6x6 map grid.

- **Turn Counter:** When the player moves in a particular direction using either the text or button, the counter is incremented.

- **Timer Equals:** The second event has had the starting location set as 0, 3.

- **Room Setup:** In the Room Setup group, we have changed all of the long and short room descriptions to match our *Wild West* game. More importantly, we

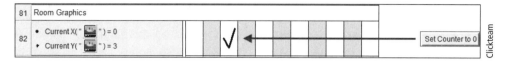

Figure 8.8
One of the events setting the Image_Counter value for a particular location.

have some new code in this group that checks which location we are currently in and then sets the Image_Counter, which we will use later in the code to display the correct animation frame for the Active object. You can see an example of the first room location in Figure 8.8 where we check the X and Y locations from the Text Adventure Map object.

- **New Location group:** When the player visits a location, we update the image for the scene, by setting the frame to the current Image_Counter value.

- **End Game:** We have updated how the game ends for the player. In our game, he either is in a jail cell or he walks out of town and collapses due to heat exhaustion.

- **15 Turns:** In event line 154, you can see that if the player takes 15 turns, he is automatically placed in the jail cell with no escape and then the game ends. This code is quite simple to create and is an interesting concept that you can use in your own games. You can use it to build tension, for example. The player might be on a sinking ship and have only so many turns to escape. You set up situations that allow the reset of this counter if the player achieves a particular task, perhaps he is underwater and running out of air and every time he finds another oxygen tank, the counter is reset and he has more time. (You could have something similar with food or water.) If you intend to use this method, you should decide how you will inform the player that he has a limited amount of turns or time left before something bad happens and how he can prevent this from happening, such as displaying text on screen, or updating a graphical health bar.

Note

You might be wondering why we set the Image_Counter to 0 in Figure 8.6 when this is the first room location, and according to Figure 8.4 that specifies this is frame 1. The animation system in MMF2 uses a 0-based index, so when you add a frame, it may say that it is frame 1, 2, 3 and so on, but when you want to display that frame within MMF2, you have to remember that the numbers start at 0. Therefore, to access frame 1, you have to ask for it to display frame 0 (always minus 1 from the actual frame you want to display).

Note

We have coded this game manually, but in Chapters 9 and 10 you will learn better ways of storing and loading this data that are easier to manage, especially for larger games. By using these methods, you will be able to drastically reduce the code you have to write, but you will also be able to transfer this code to other games.

CHAPTER SUMMARY

In this chapter, we looked at how we could add scene images to our text adventure game using a single Active object and animation frames.

We also looked at how you could implement a timer in your game that could be used to great effect in limited moves games, helping build the tension for the player. We also discussed how you could use placeholder art to ensure that you can continue coding your game while waiting for artwork to be completed by someone else.

In the next chapter, we look at how you can drastically reduce the code needed when creating your games by using an editor.

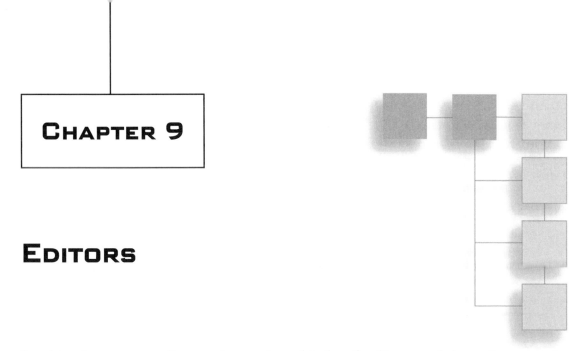

CHAPTER 9

EDITORS

In this chapter, we discuss the various kinds of editors and how they can be essential in not only making the process of creating a game easier but also in less time. In Chapter 10, we will create an editor which you can then use to load content into a game.

WHAT ARE EDITORS?

You may have not come across the term, or you may have heard gaming companies refer to the term "editor." In its most basic form, an editor is a program that can change or edit data. Most gaming companies use editors to place game content, or items, such as crates, people etc., in a game world. Editors are used to quickly change values of particular objects, such as the health of a character, the power of a sword, or the location (X, Y) of an object on-screen.

In large games, it's quite common for programmers to make an editor to a designer's specification. The designer can then change the data quickly, test it to see if it works and, if not, change it again until it does. Without an editor, the designer would have to go to the programmer to make any changes. The programmer would then have to recompile the game and give it back to the designer to test it. If there are any further changes needed, the designer goes back to the programmer. As you can see, editors put the power of changing the games' data firmly in the hands of the designer.

MMF2 has a number of editors, an Animation and a Picture editor, both of which allow you to create and change things without the need for another product or tool to do it. The Animation editor allows you to place a number of images together and instruct MMF2 to run through the animation frames at a particular speed. Without this function, you would have to code which frames need to run and at what speed.

So an editor is something that allows you to change data, and remember, changing a number in an editor is no different from moving an object in a 3D world; the object is visually being moved, but the data is still being changed.

Note

The work that you are doing will determine the kind of editor that you will create. For example, if you were working in a 3D game, you may need an editor to move and place objects, because this would be very difficult to manage just with a set of numbers. But also there is no reason to over-complicate matters if all you are doing is changing a value of an object. For example, perhaps you have a set of characters, all with their own health attribute. It would be simple to have just a simple number box where you can simply increase or decrease the starting value. In this instance, there would be no need for a fancy (and time consuming to create) editor.

WHY CREATE AN EDITOR?

If you recall from Chapter 3 when you created your *Choose Your Own Path* game, you had to manually enter data into the Event editor at the initialization stage to set up the game's text and game's links. The process would be fine for a small game, but when you start creating bigger games, the process becomes much more of a chore, and if you want to change that data, particularly time-consuming.

The great thing about MMF2 is that you can create programs as well as games, and these programs can save/load data that you can then manipulate. So you can create a nice front end to your editor, change the data, save it, and then re-load it into your game. As long as you understand how the data is used and how it is stored, you can then code your game accordingly.

There is a downside to using editors and that is the speed at which you can begin making your game. Making an editor will require you to take some time away from making your adventure games, as you need to create your app, create a data structure, and so on. But it is important to note that once you have created it, you can potentially save so much time in the long run, making the initial time you put into it worth it.

Ideas for Editors

To show you how useful an editor can be, here are some ideas for editors that can be used in adventure games or in fact any game genre that requires something similar:

■ **Objects editor:** Any adventure game requires objects, anything from food and drink to weapons and general everyday items. Each of these items needs to be created and placed within the game world, but more importantly, they need to have a set of variable data applied to them to make them useful. For example, how much health will a food item provide once consumed? Perhaps it's a positive value for an apple, but a negative value for a rotten apple. How heavy an object is will be very important when you start placing lots of objects into your inventory. Will you suddenly find you cannot carry any more? An Objects editor should also allow you to categorize objects, perhaps into associated groups, such as food, armor, and weapons. For many games, an Objects editor is one of the key editors to create. Otherwise, can you imagine adding tens or hundreds of objects to your game manually? It would be quite difficult, of course. Adding the data to an editor still needs to be done, but it can be done in such a way where you can change values, such as health benefits, quicker in an editor than you can in MMF2.

- **Character editor:** Any character you meet in a game can have a number of stats, such as a background story, available to them. For example, if the character is a shopkeeper selling items, what type of items will he have in his store to buy and will there be a discount on any of these? In text-based adventures, a character may only interact with you in a limited way, but any data for your characters should be stored in a Character editor.

- **NPC Chat editor:** Depending on the type of game you are creating, be it a text-based or point-and-click adventure, you may have NPCs. An NPC (non-player character) is a character that is controlled by the computer. You may want a character to give you hints or say something to the player. You can create an editor for the chat text, or you can also add these features to the Character editor. You may decide to make it more complicated by giving the player different chat routes, allowing the conversation to change based on the player's input. This can get very confusing, so a good system and editor will be essential for ensuring this works well.

- **Text editor:** Adventure games usually require a lot of text. You do not want to be adding all of this text manually into MMF2, so creating an editor will save you the headache. The great thing about a Text editor is that you can easily use it to create a way of entering and displaying the data, allowing you to put the data directly into the editor rather than using something like Microsoft Excel.

- **Pages editor:** In Chapter 3, we created a game called *Moon Traveller*, but we had to enter the data manually into MMF2. What if we were able to create an editor to add this text, save it, and then load it directly into the game? In Chapter 11, you will see how to do this, and we will show you how this helps reduce the amount of coding work required.

- **Location editor:** During the course of a game, players will visit various locations and, in a text-based adventure, the locations have a text description. You can create an editor to store the room descriptions (such as long and short descriptions), which you can then import directly into your game.

- **Map editor:** In Chapter 5, you created the game *Dungeon of Text*, and you manually entered the locations that the player can visit and how they were all connected. Using a Map editor will enable you to more easily edit your map data and also draw the map as you design it.

- **Words editor:** Text adventures require words, lots of words, mainly to understand what the player has typed in. Again, rather than entering this information directly into MMF2, the Words editor can easily create the required words and then hook them up into your code.

Re-using Editors

Many games developed by gaming companies use in-house game engines. This means they have programmed some code to do specific tasks. For example, if you were making a chess game, you might make an engine that handles all the code for displaying images, text, handling logic such as available moves, and AI and multiplayer code. Many of these engines go through an iterative process. Once a game has been released, the game developers look at the code and analyze what it did well and what it did badly, and then they start to improve their engine. Ultimately, the improved engine will then be used in the next version, or a similar version, of the game, resulting in the development time and cost of the game to be drastically reduced.

Editors are no different from game engines or game code. If you have made a text adventure and have already created a number of editors, and then you decide to make another text adventure, why not use the tools you have already written as the basis for your next game creation? You may need to add new features to the editors to accommodate any changes that you decide to make, but ultimately, you will be able to make your next game much quicker.

DATA HANDLING

To create an editor, you need two things: the ability to see the available values and options on-screen and to store the data in a file.

There are a number of objects that are useful for data storage:

- **Adventure Game objects:** The text adventure game objects that we have created specifically for this book allow you to save any created data and load it back in when required. The Adventure Game objects are all based on arrays, which are discussed later in this book.

- **Arrays:** Arrays are special areas of memory where you can store numbers or text against an index number. This allows you to recall data from the array at any point using the index number. Arrays are an extremely powerful item for editors, but even more importantly, they are pretty easy to use.

- **.ini files:** An .ini file is effectively a special text file containing tags to identify specific bits of data.

- **Lists:** A list in MMF2 is exactly what it sounds like; it's a list of text or numbers in alphabetical or sequential order. Lists are quite straightforward; you add a new row, with the required data, but it's surprising how useful being able to access data in real-time can be. A game called *Memory Shop: Shopping List*, available from iTunes, is a game about memory, and it uses a list to store all of the possible items that it can show. A piece of code moves three items from this list to another (blank) list at random. This second list with three randomly selected items will then be displayed in the game. So though you may initially use lists to just store object data, you may find other more complex uses for them.

Arrays in More Detail

Arrays are a way of storing and retrieving large amounts of data in an organized format. They are very efficient for storing data for many different types of reasons, but an array file can only contain either text or numbers. There are typically three types of array dimensions: single-dimensional array (or one-dimensional array), two-dimensional array and a three-dimensional array. Each piece of data is stored in a location within an array file and called upon when needed. The array can also be written when the program is running and this means it can be used to save real-time data. You can effectively class an array as a less sophisticated database, or in some respects, similar to a spreadsheet that stores data.

The most basic type of array is a single (one-dimensional) array, which is just like having a row of boxes one on top of another that contain data (either text or numbers). To access the relevant data, you would specify its location within the array. In the case of Figure 9.1, it would be [2].

Note

The image of the invader is being used to signify data and would not contain a graphic but could contain a pointer to a graphic file. (This would be the folder location and filename.) Remember the array can store either numbers or text but not both (when using MMF2's default array options).

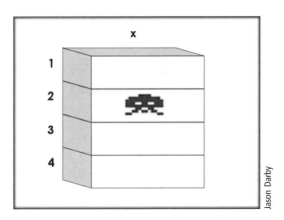

Figure 9.1
An example of an array.

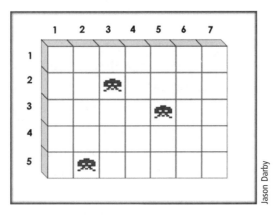

Figure 9.2
A 2D array example structure.

A 2D array is slightly more complex and allows you to have a typical grid-like data structure very much like a spreadsheet, and is usually called the [X,Y] axis as can be seen in Figure 9.2.

Because most people are familiar with programs like Microsoft Excel, a 2D array is not a difficult concept to understand. You are basically placing your data on a structure that has rows and columns (the X,Y axis).

Finally we have a 3D array, which is again a more complex type of array, which you will find to be very useful when creating your game. Think of a cube shape and that will help you understand the basic structure. With a 3D array, you need to specify three numbers, an [X,Y,Z] axis to locate the data. You can see the representation of a 3D array in Figure 9.3.

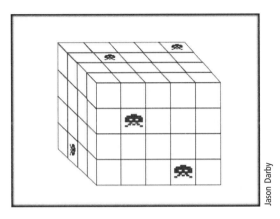

Figure 9.3
A 3D array, which looks like a cube.

The main differences to consider between a 2D and a 3D array are that with 2D you are dealing with a flat sheet of paper with rows and columns of data. A 3D array is shaped more like a cube and each block (rather than cell or face) contains the data. Though arrays are quite efficient and a basic 3D array doesn't use much hard disk space, it is a good idea to only pick the one that you need and switch back and forth unless you have to. Arrays can get quite complex and so by choosing one type of array, you will make your program understandable to you if, for example, you were to come back to it after not working on it for an extended period of time.

There is one more concept that we need to discuss with regards to arrays that you will come across: 1-based index. As you know, each array item is numbered by its axis (for example X and Y), but the 1-based index states if the numbering begins with a 1 or a 0. Figure 9.4 shows how the 1-based index works. In the first example,

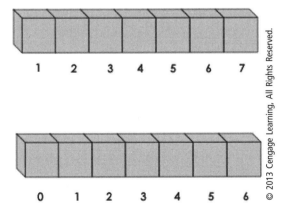

Figure 9.4
An example of a 0- or 1-based index.

the first item in that array is [1] and then [2]. In the second example, you access [0] and [1] instead. It is very important to remember which index you have selected, as if you try to read and write to a 0-based index and you have selected a 1-based index, it will not work (you will not get any error messages to suggest otherwise).

With MMF2 you have the benefit of putting multiple array files into your game, so you can break your game down into smaller and easier sections to manage files. This allows you to create a small array file and then make sure it works, and that your game is reading/writing the data correctly, allowing you to then move onto the next section. If you create a single massive array file, you might find that it doesn't work and the more data you are dealing with, the harder it will be to test. When you start to break your program down, ensure that you make a lot of comments in the program so you know what you did. This will help you when you go back to a project after a break.

.ini Files in More Detail

You may have come across the term .ini file before. This type of file was extremely common in operating systems such as Windows 95/98. They are less common today because many Windows-based applications use the Registry to store data, but for games, it can still be easier to put the data into an .ini file. An example .ini file can be seen in Figure 9.5.

Though .ini files are generally only seen in Windows-based operating systems, MMF's exporters also have support for them, in exporters such as iPhone. This is because they are treated like normal data files and so the actual .ini type is ignored.

As you can see in Figure 9.5, groups of data are separated using [ ] brackets with the keyword in the middle. Under the keywords are the items, which contain the item's name and its value. The value can be text or a number.

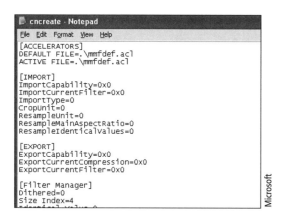

Figure 9.5
An .ini file in use showing the program configuration.

A good use of an .ini file is to store a person's high scores or particular data such as current score, lives, and level.

CHAPTER SUMMARY

In this chapter, we covered the reasons why you might want to use an editor. Even though it may take you longer to get your project started, an editor will save you a lot of time and, more importantly, effort in the long run.

We discussed where you might want to consider using an editor in your games and covered the key data objects. In Chapter 10, we will now create an editor that saves and loads information for the game we made in Chapter 3, *Moon Traveller*.

CHAPTER 10

CREATING AN EDITOR

In this chapter, we will create an editor for the game that we made in Chapter 3 called *Moon Traveller*. Even though *Moon Traveller* was a very small game, there was a lot involved in setting up the data to run the game. We set up things like text in a particular topic number, topic links, and topic link text.

For such a small game, this was a lot of work. In addition, if you want to change a small bit of data, it can be difficult to identify the particular action that needs to be changed because there is only so much space in the tool tip pop-ups.

However, we can create an editor that permits us to enter this data using an easy-to-understand interface that allows us to quickly view and change it.

DATA REQUIREMENTS

Before we start, it is important to identify what bits of data we want to store and retrieve. This will be very important when making our game, because how we set our data will define how easy or difficult it will be to program.

Note

> Before you start on this project, you may want to re-run the *Moon Traveller* game or skim through Chapter 3 to familiarize yourself with its features, especially if you do not remember how it works.

There are four key components to the *Moon Traveller* game in Chapter 3:

- **Topic number:** All topic text is associated with this number.

- **Topic text:** This creates the topic text. In the game, we put the text directly into the String object in MMF2, which is fine if you have 10-20 strings, but when you are dealing with a hundred bits of text, then it becomes unmanageable.

- **Topic links:** In each topic, there will be links to other topics.

- **Topic link text:** In each link within a topic, there will be some text, which is then placed within a button to give the user more information on what he is clicking.

The most important of these four components is the topic number. This is the unique number of each topic as you read through the story. All of the topic text and the links are associated with a topic number. When working with MMF2 and certainly when working with data in MMF2, it is important to think about assigning your data to a number that can easily be loaded into the game at the right time. What I mean by this is, we can use a counter, for example, to keep track of the current topic number, then we can load data from the array using the counter number as an index number in an array. This allows us to easily keep track of all the data and not make our coding too difficult to understand.

Note

If you are unsure about how using an array's index number will help you, don't worry because we will be making an example that should explain it further.

THE EDITOR'S LOOK AND FEEL

So now that we have an idea of the data requirements, we can start to put together a picture of what the editor will look like from a user's point of view. It needs to be simple to use, clear and concise, and store all of the information we need.

You can see an example of the editor we are going to make in this chapter in Figure 10.1.

To build this editor, we will need the following objects:

- **String objects:** The String objects will be used to identify what each part of the editor will do. It's important to mark each feature, because if you come back at a later stage, you may not remember what result you will get when entering data into a box.

- **Counter:** The Counter object is used just to display the current topic, but also to be used as a pointer to all other objects to which the topic is currently being displayed. The counter is not stored anywhere except in real-time. So in Figure 10.1, you can see it states the current topic is 1. If the user were to click

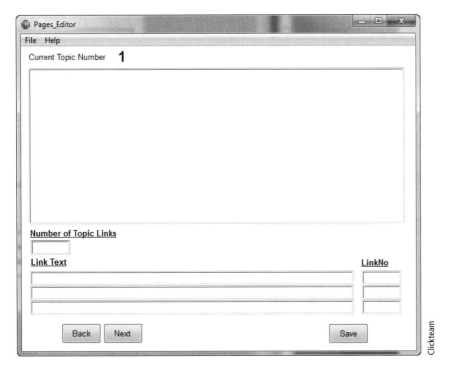

Figure 10.1
The Pages editor.

on Next, we would add a 1 onto this counter to make 2, and then tell all of the other objects to load data in for topic (2). To be able to tell the objects which topic to load, we use the current counter value.

- **Edit boxes:** Edit boxes are great for entering and displaying data. In this example, we have edit boxes for the topic text, the number of links in a topic, the topic link text, and the links from those topic buttons.

- **Buttons:** We have three buttons: one to move back a topic number, another to move forward, and one to save all of the contents to a file. We will temporarily save the data to the array in memory, but until you click on the Save button, no data will be changed.

- **Array:** An array is needed to store the number of topic links. We use this to format the data ready for the Text Adventure Pages object.

These are all of the objects that are visible to the user, but we will also need the Text Adventure Pages object to store the data. The Text Adventure Pages object is a special object made for writing and creating story-based adventure games, but also it is effectively an array, storing text or numbers in an index.

CREATING THE EDITOR

Our first task in making the editor is placing all of the component parts and setting any object properties before we begin programming. To create the editor:

1. Start MMF2, and click on the File | New option to create a blank application file.

2. Double-click on the Frame 1 text in the Workspace toolbar or double-click on the frame in the Storyboard editor. Either way, you should now see a blank frame in the Frame editor.

We need to add a few objects and, in some cases, resize them. Using the standard method of adding objects (Insert | New Object), we need to add the following (and rename them where necessary) as shown in Table 10.1.

Table 10.1 Objects We Need to Include: Names, Size Changes, and Position

Object Type	Object Name	Position X	Position Y	Size X	Size Y
Text Adventure Pages object	–	8	-44	–	–
String	String 1	13	8	133	17
String	String 2	14	286	171	17
String	String 3	15	331	150	17
String	String 4	551	333	55	17
Edit box	Topic_Text	12	34	610	246
Edit box	Topic_Links	15	305	64	23
Edit box	LinkText1	14	354	525	23
Edit box	LinkText2	14	377	525	23
Edit box	LinkText3	14	400	525	23
Edit box	LinkNo1	552	354	64	23
Edit box	LinkNo2	552	377	64	23
Edit box	LinkNo3	552	400	64	23
Button	Button_Back	65	436	64	32
Button	Button_Next	133	436	64	32
Button	Button_Save	498	436	64	32
Counter	–	171	25	–	–
Array	–	52	-43	–	–

Note

A dash in Table 10.1 indicates that it is using the default data and does not need to be changed.

Note

For the three buttons, you will need to set the button text to Back, Next, and Save. To do this, double left-click on each button from left to right and type in Back, Next, or Save.

We now need to change some of the data for these objects. First, there are a few String objects that are used as on-screen messages to describe what the data part of the screen will do, so let's change the text data for them.

Use the following table to change the display text for the specified String objects. If you don't recall how to change the text, you can either double-click on the String object and type in its new display text, or you can single-click on the String object and change the text in the Settings tab in the Properties window for Paragraph 1 (for each String object).

To make some of these items stand out more, we will also add bold and underline to the display text. You can see which text has this applied in Table 10.2. To add bold and underline to the entered text, click on the Font tab for that String object and select the checkboxes.

We also need to make a change to the Topic_Text edit object property sheet. At the moment, the edit box is a single line edit box; this means it will only display one line of text regardless of how high the object is. Ensure you click on the Topic_Text object and in the Settings tab, ensure the Multiline object is checked.

We have one additional object that we need to configure before we start programming and that is the Counter object, which should currently be displaying the number 0, but we need it to display 1 as the starting number.

1. Click on the Counter object and in the Settings tab, ensure that the initial value is set to 1 and the minimum value is set to 1.

Table 10.2 Changing the Display Text for Some of the String Objects

Object Name	Display Text	Bold	Underlined
String 1	Current Topic Number	–	–
String 2	Number of Topic Links	Yes	Yes
String 3	Link Text	Yes	Yes
String 4	LinkNo	Yes	Yes

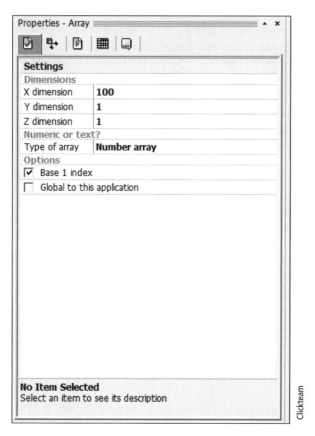

Figure 10.2
Array configuration.

We also need to configure the array file:

2. Click on the array that has been added to the frame and ensure you are on the Settings tab.

3. For the X Dimension, type **100**. Y and Z should be set to 1. Ensure the type of array is set to Number Array.

4. Ensure that Base 1 Index is selected to start numbering in the array from the number 1. We start from number 1 because our topics and its index also start from 1.

You can see the array setup in Figure 10.2.

You should now have a screen that resembles Figure 10.3, which shows the file running and the Frame editor version in Figure 10.1. If not, you can always download all of the project files from the www.castlesoftware.co.uk site. The file is called Pages_Editor_Setup.mfa.

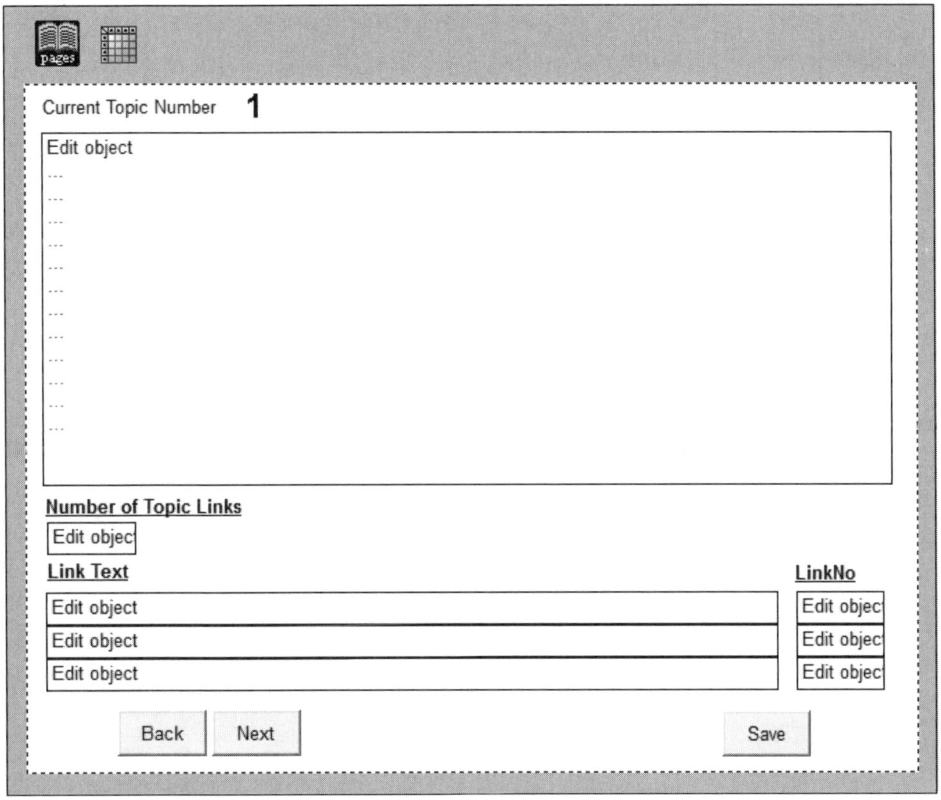

Figure 10.3
The frame setup of the Pages editor.

Note

We set the minimum value of the counter; otherwise, if the user keeps pressing the Back button, the number will continue to reduce and it may become a negative number. If we set a minimum number, we can prevent the occurrence of negative numbers.

PROGRAMMING THE EDITOR

Now that we have all of the main components in place, we are ready to begin programming the code for it to run. Hopefully from Figure 10.3 you can get a good idea of what would be entered in each section.

Note

At the moment, the editor is set up to handle a maximum of three topic links (the page links in each topic) as we programmed it in the game in Chapter 3. You can expand the editor to include more links if needed.

The first thing we need to do is go into the Event editor and set up any initializations. To launch a blank Event editor, click on the Event Editor icon.

The editors' job is to allow you to save data to an external file that you will load into your game. You also load the data into the editor so that you are easily able to scroll through it and make any changes if you need to. Once finished reviewing the editor, save any changes. You can see a simple flow of how the editor will work in Figure 10.4.

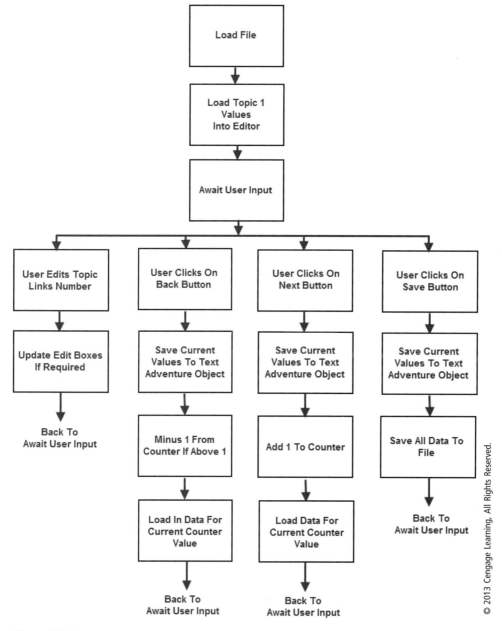

Figure 10.4
The program flow for the editor.

Creating the Files

Before we can load any files into MMF2, we have to create them first. The best way to do this is to create the files in the Event editor before you start the process of writing your editor code. You need to make a file for the Text Adventure Pages object that will store all of the data for our game. You will also need to create an array file to store the number of links within each topic.

Note

The array file is only used to help save that data in the Text Adventure Pages object that will determine how many links to add. We won't need this file in the game.

We will create the files and once we have run MMF2 (and it has auto-generated the files) we will then delete the code and start to program our editor.

1. Click on the New condition text on line 1.

2. Select the Storyboard Controls (chessboard) and select Start of Frame.

3. Move across to the Text Adventure Pages object.

4. Right-click on the action box and select File | Save. A dialog box appears as shown in Figure 10.5.

We want to store the files we create in the same location as the MMF2 editor .exe, thereby keeping the editor and its data files together, which is very important. If you

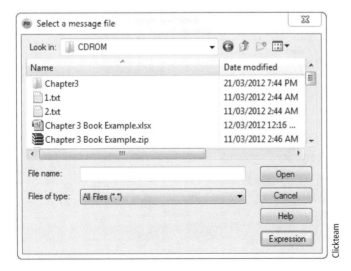

Figure 10.5
The Select a Message File dialog box.

were to select a file from the dialog box, it will remember that precise path, so if you move all of the files at a later time, the Event editor will still go back to the original location. We don't want this to occur, so we need to tell MMF2 that the Text Adventure Pages file is in the same location always as the editor.

5. Click on the Expression button, and the Expression Evaluator appears and asks for the name of the file.

If you type in a name at this point, it will save the file in the currently selected folder. So we want to tell it to load from the location of our editor application.

6. Click on the Retrieve Data from an Object button.

7. The New Expression dialog box appears. Click on the Special Object (the Computer Screens icon) and select Filenames | Application Directory.

Appdir$ will now appear within the expression box, but this only points to the location of our application. Now we need to add the filename to the end of it.

8. At the end of Appdir$, add a + sign and then the name of the file within quotes, which in this case should be "Pages.tap". You can see the completed expression in Figure 10.6.

9. Click on the OK button to save this information to the Event editor.

We will now follow a similar process for creating a save file for the array:

10. Move to the right of the Start of Frame condition until you are directly under the Array object.

11. Right-click on the action box and select Files | Save Array to File.

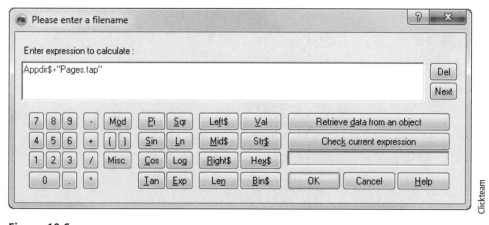

Figure 10.6
The expression to save a file in the same directory as the app.

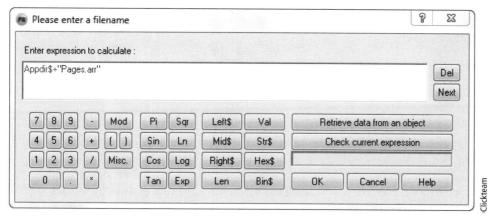

Figure 10.7
The expression to save a file in the same directory as the app for the array.

12. The Select a File dialog box appears, similar to that shown in Figure 10.5. Click on the Expression button.

13. The Expression Evaluator appears. You can either retrieve the data from the Special object or type it in directly. We will type it in directly.

14. Remove the two quotes and type in **Appdir$+"Pages.arr"**. You can see this in Figure 10.7.

15. Click on the OK button to save.

Now that we have created the code, if we run this application, it will now automatically create these two files in the same directory as the application. When you run your app, you will see the Frame editor components, but it is the Event editor that will create these two files in the background.

You can download the example from www.castlesoftware.co.uk; the filename is Pages_Editor_Saves.mfa.

Once you have confirmed the two files you have created, you can delete the whole event since we will now begin to create the editor.

Loading the Data Files

We will start programming our editor by loading in both the Text Adventure Pages file and the array file; this will then allow us to load any current data into the editor.

Before you start, make sure there are no events in the Event editor. If there are items from the previous example where we saved files, please delete them.

Our first condition will be a Start of Frame condition, which we will use to load our files and for initialization.

1. Click on the New condition text on event line 1.

2. Select the Storyboard Controls object and then choose Start of Frame.

Let's now add the code for loading Text Adventure Pages object and the Array object files. We can use the same principle as we did for the saving of files, ensuring that we specify the application path.

3. Move across from the Start of Frame condition until you are directly under the Text Adventure Pages object, right-click on the action box, and select File | Load.

4. When the Select a Message File dialog box appears, click on the Expression button.

5. The Expression Evaluator dialog box appears. Click on the Retrieve Data from an Object button, then select the Special object and Filenames | Application Directory.

6. Appdir$ appears in the Expression box. At the end of the text, type a + sign and **"Pages.tap"**. The contents should match Figure 10.6.

7. Click on the OK button.

Now that we have added the pages file, let's now add the array file.

8. Move across from the Start of Frame condition until you are directly under the Array object. Right-click and select Files | Load Array from File.

9. In the Selection dialog box, click on the Expression button.

10. Click on the Retrieve Data from an Object button, select the Special object, and then choose Filenames | Application directory.

11. On the end of the Appdir$ text, add a + sign and then **"Pages.arr"**. It should now look like Figure 10.7. Click on OK.

You have now added the code to load both files. At the moment both files contain no data, so all we have done is create a link between the file and MMF2.

Initializing the Data

Now that you have created both files and instructed the application to load them at the start of the frame, you now need to set up the editor with the correct data. Even though we haven't actually placed any data in the data files, we still need to set it up correctly so later on it will display the data.

If you look at the Figure 10.2, you can see all of the edit boxes that need data placed within them, so now we have to read information from the Text Adventure Pages object and place that data into the edit boxes.

First you need to set up the topic text, which is the story content to your adventure. You will get the data from the Text Adventure Pages object and place it directly into the Edit box.

1. Move across from event line 1 (Start of Frame) until you are directly under the Topic_Text edit box.

2. Right-click on the action box and select Editing | Set Text.

3. The Expression Evaluator appears asking for some text. You need to retrieve the data from the Pages object, so click on the Retrieve Data from an Object button.

4. When the New Expression dialog box appears, right-click on the Text Adventure Pages object and select Get Topic Content.

The Set text box will now be filled with an expression, but it will have the word >Topic< highlighted indicating that you are supposed to type in a topic number. Because this initialization will always load in topic one, you could type in the value 1. But to give you some practice with another method—which will be used quite a lot in this section—we will retrieve data again from the Counter object and get its current value. Since the counter is set to the value 1 at the start of the frame, it achieves the same goal:

1. Ensure that >Topic< is highlighted and then click on Retrieve Data from an Object.

2. Find the Counter object in the New Expression dialog box, right-click, and select Current Value.

3. Click on OK to continue.

If there is an error, confirm your expression looks like the following:

```
Topic Content$( "Text Adventure Pages", value( "Counter" ))
```

Topic Links

Topic links are numbers that indicate to the editor how many links will be in each topic.

Once you have added content to the Pages object, it knows how many links there are, but it does not know how many links you're going to add. When you add topic links into the Pages object, it is formatted as follows:

"14,8,2" = 3 topic links

"6, 91" = 2 topic links

We have set up our editor to handle a maximum of three links. However, if we were to copy all three bits of data to the Pages object, but we only wanted two links, the following would appear:

"6,91,0"

The Pages object believes 0 is a valid link, and so when you run the game from this data, it creates a third button, even though you only want two links.

So we have to find an alternative way of placing the link data into the Pages object since you cannot just paste the data in the three link boxes directly into the object. By using the Topic_Links edit box, the user will type in the number of links for this current topic, and we will write some additional code for it that will only place that data into the Pages object. Hopefully this will become clear as we begin to write the code.

Because we cannot store the number of links in the Pages object, we will be loading it in from the Array object:

1. On the Start of Frame event line, move across until you are directly under the Topic_Links edit object.

2. Right-click on the action box and select Editing | Set Text.

3. The Expression Editor appears. You need the contents of the array, so click on Retrieve Data from an Object.

4. Find the array object in the New Expression dialog box, right-click, and select Read Value from X Position.

We set the array to handle numbers, which is why we use the read value and not read string.

You will see the expression in place, but you are now being asked for >Enter X offset<. This is what index number you want to look up in the array. We are going to use the counter as the index, because this will always be pointing to the correct topic.

5. Ensure that >Enter X offset< is highlighted and click on Retrieve Data from an Object.

6. In the New Expression dialog box, right-click, and select Current Value.

If you were to click on the OK button now, an error message will display. If you click on the Check Current Expression button, it will give you some information about the problem. It asks, "Please enter an alphanumeric expression," which means that it is expecting text and not a number. In this case, because MMF2 was expecting text, it cannot handle a number, so you need to convert the number into text so that it can understand it.

Select the current expression in the Expression Evaluator and press the Ctrl+X keys to cut it. The text will be stored in memory.

7. Click on the Str$ button to convert a number to text.

8. You will now see Str$(>Enter number here<). Ensure the >Enter number here < is selected and then press the keys Ctrl+V to paste the original expression you created.

9. Your expression should now look like Figure 10.8. If so, click on OK to continue.

Link Text 1, 2, & 3

When you play the game, the text you see on each button is called the link text. We need to load in the text from the Pages object into the three edit objects of LinkText1, LinkText2, and LinkText3:

1. Move across from the Start of Frame condition on event line 1 until you are directly under the LinkText1 edit object. Right-click on the action box and select Editing | Set Text.

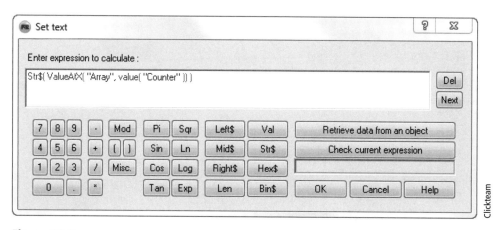

Figure 10.8
The expression to read a value in an array at a particular index.

2. When the Expression Evaluator appears, click on the Retrieve Data from an Object button.

3. In the New Expression dialog box, right-click the Pages object and choose Get Text of Nth Link.

4. You will be returned to the Expression Evaluator and have two bits of information to fill in: >Topic< and >Index<.

The topic will be retrieved by the current counter value, while the index will be a specific number you enter. Since this is the first of the three topic link texts (as it's in the first edit box), we know that we can specify a number for the first link number in the Pages object.

First, you need to replace the >Topic< with the counter value:

1. Ensure that >Topic< is highlighted and click on Retrieve Data from an Object. When the New Expression dialog box appears, select the Counter object, right-click, and choose Current Value.

You will now be back at the Expression Evaluator, but this time you need to specify a value for the index of the link topic number. You want to retrieve the data for the current topic for the very first topic link. You need to be careful here, because it would seem logical to put the number 1 in the >Index< area, but the topic links uses a 0-based index, which means it starts its numbering from 0. First link is 0, then 1, and then 2.

2. Ensure the >Index< option is highlighted and type in the number **0**. You can see the full expression in Figure 10.9.

3. Click on OK to save the information to the Event editor.

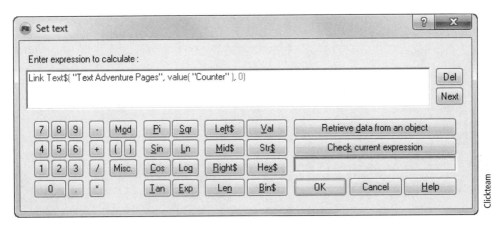

Figure 10.9
The expression to retrieve the first link number from the current topic.

Table 10.3   Expressions for Each of the LinkText Action Boxes

Object	Expression
LinkText1	Link Text$("Text Adventure Pages", value("Counter"), 0)
LinkText2	Link Text$("Text Adventure Pages", value("Counter"), 1)
LinkText3	Link Text$("Text Adventure Pages", value("Counter"), 2)

Now that you have entered the data for LinkText1, you can manually do the same again for LinkText2 and LinkText3, with the only change being the index value of 1 and 2. But obviously there is a faster way, which is to drag and drop the action from the one box to the other two.

1. On the action you just created in the LinkText1 box, press the left mouse button and hold, then drag and release over the LinkText2 action box.

2. By dragging and dropping the action, you have created a new action under LinkText2, but the index number is incorrect. So hover the mouse over the action box of LinkText2 and right-click and select Edit.

3. The Expression Evaluator appears. At the end of the expression, change the 0 to a 1 and then click on OK.

4. Repeat for LinkText3 and change the index number in the expression to a 2.

So you should have the following expressions in each of the actions as shown in Table 10.3.

Link Text Numbers

You need to follow a similar process for the action boxes for the text numbers LinkNo1, LinkNo2, and LinkNo3.

The link numbers provide you with a way of keeping track of which topics you can jump to.

1. Move across from the first event line until you are directly under the LinkNo1 object. Right-click on the action box and select Editing | Set Text.

2. The Expression Evaluator appears. Click on the Retrieve Data from an Object button, and from the New Expression dialog box, right-click on the Text Adventure Pages object and choose Get Nth Link.

The expression will be filled but will be asking for two bits of information, the topic and the index.

3. Ensure that the >Topic< text is highlighted and then click on Retrieve Data from an Object. Right-click on the Counter object in the New Expression dialog box and select Current Value.

4. Ensure that the >Index< item is highlighted and then type the number **0**. Again we are using a 0-based index and so we need to start from 0 for the first value.

5. You can't use this current expression because it is a value (link number) and you are trying to load it into a text box. Cut and paste the expression so that the expression box is empty.

6. Click on the Str$ button to enter the command to convert a number to text. Replace >Enter number here< by pasting the cut expression into the box (by pressing Ctrl+V).

Your expression should read:

Str$(Link("Text Adventure Pages", value("Counter"), 0))

7. Now click on OK to save the information to the Event editor.

We can follow the same process as the LinkText items by dragging and dropping the LinkNo1 action over to the LinkNo2 and LinkNo3 items.

8. Ensure your mouse cursor is over the action box for LinkNo1, hold down the left mouse button, and then drag the action to the LinkNo2 action box and release the left mouse button to copy the action.

9. Drag the action now in LinkNo2 and drop it on LinkNo3.

10. Right-click on the action in LinkNo2 and select Edit, change the index number (the last number) from 0 to 1, and then click on OK.

11. Right-click on the action in LinkNo3 and select Edit, change the index number (the last number) from 0 to 2, and then click on OK.

You should now have changed the three expressions to read the same as Table 10.4.

You can see all of the actions as shown in the Event List editor in Figure 10.10.

We have now completed the first event line and will move on to the button clicks.

Table 10.4 Link Text Numbers

Object Name	Expression
LinkNo1	Str$(Link("Text Adventure Pages", value("Counter"), 0))
LinkNo2	Str$(Link("Text Adventure Pages", value("Counter"), 1))
LinkNo3	Str$(Link("Text Adventure Pages", value("Counter"), 2))

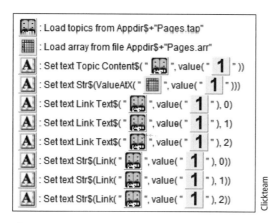

Figure 10.10
All of the actions for the Start of Frame event.

Creating Button Clicks

In this section, we will be creating a comment line and three conditions to check for when the user of the editor has clicked on the Back, Next, and Save buttons.

First, we will create a comment line that describes what this bit of code is doing.

1. Right-click on the number 2 in the Event editor and select Insert | A Comment.

2. In the comment box, type **Button Clicks** and then click on OK.

Let's now create our three buttons:

3. Click on the New condition text on line 3, right-click on Button_Back, then choose Button Clicked.

4. On event line 4, click on the New Condition text, right-click on Button_Next, and then choose Button Clicked.

5. Finally, add the last of the buttons: on event line 5, right-click on Button_Save, then right-click and choose Button Clicked.

You have now created the conditions that we need to create the actions.

Back Button Code

Now that you have your buttons in place, you can start creating your code for pressing the Back button. Pressing the Back button needs to result in two things: to save anything on the current topic number into the Text Adventure Pages object and to change the topic number and reload all data back into the edit boxes. This is so you save your current work but then it updates the data to present you with the previous index data results.

Note

> When you place data back into any objects, it saves it into memory. This means that if you close the application, it will lose any updated content. If you want to save anything that has been updated, you will need to save it to an actual file, which we will do later in this chapter.

The first thing we need to do is get the value from the Topic_Links edit box and store it in the array. We will be storing it in the X index, with a value that is the same as the current counter value.

1. On event line 3 (Button Back Is Clicked), move across until you are directly under the Array object. Right-click and select Write | Write Value to X.

2. The Expression Evaluator appears. You need to write the value that is currently stored in the Topic_Links edit box, so click on the Retrieve Data from an Object button.

3. In the New Expression dialog box, right-click on the Topic_Links object and select Get Text.

The problem we have now is that the text in the edit box is a string, but we are writing a number to the array, so we need to convert this string into a number. The process is very similar to converting a number to a string, but instead you use the Val option.

4. Cut the text from the expression box using Ctrl+X keys.

5. Click on the Val button and a piece of text will appear saying Val(>Enter string here<). The >Enter string here< will already be highlighted, so use Ctrl+V on the keyboard to paste the text from the clipboard.

The text should now read:

Val(Edittext$("Topic_Links"))

6. Click on the OK button.

You will now be asked where in the X index you want to save this information. Because we are saving all information based on the current counter value, you can retrieve the data for this.

7. Click on the Retrieve Data from an Object button.

8. In the New Expression dialog box, right-click on the counter and select Current Value.

9. Click on OK again to close the Expression Evaluator.

Now that we have saved the Topic_Links text to the array, we now have to save any other useful information that may have been entered or changed on this current page before we change pages. If we don't, then the data will be incorrectly placed into the Pages object and will appear incorrectly when viewing it.

First, we need to set the topic content (the story text) from the edit box into the Pages object.

10. Move to the right of event line 3 until you are directly under the Text Adventure Pages object.

11. Right-click on the action box and choose Set Topic Content.

12. The Expression Evaluator will appear asking for a topic number. Click on the Retrieve Data from an Object button and in the New Expression dialog box, select the Counter object and choose Current Value.

13. Click OK.

You will still be in the Expression Evaluator, but it will be asking for the topic content. You need to take it from the edit box.

14. Click on the Retrieve Data from an Object button.

15. In the New Expression dialog box, right-click on the Topic_Text object and choose Get Text.

16. Click on OK to save the information to the Event editor.

Next we need to create three actions that store the link text into the Pages object:

17. Move to the right of event line 3 (Button Back Is Clicked) until you are directly under the Text Adventure Pages object. Right-click in the action box where there is already a tick icon, and select Set Topic Link Text.

18. When the Expression Evaluator appears, it will ask you for a topic number. Click on Retrieve Data from an Object, right-click on the Counter object, and select Current Value. Click on OK.

19. You will now be asked for the Index of Nth Link. Because this is a 0-based number, leave the value as 0, which specifies the first slot in the Pages object. Click on OK.

Now you will be asked to enter the text associated with this link. Since the text is stored in the edit box, you just need to retrieve that from the edit box in question.

20. Click on Retrieve Data from an Object. From the New Expression dialog box, find the LinkText1 object, right-click on it, and select Get Text.

21. The expression now appears in the Expression Evaluator. Click on the OK button to save the action to the Event editor.

You now need to repeat this process to create two more actions, but with different link indexes of 1 and the last one of 2.

You can do this manually or you can use the Event List editor to help you quickly create the actions.

22. Double-click on the tick mark in the Text Adventure Pages object action box to the right of the Button Back Is Clicked event (event line 3).

This will take you into the Event List editor that shows a list of all actions on this event line.

23. Highlight the action you just created and press Ctrl+C, and then press Ctrl+V twice to create two copies of this action.

24. If you double-click on the second Set text of topic values action (which should be the fourth action in the list), you will be taken back into the Expression Evaluator.

25. Click OK until you get to Index of Nth link, and replace the 0 with a 1. Click the OK button twice to save the information to the Event Editor.

Now do this for the final action in the list, where we need it to say link 2 rather than link 0. You can see what it should look like in Figure 10.11.

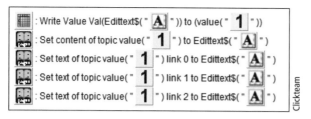

Figure 10.11
The list of actions currently created.

Once you have confirmed that the actions are correct, go back to the normal Event editor view, click on the Event Editor button, or while in the Event List Editor, click on the small X button in the top right-hand corner.

Note

Be careful not to click on the outmost X icon in the window, because it will close the application.

You now have set all of the current data into the object, so now you need to tell MMF2 to reduce the counter by a value of 1. If the counter is already at 1, then nothing will happen because we had previously configured the counter to have a minimum value of 1.

26. From event line 3, move across until you are directly under the Counter object.

27. Right-click the action box and select Subtract from Counter.

28. When the Expression Evaluator appears, type the value **1** and click on OK.

Now that you have reduced the counter, you need to update the editor screen to display the current topic content, updating all of the edit boxes with data that has been stored in the Text Adventure Pages object. This means going through all relevant edit objects and updating their content.

We will start with updating the topic content, which is our game's story line.

29. From event line 3, move across to the right until you are directly under the Topic_Text edit object.

30. Right-click on the action box and select Editing | Set Text.

31. When the Expression Evaluator dialog box appears, click on Retrieve Data from an Object. The New Expression box appears, so right-click on the Text Adventure Pages object and choose Get Topic Content.

32. An expression will fill the dialog box, asking you for a topic number. Ensure >Topic< is highlighted and then click on Retrieve Data from an Object.

33. From the New Expression dialog box, right-click on the counter and select Current Value.

34. You will now be back at the Set Text dialog box and the expression. Click on the OK button to save to the Event editor.

Now we need to update the number of links in a topic from the array file:

35. Move across from event line 3 until you are directly under the Topic_Links object. Right-click on the action box and select Editing | Set Text.

36. Click on the Retrieve Data from an Object button.

37. In the New Expression dialog box, right-click on the Array object and choose Read Value from X Position.

38. The expression is asking for a >Enter X offset<, so ensure this is highlighted and click on Retrieve Data from an Object. Right-click on the Counter object and choose Current Value.

39. Because this is a number being placed into a text box, you need to convert it first to a string. Cut the whole expression from the Expression Evaluator and then click on the Str$ button. You should see that >Enter string here< is already highlighted. Press Ctrl+V to paste your code here.

Your expression should now look like this:

    Str$(ValueAtX("Array", value("Counter")))

40. Click on the OK button to save it to the Event editor.

Your current list of actions in the Event List editor will look like Figure 10.12.

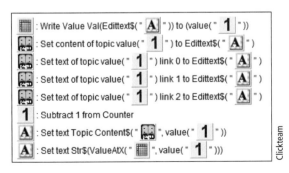

Figure 10.12
The current actions for the Back button.

We have six actions left to create; the first set of three is to load the topic link text into the edit boxes, while the last three actions involve loading the topic link numbers.

Fortunately, the code that we used in the Start of Frame event on line 1 is exactly the same code we need to create these actions. You will need to drag and drop the action boxes from event line 1 to event line 3 in the following order:

■ LinkText1

■ LinkText2

■ LinkText3

■ LinkNo1

■ LinkNo2

■ LinkNo3

Now that you have dragged and dropped these into your actions, the Event List editor should look like Figure 10.13.

You have now completed the code for the Back button.

Next Button Code

The Next button code is the same as the Back button code in terms of it needing to write and update the same objects. The only thing that changes is the counter. When

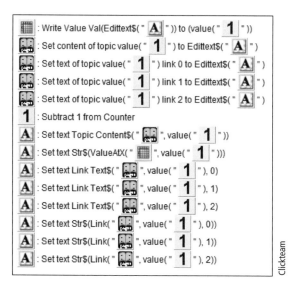

Figure 10.13
The actions for the Button Back condition.

we are moving back through the data, we subtract from the counter. Likewise, if we move forward, we add to the counter.

We could manually create all of this code and then drag and drop the relevant items in place. Or another solution is to copy the whole event line and then paste it. If we use the copy-paste method, it is important to keep these two potential drawbacks in mind: first, the button would be saying Button_Back is being clicked, and the counter would obviously be subtracting rather than adding. Fixing these two problems, however, takes much less time than re-adding all of the code and in the right order.

So let's start by copying and pasting:

1. Click on event line 3 to highlight the entire line. Press the Ctrl+C keys to copy the line into memory.

2. We already have a Button_Next event line with no actions in it. Press the Ctrl+V keys to paste the event line. This should now appear directly below event line 3.

3. Click on event line 5, which contains the blank Button_Next Clicked event, and delete it.

Now you need to amend your copied Button_Back event so that the action changes when the user clicks on Button Next.

4. If you hover your mouse cursor over the small button object icon on the condition on event line 4, you will see that it says Button_Back. Double-click this icon to bring up the dialog box, and then double-click on Button_Next to change the object. (Remember to hover your cursor over the object to find out which one.)

5. Now move across from event line 4 until you are directly under the Counter object, right-click on the action box, and then select Add to Counter.

In the Expression Evaluator, enter the value of **1** and click on OK.

You now have two actions for the counter and need to delete one of them. But because the order of the actions is based on when you added them, if you double-click on the counter action box and view it in the Event List editor, you will see a problem shown in Figure 10.14.

In Figure 10.14, you can see we have one action (subtracting from the counter) in the middle of the actions, and the one we just added at the bottom of the list. We cannot leave our action at the bottom because the code will not work correctly as it will update the data with the current counter value before displaying the same data.

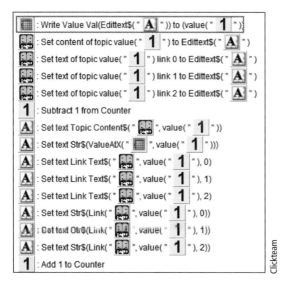

Figure 10.14
The order of the actions and two counter actions.

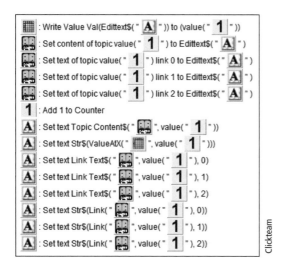

Figure 10.15
The completed actions for the Button_Next event.

So drag and drop the Add 1 to Counter to just below the Subtract 1 from Counter, and then delete the Subtract 1 from Counter action. Your actions should now look like Figure 10.15 in the Event List editor.

Your Event editor will now look something like Figure 10.16.

	All the events / All the objects							1				A	A	A	A	A	A	A	A	abc	abc	abc	abc	
1	• Start of Frame			✓								✓	✓	✓	✓	✓	✓	✓	✓				✓
2	Button Clicks																						
3	• Button ▭ clicked		✓	✓					✓	✓	✓	✓	✓	✓	✓					✓
4	• Button ▭ clicked		✓	✓					✓	✓	✓	✓	✓	✓	✓					✓
5	• Button ▭ clicked																			
6	• New condition																			

Figure 10.16
The Event editor with its events and actions so far.

Clickteam. Game: Jason Darby.

Button Save

The Save button will ultimately have two actions: to save the current topic number to the array and to activate a group called Update Values, which will tidy up the editors edit boxes.

We cannot add the group actions since the group is not currently created, so we will do this a little later.

Let's update the array by moving across from event line 4 until you are directly under the Array object. Drag and drop the array action into the action box below it on event line 5.

We will come back to the Button Save event later after we have created the rest of our code.

Reset Modified Flag

The next section of code will be a check to see if any of the edit boxes has been edited. If they have, we will reset any flags (so that it's not always true), and then we will activate the Update Values group. Obviously, we haven't created the group yet, but we will add all other code in place.

1. First create a comment line called "Reset Modified Flag".

2. Click on the New condition text on event line 7.

3. In the New Condition dialog box, right-click on the Topic_Links Edit object, and select Has Entry Zone Just Been Modified.

You now have one condition, but we want to check if any of the other edit boxes have been updated. We could create lots of conditions that do this, but it creates a lot of code. To solve this problem, we can use the OR (logical) condition. The OR (logical) condition will check if any of the conditions are true and then run the actions.

4. Right-click on the condition you have just added in event line 7 and select OR operator (logical).

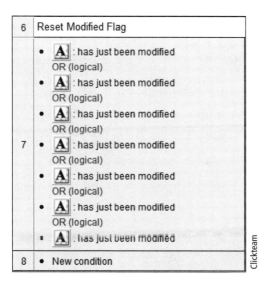

Figure 10.17
The Reset Modified Flag condition.

5. Now you need to add all of the topic links and link number edit boxes (LinkText1, LinkText2, LinkText3, LinkNo1, LinkNo2, and LinkNo3) until you get a condition that looks like Figure 10.17.

Now that you have a condition that lets you know when an edit box has been edited, we need to reset the flag on each of the edit boxes.

6. Move across from event line 7 until you are directly under the LinkText1 Edit object, right-click the action box, and select Control | Force Text Modified Flag | Off.

7. Now drag and drop this action across to the following action boxes of LinkText2, LinkText3, LinkNo1, LinkNo2, and LinkNo3.

Updates Group

The Updates group will be disabled at the start of the frame and will be activated every time the user edits one of the edit box's contents. It will then update the data that is stored in the Text Adventure Pages object, ensuring that it is always the latest data. It's important to ensure the latest data is being stored before saving off to a file; otherwise, you may have data issues.

1. First, create a comment that says "Update Values". To create a comment, right-click on an event number and select Insert | A Comment."

2. Create a group called Update Values, and ensure that it is disabled by verifying that the checkbox for Active When Frame Starts is not selected. To create a group, right-click on an event number and select Insert | A Group of Events.

We now need four events that are similar. We need an event that will check what the value is in the Topic_Links edit box. As we are only going to have a maximum of three links, the only possible number of links in each topic will be 0, 1, 2, and 3.

3. Click on the New condition text in the Update Values group (event line 10).

4. In the New Condition dialog box, right-click on the Special Conditions object and select Compare Two General Values.

We want to compare the number stored in the Topic_Links box, but remember that the Topic_Links box is an edit box, so we have to ensure we convert it to a value so that it can be compared to another value.

5. Click on the Val button in the Expression Evaluator.

6. It will now say >Enter string here<. Ensure this is highlighted and click on Retrieve Data from an Object.

7. When the New Expression dialog box appears, right-click on the Topic_Links object and select Get Text.

8. Ensure the operator stays at Equal in the drop-down list. In the bottom box, change the value to **3**. You can see an example of this in Figure 10.18. Click on OK to save this to the Event editor.

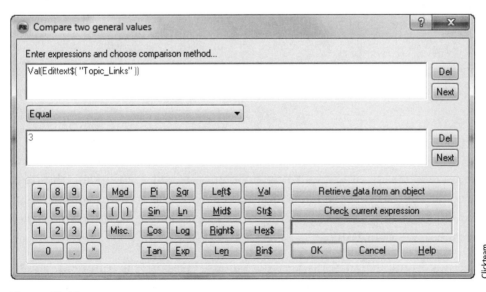

Figure 10.18
The expression to compare two values.

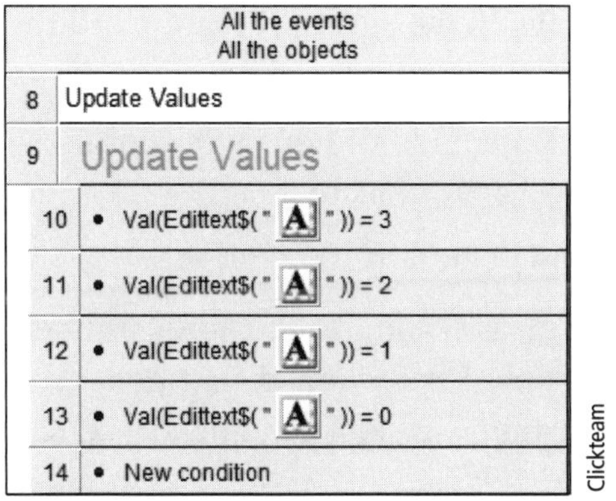

Figure 10.19
The conditions to compare the edit box to a number.

9. Drag and drop this condition line to the New condition text below it, and repeat until you have four of them.

Now you need to change the final numbers in each of the event lines so that they read =3, =2, =1, and =0.

10. Double-click on the condition in event line 11.

11. Change the number 3 to the number **2**, and click on OK.

12. Double-click on the condition in event line 12, change the number 3 to **1**, and click on OK.

13. Double-click on the condition in event line 13, change the number 3 to **0**, and click on OK.

You should have four events that look like Figure 10.19.

Now that you have the four events in place, you need to program each one to set the topic text and the link numbers to the Text Adventure Pages object and then reset any edit boxes (using "") that should not contain any data.

Note

The link numbers are formatted in the Text Adventure Pages object by placing each number into the Expression Evaluator using commas to separate them, so "4,85,15" indicates that there were three links.

Let's set up the saving the information to the Text Adventure Pages object action for event line 10, which is when the number of links in the Topic_Links box equals 3. We will update the topic content, the topic links, and then clean up edit boxes.

1. Ensure that you can see the events in the Update Values group before continuing. If not, double-click on the group to expand the contents.

2. Move across from event line 10, which is the Topic_Links Equals 3 condition, until you are directly under the Text Adventure Pages object.

3. Right-click on the action box and select Set Topic Content.

4. When the Expression Evaluator appears, it will ask you for a topic number. Click on Retrieve Data from an Object. In the New Expression dialog box, right-click on the Counter object and select Current Value. Then click on OK.

5. The Expression Evaluator will then ask for the topic content, so click on Retrieve Data from an Object, right-click on the Topic_Text edit object, and then Get Text. Click on the OK button.

Now that the topic content has been set, you now need to save the topic links, and the first will be for three links.

6. Move across from event line 10 until you are under the Text Adventure Pages object. Right-click on the action box with a tick mark in it.

7. Select Set topic links.

When the Expression Evaluator appears, it will ask you for a topic number, which you will get from the Counter object.

8. Click on Retrieve Data from an Object. In the New Expression dialog box, right-click the Counter object and choose Current Value. Click on OK when back at the expression to continue.

You will now be asked to enter the topic links separated by commas. We know we can get the data from the three edit boxes, but we need to format it precisely.

9. Ensure that the quote marks are selected and then click on Retrieve Data from an Object. Right-click on the LinkNo1 object and select Get Text.

You will now have a single edit string in the Expression Evaluator. You can add additional text to this line. If you were to just add additional edit boxes, you would end up with all of the numbers in a row, so you need to add a comma. Do this by typing in a + sign, then a quotation mark and a comma then another quotation mark:

1. At the end of the expression, type a + sign, then "," so you should have a line that looks like the following:

Edittext$("LinkNo1")+","

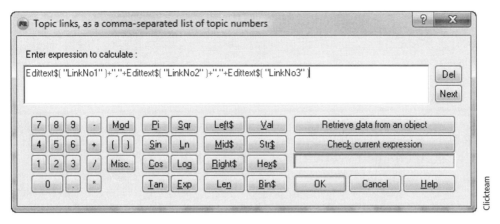

Figure 10.20
The expression to create all of the links for the Text Adventure Pages object.

Now we need to add LinkNo2:

2. At the end of the expression, type another + sign and then click on the Retrieve Data from an Object button. Right-click on LinkNo2 edit object and then select Get Text.

3. Now add a further +"," text to the end of LinkNo2.

4. Finally add another + sign and then click on Retrieve Data from an Object, right-click on LinkNo3, and select Get Text.

Your expression should now look like Figure 10.20.

5. You can now click on OK to save the information to the Event editor.

Now that you have done that, you can quickly create the other actions for the 2, 1, and 0 comparison conditions (event lines 11, 12, and 13).

6. Drag and drop the actions from event line 10 from the Text Adventure Pages object and drop it onto the action boxes for events, 11, 12, and 13.

We now need to edit the links in each of the events (11, 12 and 13) so that it stores the correct number of links at the moment you are storing 3, but we need to only store 2 in event line 11, 1 in event line 12 and 0 in event line 13.

7. Right-click on the action box for the Text Adventure Pages object on event line 11. From the pop-up box, choose Edit and then select the second item in the list that is the Set Topic Values.

8. Click OK on the topic number as this is correct.

When it displays the three topic links, you need to remove everything after the second LinkNo2 edit expression.

This will leave you with:

Edittext$("LinkNo1")+","+Edittext$("LinkNo2")

9. Click on OK to save.

We now need to do the same for event line 12, but you need to delete the two end topic links, which will leave you with:

Edittext$("LinkNo1")

Finally, you need to repeat the same process but for event line 13, but this time delete all of the LinkNo's and leave just "" in the expression box for topic links.

You should see the following actions for each of the conditions as shown in Figure 10.21.

Now that we have put our data into the Pages object, we need to ensure that any edit boxes that had data in them are removed if they are not a valid link. In other words, if the user of the editor indicates that there is only 1 topic link, then topic links for 2 and 3 should be cleared of any data. We will do this by setting the edit boxes of those objects that are no longer needed to "", which is effectively empty.

We don't need to reset any edit boxes if the user has entered 3 links, but we do for all of the others.

10. From event line 11, move across until you are directly under the LinkText3 object, right-click on the action box, and choose Editing | Set Text.

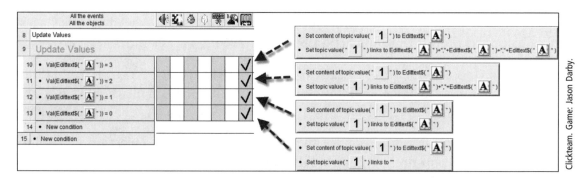

Figure 10.21
The storing of information to the Text Adventure Pages object.

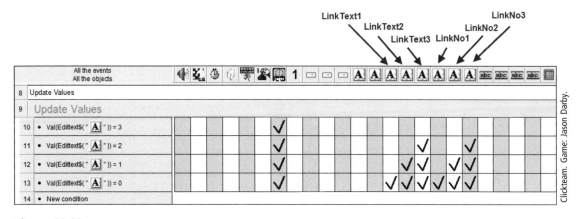

Figure 10.22
Clearing the edit boxes of data.

11. In the set text Expression Evaluator, leave it as "" and click on the OK button.

12. Drag and drop this action to the LinkNo3 object on the same event line.

Now you can drag and drop this to the other lines that need data clearing. See Figure 10.22 for how this should look.

Now that you have added all of the required actions to this group, you need to disable the group so that only when something has been edited will the group be activated. If it is activated all the time, it will always be updating the objects and may cause your editor to slow down.

13. Click on the New condition text in the Update Values group (event line 14).

14. Click on the Special Object, and then click on Always.

Now that you have the Always condition, you can create an action to disable the group:

15. Move across from the Always event line (14) until you are directly under the Special Conditions object.

16. Right-click on the action box and select Groups of Events | Deactivate.

17. When the Deactivate dialog box appears, select Update Values and click on OK.

Save Code

Now that you have the majority of code in place, you can finally create your code to save both the data in the Text Adventure Pages object and the array files to an actual file. This will overwrite the file that we loaded at the start of the frame.

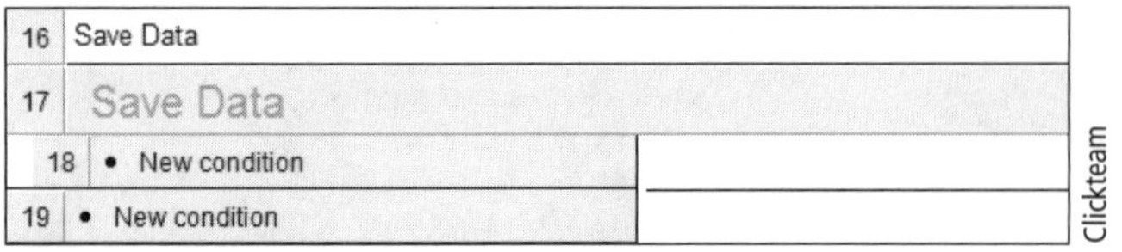

16	Save Data	
17	Save Data	
18	• New condition	
19	• New condition	

Clickteam

Figure 10.23
The Save Data group.

1. First, create a comment called "Save Data".

2. Then create a group (deactivated) with the name ("Save Data").

It should look like Figure 10.23.

We only need a single condition in the Save group, which will be an Always condition. Within this group, we will set all current data to the Text Adventure Pages object from the edit boxes. To ensure that we have the latest data, save for both the Text Adventure Pages object and the array, and then we will deactivate the group so that it will only be activated when required.

First let's create our condition:

1. Click on the New condition text in the Save Data group.

2. In the New Condition dialog box, right-click the Special Object and select Always.

Next, we will set the content to the Text Adventure Pages, but since we already created these actions before, we can drag and drop them from another action box.

3. Go back to event line 3, and move to the right of the Button_Back Clicked event. Drag and drop the content from the Text Adventure Pages object on this event to the Text Adventure Pages object on line 18.

Now we need to save all of this content to the Text Adventure Pages object.

4. Move across from event line 18 until you are directly under the Text Adventure Pages object, right-click on the action box, and select File Save.

5. When the dialog box appears, click on the New Expression dialog box.

6. When you are asked to enter a filename, click on the Retrieve Data from an Object button.

7. In the New Expression dialog box, right-click on the Special object and choose Filenames | Application Directory.

8. You will now be taken back to the Expression Evaluator where you will see Appdir$ already entered. Add the following +"**Pages.tap**" and then click on the OK button.

Now we need to save to the array file using a similar process.

9. Move across from event line 18 until you are directly under the Array object, right-click on the action box, and select Files | Save Array to File.

10. When asked to select a file, click on the Expression button.

11. When asked to enter a filename, click on the Retrieve Data from an Object button.

12. In the New Expression dialog box, right-click on the Special object and select Filenames | Application Directory.

13. When you are in the Expression Evaluator and can see Appdir$, add +"**Pages.arr**" to the end of it and click on OK.

The last thing we need to do is deactivate the group.

14. Move across from event line 18 until you are directly under the Special Conditions object, right-click on the action box, and select Group of Events | Deactivate.

15. The Deactivate dialog box now appears. Ensure that the (2) – Save Data option is selected and then click on the OK button.

You have now completed the actions for the Save Data group. You can see the actions in the Event List editor in Figure 10.24.

Group Activations

Now that you have your groups in place, you can set up the activation for the Update Values and the Save Data groups. This means the groups will be called, process any actions, and then deactivate.

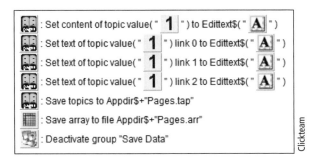

Figure 10.24
The actions for the Save Data group.

Let's start with activating the Save Data group when the Button_Save has been clicked.

1. Move across from event line 5 until you are under the Special Conditions object.

2. Right-click on the action box and select Group of Events | Activate.

3. When the Activate dialog box appears, ensure the (2) – Save Data option is selected and click on OK.

4. Now activate the final group and enable the Update Values group when the edit boxes have been modified.

5. Move to event line 7; move across until you are under the Special Condition object.

6. Right-click on the action box and select Group of Events | Activate.

7. When the Activate dialog box appears, ensure (1) – Update Values option is selected and click on the OK button.

Congratulations! You have now completed all of the programming for the Pages editor. You can now run this program and store your data in data files. Next, we will show you how to update the game created in Chapter 3 to load in this data.

The completed editor can be downloaded from the Castle Software website and is called Pages_Editor_Complete.mfa.

UPDATING THE ORIGINAL GAME

In Chapter 3 we made a simple adventure game called *Moon Traveller* where you were tasked with setting up a moon base. If you recall, there was a large amount of data entry for just 15 different topics. Now that you have created an editor that has stored all of this data, you can replace some of the code and use the data from the editor instead.

Load up the file MoonTraveller.mfa, which contains all of the old code that we had in our game. We now need to make a few changes.

Previously, we had a String object displaying 15 paragraphs of text that had to be manually placed in the game. We no longer need this file as it will be replaced by an edit box. This will be the only change we need in the Frame editor, so ensure that you are looking at the frame before proceeding.

1. Delete the String object from the Frame editor. You will see a Delete Objects dialog box that advises you that there are events associated with this object you are about to delete. Since we already know that we won't be using these events for this object, we are safe to delete them, so click on the Yes button.

2. Insert an edit box onto the frame and place it anywhere on the screen.

3. In the edit box Properties Settings tab, ensure multiline is ticked and that Border and 3D Look are deselected.

4. Go to the Size/Position tab for the new edit box and change its position to X to **24** and Y to **52**.

5. Change the size of the edit box to **585** and **257**.

Now go into the Event editor to make some small changes to allow you to load the data in and display it.

We don't need some of the content that is in this screen as it's all being done via the loading of a file.

6. Delete all the actions currently under the Text Adventure Pages object on event line 2.

7. Delete event lines 3 and 4. This is a comment and a timer equals 00.05 line.

Now we need to load in the data file for the Text Adventure Pages object and set the topic content to the newly added edit box.

8. Move across from event line 2 until you are directly under the Text Adventure Pages object, right-click on the action box, and select File | Load.

9. Click on the Expression button.

10. Click on the Retrieve Data from an Object button.

11. Right-click on the Special object and select Filenames | Application Directory. You will now see Appdir$ in the Expression Evaluator. Add +"**Pages.tap**" to the end of the expression and then click on OK.

Now we need to load this data into the new edit box we created.

12. Move across on event line 2 until you are under the edit box.

13. Right-click on the edit box and select Editing | Set Text.

14. Click on the Retrieve Data from an Object button.

15. Right-click on the Text Adventure Pages object and choose Get Topic Content.

16. The text >Topic< will now be highlighted. Click on Retrieve Data from an Object and then right-click on the Counter object and select Current Value.

17. Click on OK to save this information to the Event editor.

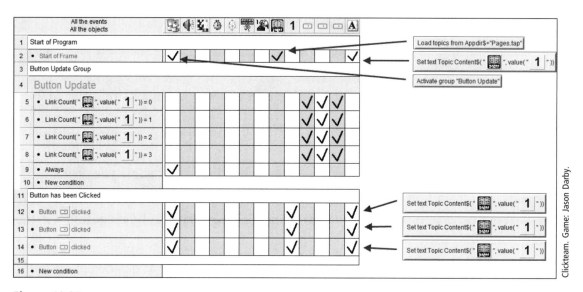

Figure 10.25
The changes made to *Moon Traveller* to allow for external data.

Then we need to activate the Button Update group.

18. Move across from event line 2 until you are under the Special Conditions group.

19. Right-click on the action box and select Group of Events | Activate.

20. When the Activate dialog box appears, choose (1) Button Update and click on OK.

Now that we have loaded the file in and, set its contents on-screen, there is one final thing we have to do, and that is to update the content in the edit box every time one of the three buttons has been clicked. We already have the action for this from event line 1 under the Edit object.

21. Drag and drop the action from event line 2 under the edit box and place a copy of it in the edit box for all three buttons; this is event lines 12, 13, and 14.

You can see these changes in Figure 10.25.

CHAPTER SUMMARY

Though the code may have taken you a while to get through, the actual work to create this editor was only a few hours. If you were creating a longer game than *Moon Traveller,* you would have certainly spent more time trying to add the data to MMF2 directly through the Event editor. Viewing and changing that data would also have become more and more complex as the game became larger. So hopefully you will now see why creating editors is extremely important to improving how you work with your game. The great thing with an editor is that you can also give the files to someone else to work on while you work on something else, which is especially important if you are working on a team.

In the next chapter, we will be looking at the features required for a point-and-click adventure game.

CHAPTER 11

POINT-AND-CLICK ADVENTURES

In this chapter, we will look at point-and-click adventures and the various features that make up these types of games. We will also look at how to create these various features in MMF2. In Chapter 12, you will create a simple point-and-click game that will incorporate the features you learn about in this chapter.

WHAT IS POINT AND CLICK?

In Chapter 1, you learned about the various kinds of adventure games that are currently on the market as well as those from the past.

Point-and-click games normally place you within an environment with a plot or story. Working from within this environment, you are then expected to figure out the clues and move around the game world using the mouse or touch (in iOS games). You will then navigate the world by pointing and clicking (or touching if using a touch device).

Point-and-click adventure games are still extremely popular, with games such as *Broken Sword* and *Monkey Island* appearing on iOS devices such as iPhones and iPads. Companies, such as Telltale Games, continue to make point-and-click adventure games, such as *Jurassic Park* and *The Walking Dead*, for PC and PS3/Xbox.

Note

The *Walking Dead* game from Telltale sold over one million copies within two weeks of release. Telltale releases games in an episodic format, very much like a TV series where a part of the story is released over a period of time. For example, there may five episodes, each providing a part of an ongoing story arc.

POINT-AND-CLICK FEATURES

Even though point-and-click adventure games have many different features and are generally more complicated than normal text-based games discussed earlier in this book, they can still be pretty easy to make if you break the game into the various systems needed to create your game.

Some of the core concepts and features of a point-and-click adventure game are as follows:

- **Rooms/locations:** Very much like the text-based adventure games you made earlier in the book, rooms and locations play an important role in point-and-click adventure games. As the player explores the game world and figures out puzzles, he is allowed to travel farther into the game world, being introduced to new and interesting locations. For example, you may start out in a single boring room in your adventure game. Perhaps the player has to figure out how to get out of the room and solve a puzzle. At this point, the player is feeling that he wants to figure out how to get out of the room. Once the player has, he is then presented with a new room, perhaps with a twist. What happens if he opens the door to his room and finds that he is now in a prison cell, and the room was just a fake location to give the player a false sense of security? You don't necessarily have to go for a surprise or shock; just revealing a new location to move to and from is a good starting point in an adventure game. Just remember not to confuse the player with too many directions and rooms at the very beginning. Instead, build up to opening the game world.

- **Characters:** Characters are extremely important in building a believable game world. Characters will also help your player by pushing the story forward in terms of what the current issues are that need to be solved. When creating characters for your game world, ensure they fit into your story and your world. If you are making a game about being on a moon base, you might find workers, security personnel, and scientists, but you wouldn't necessarily expect a clown or a pirate to appear. This doesn't mean you can't have these types of characters, as it all depends on context. If you are making a game about space, then perhaps you might have space pirates, and if you are making it a comedy-based adventure game, then including a pirate might actually work.

- **Plot:** You can create a game that has a very simple concept, such as getting your brother's stolen toys back from a bully, or retrieving your homework that was stolen by a dog before you get into trouble. It's important for the player to be able to get hooked by the story or concept as early on in the game as possible so that he is inclined to play more of it.

- **Conversation trees:** You may want to allow your character to talk to NPCs (non-player characters), and these are normally in the form of a simple selection and reply. For example, you click on the Talk button and then on a character on-screen. You might then get a selection of three questions to ask, and you select one to elicit a particular response. You might decide to keep the conversation trees as text only or add a voice-over response.

- **Animations:** An animation is a set of graphics that make a character or object appear animated. For example, you create a dog which is going to be controlled by the player; you may need a moving up, down, left and right walking animation. You may decide you want the dog to wag its tail and, if it stays in one place too long, to sit. Objects can also be animated, such as fountains, clock faces, or background scenes. Animations are very important in point-and-click games to provide an extra element of quality.

- **Mouse cursors:** There are a number of ways you can present the mouse cursor to the player: you can continue to use a Windows-based arrow pointer, which is very good for fine control, or you can replace the cursor with a graphical object, which can be changed to a particular action that you want the character to do on-screen. A good example of this is in *Monkey Island* or *Gabriel Knight* where you can change the cursor to a graphic that looks like a mouth (to represent speaking). You would then click on the person you want to speak to.

- **Inventory systems:** You cannot make an adventure game without an inventory system. Inventory systems are essential to allow the player to collect items that may help him solve puzzles later on in the game. An inventory system is effectively a bag or box that the player carries around the game world, which he can access at any time. To add a level of difficulty to some point-and-click adventure games, it's quite common to only allow a limited number of objects to be carried at any one time. The player may have to solve one mystery and go back for an object once he has made more space in his inventory.

- **Layers:** If you have used programs like Photoshop, you may have already heard of a layer. A layer is like placing a number of graphic objects on top of one another. Each layer has a number and it is ordered from front to back, so a layer at the front will appear on top/in front of another object. You can then place a character at a different layer between the two objects and have him walk between the objects. Layers are used to create a perspective. We will discuss how to use layers later on in this chapter.

- **Graphic bars and buttons:** You may want the player to be able to interact with the game using a graphic bar, icon, or buttons. You may want to allow the player to access special in-game features using these graphic bars, such as the inventory system and help systems.

■ **Pop-up menus:** In games such as *Future Wars*, you would use a pop-up menu to select a particular option such as talk or use.

■ **Hint systems:** If you have difficult puzzles in your games, you might want to provide some form of help or hint system. This can be in the form of providing more information via text or voice-activated when a player repeats the same action more than once.

Now that we have some of the basic features of a point-and-click adventure game, let's explore some of them in detail and how they can be implemented in MMF2.

ORDERING OF OBJECTS

Ordering of objects is a basic version of layering. The order in which you place the objects within MMF2 will define their order within the game world. In the following example, we have inserted three colored active objects into the MMF2 Frame editor as shown in Figure 11.1. Because the objects are not overlapping each other, everything seems as expected, but if you select each of the objects (by dragging the cursor over all the objects or by holding down Ctrl and left-mouse clicking), you will notice that each object has a number in the top left-hand corner as shown in Figure 11.2.

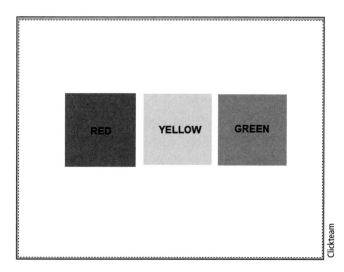

Figure 11.1
Three simple active objects placed on the Frame editor.

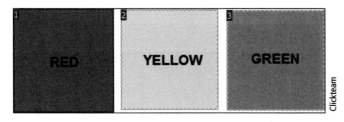

Figure 11.2
The order numbers on each square.

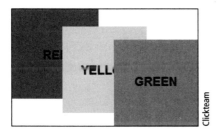

Figure 11.3
The order of the objects when they are overlapping.

The numbers are assigned to each object as they are created and placed on the Frame editor, and more importantly, the lower the number the order of the object will be placed at the back. What this means is that if you had 10 pieces of paper all with numbers on them and you placed them in a pile, the number 1 piece of paper would be at the bottom, while the number 10 paper item would be on top.

When all objects are separate on the screen such as the objects in Figure 11.2, they all appear to be at the same level. But when they start to overlap, the ordering begins to take precedence as shown in Figure 11.3.

As you can imagine in a point-and-click adventure where you have a character walking around a scene, the ordering of objects can be very important to ensure that the right graphical object is at the right level at the right time; otherwise, you could make a character disappear when you only wanted them to walk between objects. Figure 11.4 shows an example of the ordering working correctly where you have two characters: one at the front of a shelf, while the other is running behind it. In contrast in Figure 11.5, you see that the second character is placed incorrectly in front of the shelf and appears to be running on top of it.

Note

All backdrop objects will appear behind any other objects regardless of when they were added to the frame.

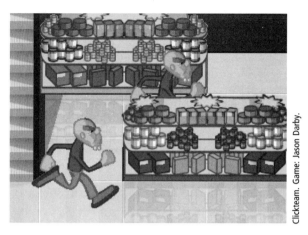

Clickteam. Game: Jason Darby.

Figure 11.4
Example showing ordering working correctly.

Clickteam. Game: Jason Darby.

Figure 11.5
Example showing ordering working incorrectly.

Changing the Order of Objects

Development of games is never totally straightforward, and though you may start out adding graphics on the Frame editor in the correct order, you may add new objects and find they are out of sync.

You can change the order of any object by doing the following:

1. Select the object with a single left-mouse click.

You now see the objects order number. Right-click on the object that you just selected to reveal a pop-up menu as shown in Figure 11.6.

2. Select the relevant option.

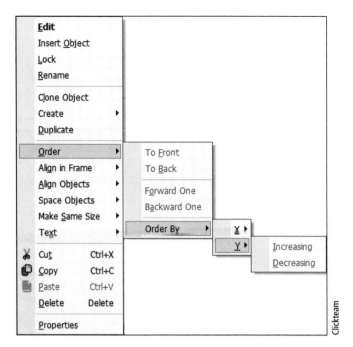

Figure 11.6
The ordering pop-up menu options.

Note

The options available in the pop-up menu are all related to the object currently in the editor. If you want to make the changes in real-time while the application is running, then you will need to use the Event editor.

Some important options that you can use in the pop-up menu (which are also within the Event editor) are as follows:

- **To Front:** Bring an object to the front of the screen, which means it will replace its current order number with a higher number.

- **To Back:** This will place the object at the back of the screen, so it will get a lower order number.

- **Forward One:** This will move an object forward in order, so that it appears on the top of the screen.

- **Backward One:** This will move an object backward in order, so that it will appear toward the back of the screen.

In Figure 11.7, you can see how to move an object forward and backward in order by using the Event editor. The benefit of moving objects in real-time is that you can write code that will move an object at a specific time.

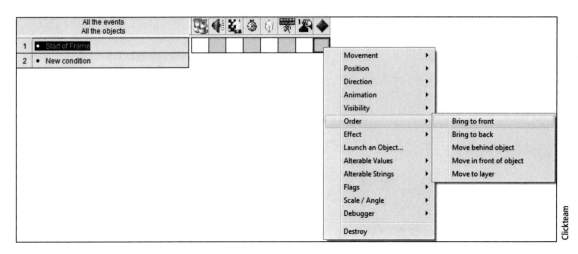

Figure 11.7
The Order options in the Event editor.

LAYERS

Layers are the next step up from ordering objects. Rather than having all images on the same level, you have multiple levels on top of each other. On each layer, you can place specific images and then order them within that level. Think of it as having multiple pieces of transparent paper, one on top of another, and you place a set of image objects on each piece of paper. The level of the layer will define the order on the screen where the objects will appear.

The layers system is not always apparent in MMF2, and you may have it switched off (which means any objects that you add are all on the same layer). To ensure that you have it enabled, click on View | Toolbars | Layers Toolbar. You will know if it's enabled if you can see a single layer as shown in Figure 11.8; a close-up can be seen in Figure 11.9.

Below is a list of the icons that appear on the Layers toolbar and a description of what each command does:

- **Plus Sign:** Adds an additional layer.
- **Red X:** Deletes the currently selected layer. You must always have a single layer, so if there is only one layer, the red X icon will be disabled.
- **Eye:** Changes the visibility of the layer; to make a layer invisible, you must have more than one layer present.
- **Padlock:** Locks the currently selected layer, meaning that you are unable to delete or edit any objects; however, you are still able to add new objects to the layer.

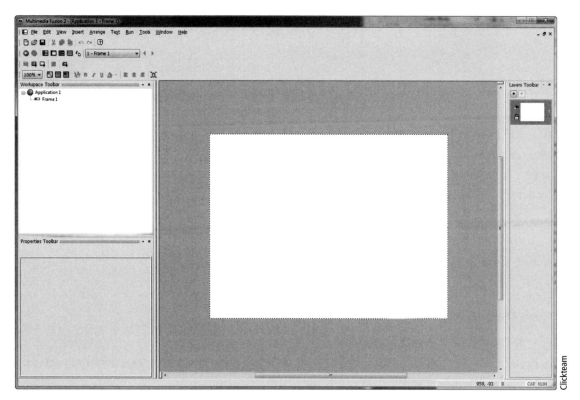

Figure 11.8
The Layers toolbar on the right-hand side of MMF2.

Figure 11.9
A close-up of the Layers toolbar.

- **White Page:** Displays a thumbnail image of the frame.
- **Number:** Indicates the current layer number.

To add an object to a layer, ensure that it is selected first. When you use more than one layer, you will see that objects are given a new order number as shown in Figure 11.10. In Figure 11.10, we have created two layers and placed a colored box on each layer.

Figure 11.10
Two boxes with their layers and order numbers displayed.

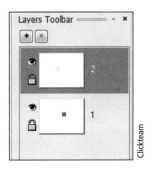

Figure 11.11
Two layers with an image on each layer.

In Figure 11.11, you can see how this is represented in the Layers toolbar. As you add layers, the most recent layer that is added appears on top. From a graphical position point of view, those objects on the highest layer will always appear at the front of the frame.

In a point-and-click adventure, you can have three layers (but it's perfectly fine to have more layers depending on your game) and have the walls of a room on layer 1, the character on layer 2, and some objects that will appear in front of the player on layer 3.

Pop-up Menus

A pop-up menu is a menu bar that appears when you right-click on the mouse in a point-and-click adventure game.

The pop-up menu appears at the location where you clicked the mouse and provides you with a list of possible options to choose from. You can see a simple graphical representation of a pop-up menu in Figure 11.12.

We can create a pop-up menu system in MMF2 by using the Popup Menu object. The only disadvantage of this object is that it is for Windows platforms only, so if you intend on making your games for other platforms, you will have to look at alternative options such as creating your own pop-up menus.

Figure 11.12
Simple example of a pop-up menu.

Note

You don't have to use the right mouse button to activate a pop-up menu. You can activate it by a keyboard press or button press.

Note

The biggest issue with pop-up menus is that they are slower to use for the player than the cursor icons/ selection system we are going to talk about shortly. Pop-up menus are discussed here for completeness, and you may decide they are still useful in particular situations within a point-and-click adventure game.

We will now take a quick look at the options for the Popup Menu object.

1. First, create a blank application and then insert an object onto the frame. Find and select the Popup Menu object as shown in Figure 11.13.

2. As soon as you place this on the frame, you will see a Popup Menu dialog box as shown in Figure 11.14.

3. You can click on the Add button to create a menu option and use the Left and Right options to create submenus.

Figure 11.13
The Popup Menu object in MMF2.

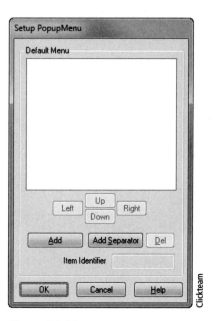

Figure 11.14
The Popup Menu dialog box.

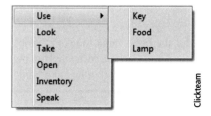

Figure 11.15
Additional menu levels.

You are also able to access the Popup Menu object through the Event editor, which is extremely useful as you are able to create menus on the fly based on what is happening in your game.

For example, you could have a Use option in your menu that would allow you to use an object from your inventory in the game world. By keeping track of your objects, you can place an object name in the menu. An example of this is shown in Figure 11.15. You would add these inventory items to the menu as they are required.

In the Event editor, you have some useful conditions to check when an item has been selected, and there are a large number of actions such as:

■ Adding an item

- Setting item text
- Showing the menu at the clicking location or a different location on-screen

GRAPHIC CURSORS

One of the common point-and-click adventure game features is using the mouse to create an in-game action. For example, if you want to talk to a character or pick up an object, you can use the pop-up menu option covered in the previous section. The main issue with pop-up menus is that they are quite slow when a lot of things are happening on-screen, so an alternative is to use the mouse to select the game action instead. So, if you want to open a door, you can right-click on your mouse to change the mouse cursor until the Open graphic appears, and then you can specify that you want to open the door by clicking on it.

To create a graphic cursor, you need the Cursor object as shown in Figure 11.16.

1. Create a blank application and insert the Cursor object on the frame.

2. Double-click on the Cursor object to access its properties; you will see the cursor dialog box as shown in Figure 11.17.

Figure 11.16
The Cursor object.

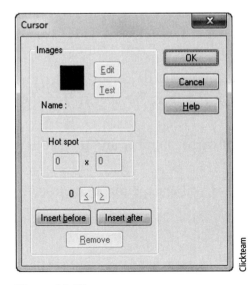

Figure 11.17
The Cursor dialog box.

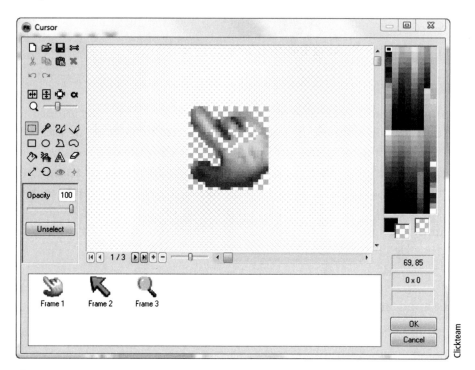

Figure 11.18
The Picture editor with our mouse cursor images.

Within this dialog box, you create the images that you wish to display instead of using your mouse cursor. By clicking on Insert, you can create images that you can use. Clicking on the Edit button enables you to use the standard picture editor to import or draw your own images. In Figure 11.18, you can see the three images that you have assigned to the Cursor object.

To access the different animation frames, you need to use the Event editor:

3. First we added a Start of frame condition that then sets the cursor to our first animation frame using Set Cursor Shape | Image Number. We specify 0 as the image.

4. Next, we create a condition that gets the current cursor number and then adds 1 to it.

5. Every time we click on the right mouse button, it will change the animation.

You can see the code in Figure 11.19.

Note

We can set an image from a number, name, or an active object already placed on the Frame editor.

	All the events All the objects									
1	• Start of Frame								✓	→ Change cursor to image number 0
2	• User clicks with right button								✓	→ Change cursor to image number CurrentImage(" ⬚ ")+1
3	• New condition									

Figure 11.19
The code to change our mouse cursor.

Note

You cannot create conditions for the Cursor object, so you will need to use a counter to keep track of the current cursor so that you can create conditions when the player has clicked on an object with a particular cursor set.

CONVERSATION/DIALOGUE TREES

Having the player initiate conversations between characters is an important part of point-and-click adventures. The player will ask a character a question and get either a text or voice (sound sample) response.

A dialogue tree is a system that is often used in games to create multiple conversation paths. Think of a tree and its roots that start from a single point and branch out into various strands; each strand is a topic of conversation. A basic drawing of a conversation tree is shown in Figure 11.20. One question may generate another set of questions, which can in theory create multiple other branches of questions. You might also start with multiple trees. Therefore, as you can imagine, if you are not careful it can become very confusing.

Before we talk about how a conversation tree might work and how to create one, let's take a look at the example file called SimpleTalk.mfa where we have created a simple three-question conversation. Each of the questions is a single tree, with a single

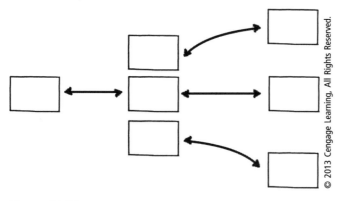

Figure 11.20
A simple drawing to show a conversation tree.

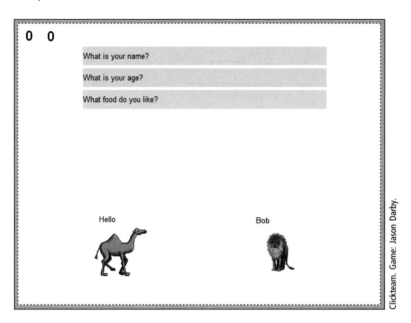

Figure 11.21
Frame setup for the SimpleTalk example.

branch. It is not very complicated in terms of conversation but a good starting point at looking at the complexities of creating a system.

In Figure 11.21, you can see the basic setup of the Frame editor of a simple three-question conversation. It has the following elements:

- **Counter:** A counter used to keep track of which text question has been selected by the player.

- **Counter2:** A counter used as a timer to display and remove text elements based on the progress of time.

- **Static Text:** Three Static Text objects used for the three questions that the player can ask.

- **String Objects:** Two String objects that will display text about the two animals to show the conversation progression.

- **Active Objects:** Two Active objects being used as characters that are talking to each other.

The example file works by displaying the three questions to the player, the player selects a question, which is then asked by the camel and after a short while is then answered by the lion. Once the lion has answered, any questions that still remain appear on-screen and the player is then able to ask another question.

Note

The two counters are on the frame for testing purposes and in a real game would be hidden from view.

Code for SimpleTalk Example

If you load the example file called SimpleTalk.mfa and access the Event editor, you will see the code as shown in Figure 11.22.

The code can be broken down in to the following sections:

- **Start of Frame:** At the start of the frame, we hide the three Static Text objects because we only want them to display when the user selects a text option.

- **Timer – Every Second:** Every second we want to update our timer counter by 1, which allows us to create our very own timer that we can reset at any time. We will be using this counter to handle specific timings for displaying text.

- **Timer – Specific times:** Display the text Hello and then hide it. After 3 seconds, display the questions.

- **Cursor over Text:** When the cursor is over one of the three pieces of text, change the background to a different color.

- **Cursor Not over Text:** If the cursor is not over the text, then change the background color back.

- **Text Selection:** The code makes a note of which question is selected and then hides all of the other questions.

- **Ask Question group:** This group allows us to display text from the first animal so that we can ask the question, "What is your name?"

- **Timer group:** The Timer group waits a specific amount of time and then displays the text answer.

The biggest problem for SimpleTalk is that it works well for a small number of questions, but if you were looking to create a complex conversation tree, it would expand the amount of code required considerably if you continued with this route. In Chapters 9 and 10, we looked at the role of editors and data, and a conversation tree system would benefit greatly from such a system.

The things you need to effectively manage a more complex conversation tree would be as follows:

- **Questions:** A set of questions you can ask a character that can be stored in a file and loaded when required. Each question will need an ID number so that you can ask the right question at the right time.

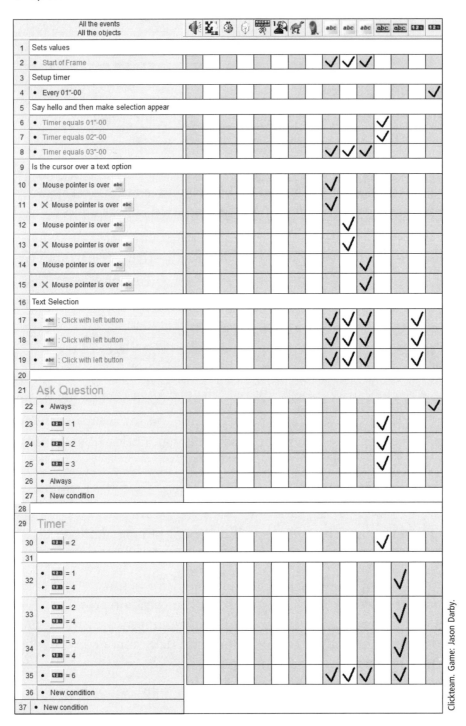

Clickteam. Game: Jason Darby.

Figure 11.22
The code for SimpleTalk.

- **Answers:** A set of answers based on the questions. Again these should be stored in a file such as an array. The answers should point to the question ID, but they may also have multiple answers. What if the person you are speaking to does not like you; perhaps you can give a different answer? In games, such as *Mass Effect* and *Fallout*, your status can define which answers are given, and sometimes they are not the answers you might be hoping for.

- **Unlocks:** A flag(s) to unlock further questions or indeed to keep specific questions locked.

- **Question Flow:** The ability to connect questions together. When asking one question and getting an answer, you may get a new group of questions.

- **Different Replies:** One issue in many conversation-based games is repetitive answers. It's more of a problem in RPG/open world–based games where you ask a character a question and then ask her again, and the response is exactly the same, as though you had never asked the original question. One way around this is a bit like the long and short room descriptions in text adventure games. When a question is asked the first time, they get a particular response. When they ask again, they get a different response. The only downside to this system that you need to be aware of is if a player comes back to a character to hear the answer to the question again and she gets only get a shortened (or "You've asked me that") type response. So it's important to build that into your answers and ensure that you have multiple replies. Adventure games get around this by having a journal or some method of reviewing comments made by characters, perhaps a notebook that states the key help information gathered from a conversation.

CHAPTER SUMMARY

In this chapter, we looked at the various features of a point-and-click adventure game and how you might consider implementing them in MMF2. In the next chapter, we will make a simple game using some of these features. It is important to note that a good point-and-click adventure game requires many different locations/rooms and puzzles, which is beyond the scope of this book. However, the features discussed here and the game in Chapter 12 will certainly give you enough code and ideas to get started on your own point-and-click adventure.

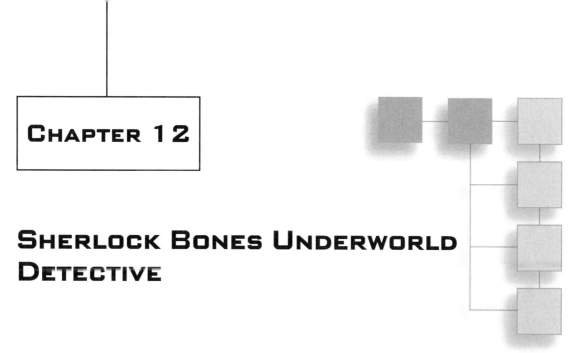

CHAPTER 12

SHERLOCK BONES UNDERWORLD DETECTIVE

In this chapter, we will look at putting together what we have learned in Chapter 11 and create our very own point-and-click adventure game called *Sherlock Bones Underworld Detective*. You play Sherlock the Skeleton who lives in the underworld and his job is to solve mysteries.

In this game, the mystery is to explore the two rooms within the game and interact with the items that the character comes across. The game will contain the following:

- Character movement
- Mouse cursors
- Movement masks
- Connecting frames and fades
- Item interaction
- Layers
- Inventory
- Trigger zones

You can find the file that we are using for this game, called Sherlock2b.mfa, with the other downloadable files. from www.castlesoftware.co.uk or from www.courseptr.com/downloads.

Note

In most point-and-click adventures, there are many places to visit, puzzles to solve, and characters to interact with. In a book that is devoted to many different adventure games, it would be impossible to provide a fully complete game as it would require a book of its own. The example in this chapter should provide you with a good introduction to the different features that you will need to include in your own games. Eventually, you will be able to build up to bigger and more complex games.

Sherlock Introduction

In this part of the chapter, we will look at the game frames and discuss the features that we have implemented to make this game work. In this game we have two frames: you can see the first in Figure 12.1 and the second room in Figure 12.2.

The aim in *Sherlock* is quite simple; you must control the movements and actions of Sherlock within two rooms in the underworld. You will control Sherlock using a Footprints mouse cursor. In the first room, you can interact with items around the room, pick up some items, and see a description for others. To move into the second room, you must first open a secret compartment on the picture frame and retrieve the key, which you will need to open the door on the left.

Figure 12.1
The first scene in our game.

Figure 12.2
The second scene in our game.

If we look at the contents for the first scene, which is Sherlock's living room, we can see the following things:

- **Counters:** Above the frame there are a number of counters for various tests and checks in our game.

- **Mouse cursor icons:** On the left of the frame, we have four icons that will replace the mouse cursor. The four icons represent four actions.

- **Orange box:** Below the mouse cursor icons we have an orange box. This box will be placed under the skeleton character and will be used to check when Sherlock collides with various trigger boxes in the game.

- **Trigger boxes:** We have four objects on-screen: three box shapes and a diamond. These are used to trigger conditions in the Event editor when the orange box collides with them. This will mean that the player has walked into the area, and we can trigger animations, sounds, and game play mechanics using this simple system.

- **Objects to pick up:** There are three objects that the player can pick up from the table, and there is a key hidden behind the picture on the wall.

- **Animations:** There are a number of animations: the first is the skeleton walking up, down, left, and right. The second animation is activated when the player opens the secret compartment on the picture, and we also have an animation of an opening door that will play once the player has retrieved a key and clicks to open the door.

- **Layer graphic:** For the opened door animation, we require that the player walk behind it. We can do this by having a graphic that appears after the door animation has played that will be layered in front of the skeleton.

- **Footprint marker:** When the player clicks on an area on the screen, we place the footprint icon, which allows us to use this as a marker for our code, so that we can work out how to move the skeleton and in which direction.

- **Detectors:** We have a number of red squares that are used to control the skeleton's movement.

- **Inventory bar:** This will contain any objects that the player will pick up. Initially this will be hidden. The player will be able to access this using the "I" key.

Note

The second scene in an underground room contains a subset of the first room.

Note

The trigger boxes in Figures 12.1 and 12.2 will be hidden from view from the player. For the purposes of this example and to show how trigger boxes work, we have initially made them visible.

Layers

We have two layers in both frame 1 and frame 2. The first layer in both frames is a cut-out image of the scene that shows where the player is able to walk. The second layer is the scene that contains all of our game graphics.

You can see these layers in Figure 12.3. If you cannot see these, you can switch on the layers by selecting View | Toolbars | Layers Toolbar. You can hide the second layer in a frame by clicking on the small eye icon for frame 2 (the top frame). You can see what the frame will look like if you hide layer 2 in the first frame in Figure 12.4. The colored area of the layer will be the area where the player cannot walk, while the transparent area is where he will be able to walk.

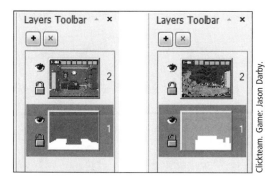

Figure 12.3
The layers for both frames.

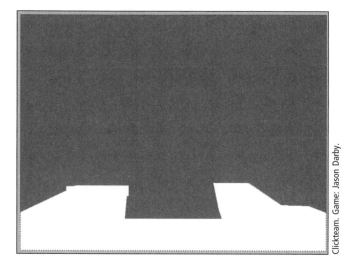

Figure 12.4
The walk layer.

We will check if the mouse pointer is over the colored area when the player clicks on the mouse. If it is, then we will not move the skeleton; if it's over the transparent area, we can then select some code that will move Sherlock.

Inventory Box

The inventory box will contain all of the objects that the player picks up in his adventure. We have seven slots in our inventory; you can create more or less depending on how much space you want to provide the player. In the first four inventory slots, we have an active image hidden in each of the boxes that contains six frames as shown in Figure 12.5.

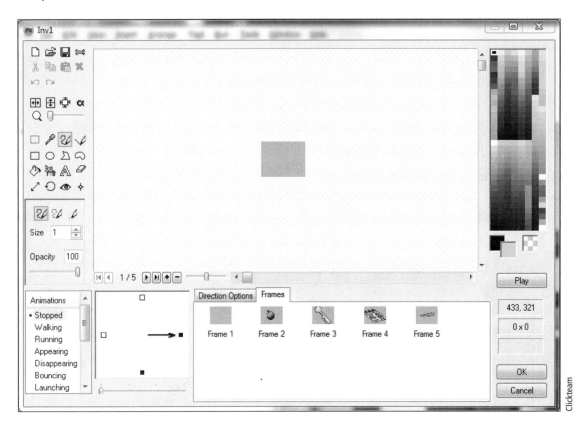

Figure 12.5
The six frames needed for our inventory.

By default at the start of the game, we have a blank image of just an orange background, so that when the player has nothing in the inventory he does not see anything different. As the player picks up objects, we find out what object is in the
inventory and then change the frame image to match the object.

We have set up a set of alterable values for the Inventory_Bar active object, which is
set to 0. As the player picks up the objects, we set the Alterable Value slot to the
value of that particular object. We then have some code that changes the frame
depending on the value in the Alterable Value property. You can see the alterable
values in the Inventory_Bar object as shown in Figure 12.6.

Counters

We are using quite a few counters in this example game to keep track of temporary
values. We have the following counters:

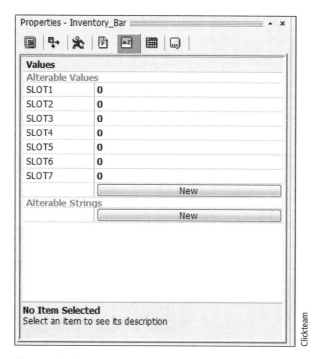

Figure 12.6
The alterable values needed to keep track of inventory items.

- **InventoryCounter:** We need to know when the inventory screen is being displayed or when it needs to be hidden. We have a counter that keeps track of the visibility of the inventory bar and refreshes the items in the inventory when it is displayed.

- **MouseCounter:** This counter keeps track of the current mouse icon that is displayed. We have four icons, each represented by a number stored in the MouseCounter. This ensures that we can prevent the player from picking up an object unless they currently have the Pickup_Icon currently selected.

- **TimerCounter:** When you look at an object, or view an object, a piece of text appears at the bottom of the screen to ensure that any text stays on-screen a set amount of time. TimeCounter is updated by MMF's inbuilt timer.

- **InventoryItemsCounter:** Keeps track of the number of items in the inventory, so that when you pick up an object it knows which image to display.

- **BetweenRoomCounter:** If Sherlock moves from the living room to the underground area and then back again, as they are on two separate frames, the game will start the frame as if it started for the first time. This means the skeleton will be placed on the right-hand side of the room, all animations will be reset, and the objects will be placed back on the table. Using this counter we can check if the player has left the room and returned, and if so, make any necessary changes to update the game so that it looks as if the player left it.

Note

The counters in this example file have been moved off the frame and so can no longer be seen, but it is useful while developing your games to leave them on the frame so you see their values. Once you have completed the game and everything is working correctly, you can move them off-screen.

SHERLOCK CODE

We will now look at the code for *Sherlock Bones Underworld Detective*, starting with the first frame, which is the starting location for our adventure.

Ensure that you have Sherlock2b.mfa loaded into MMF2 and that you are currently on frame 1, then click the Event editor to display all of the code for this frame. You will see 86 lines of code for this example and a number of groups. This isn't a large amount of code for a game like this, and many of the features in this game are easily transferable into other point-and-click adventure games.

Start of Frame Initialization

As with all games, we begin with some simple initialization and configuration of our game code. In line 1, you will see a Start of Frame condition and a comparison of the BetweenRoomCounter equals 1. This code will only run when the frame is loading and this counter is 1. The counter will only ever be 1 when you have moved into the second room and walked back to the original room. The BetweenRoomCounter is a global value, which means that it exists through the whole of our game, so we can set this counter in another frame and the value will continue to exist when we move into another frame.

You can see the actions for this event in Figure 12.7.

- The first three actions involve hiding or displaying the mouse cursor. The Walk_icon is the starting icon, so we want to have that visible at the start of the game.

- The fifth action is to activate the group "Inventory Fill." This group handles displaying the correct image in the inventory. It will also destroy any objects from the table or behind the picture if the player has already picked them up. If he re-enters the room, he will not see any of the destroyed objects.

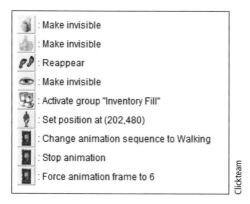

Figure 12.7
The actions for setting up the room when previously entered.

- The sixth action moves the skeleton to the left-hand side of the room. Otherwise, when the player re-enters the room, Sherlock would be positioned on the right side.

- The final three actions are to set the animation of the picture frame to "open." Otherwise, re-entering the room will reset the picture frame to "closed."

Hide Mouse Pointer

We can only have one Start of Frame event in a game, so for our second event we have set up a simple timer event that will run when a quarter of a second has gone by. In our game, we can make other changes that are implemented quickly without the user noticing.

For event line 2, the Windows mouse pointer can be hidden with a single action to hide, allowing us to replace it with our own graphics.

Pressing Escape

Hiding the Windows mouse cursor is very useful when you want to display your own icon for the mouse, but it also presents an issue when running a game in a windowed environment rather than full screen. This is because when you move the mouse between your game window and the Windows desktop, your mouse cursor will disappear. To allow the user to easily quit the game instead of trying to click on the red X in the top right-hand corner, the player can use a key to quit the game. For this game, we have used the Escape key.

Always Setting Icon Position

In event line 4, we have an Always event, which will always be run when MMF2 loops through the code. We have nine actions for this event, as shown in Figure 12.8. You will notice that the first eight are similar. They are in groups of two for each of our mouse icons: the first two, for example, are setting the Look_icon's X position on-screen to that of the X position of the mouse, while the second of the two sets the Look_icon's Y position on-screen to the Y position of the mouse.

This code means that all four icons will always be positioned in the exact location of the mouse cursor. Even though the Windows mouse cursor is hidden, it still moves around the screen and checks for left and right mouse clicks.

The final action in the Always event is setting the Overlapper box at a particular position from the Sherlock character. This means that wherever Sherlock moves, the Overlapper box will always be –29 (X) and –25 (Y) from its position. This will be placed at the bottom of Sherlock's feet and will be used to check when the character has moved into a particular location on screen.

Inventory Visible and Invisible

When the player presses the "I" key for the first time, the inventory bar will appear showing the player what items are currently in his possession. In event lines 6 and 7, we have two events for handling this visibility of the inventory bar.

The first of the two events checks if the player has pressed the "I" key and Inventory-Counter equals 1. If so, we hide the Inventory_Bar, add 1 to the InventoryCounter counter, then activate the Inventory Reset group, and finally we set all four inventory icons to hidden. The Inventory Reset group is used to reset the InventoryCounter back to 0.

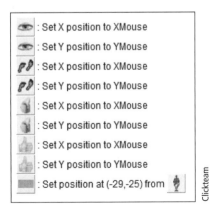

Figure 12.8
Actions for the Always event.

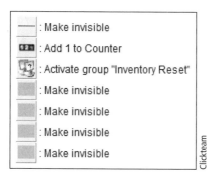

Figure 12.9
The actions for hiding the Inventory_Bar.

You can see the actions for this event in Figure 12.9.

The second of the two events (event line 7) will check for the key press and if the counter equals 0, then make the Inventory_Bar appear, add 1 to the InventoryCounter, and display all four of the inventory icons. Finally, we activate the group Inventory Fill, which will change the four icons to display the correct graphic. If the player has not currently picked up any objects, then it will set them to the blank (orange) default animation frame.

You can see the actions for displaying the Inventory_Bar in Figure 12.10.

Changing the Cursor

In point-and-click adventure games, it is important to implement a system that allows the player to interact with his surroundings. In this example, we are using graphical icons to depict a set of common actions, such as looking, walking, and picking up objects.

Figure 12.10
The Inventory_Bar displayed.

When the player clicks on the right mouse button, the icon will change. Once the player has a particular icon selected, they will be able to perform the corresponding on-screen action, such as picking up an object or walking to the other side of the screen.

Event line 9 will be true whenever the player clicks on the right mouse button. It only has two actions: the first to increment the MouseCounter counter, which is used to decide which icon graphic to show, and then to activate the group mouse cursor, which will update the actual visibility of the graphic.

Additional Cursor Events

Event lines 11 and 13 check the current value of the MouseCounter and will run if the player presses the left mouse button. Clicking the left mouse button means that the player wishes to do something on-screen.

Event line 11 is checking if the MouseCounter equals 2, which means that the cursor icon is currently the Look_Icon. If so, it will reset the timer to 0 seconds and then activate the group Look.

The timer is used to keep track of how long we want to display a message on-screen. We reset the timer before activating the group as we want to run the group for a set number of seconds, and we know that by resetting the timer we will always have the correct amount of time to display any messages.

Event line 13 checks when the MouseCounter equals 3, which means that the player has selected the Pick_Icon and indicates that the player wants to pick up objects in the game world. The action for this event is a single activate group Pickup action that handles the action of picking up of objects.

Groups

The groups within frame 1 are the core code for our game—most are run only when we tell them to be run—while the movement group is active all the time. The groups that we have are as follows:

- **Movement:** Handles the movement for our Sherlock character.
- **Inventory Reset:** Resets the inventory by resetting the counter that keeps track of making it visible and invisible.
- **Inventory Fill:** Handles the inventory contents, which items to display, and in what order of the Inventory_Bar.
- **Mouse Cursor:** Displays the correct mouse cursor and hides all others using the MouseCounter.

- **Look:** Checks if the player has the Look_Icon selected and has clicked on a particular object; if so, displays a message.

- **Message Timer:** After a set period of time, removes any text.

- **Pickup:** When you have the correct mouse cursor and you click on an object, picks up the object by removing it from the scene and adding it to the inventory. In our game, we will also display a message to the user letting her know that she has picked up an object.

Movement Group

The movement group contains the hardest code in the game, as it handles how Sherlock moves around the two rooms. You can see the events in Figure 12.11. There are a number of key components to how Sherlock moves: the first is the graphic icon called Footprints. When the player clicks on an area in the game where the skeleton can move, the Footprints image is placed. This Footprints image is used to calculate how Sherlock will move across the room. We also have the Mask No Walk graphic that will prevent the player from moving into an area with this image present, and we also have a number of alterable values assigned to Sherlock himself. If you are in the Frame editor and click on Sherlock and then click on the Values tab in the Properties window, you will see three alterable values as shown in Figure 12.12. We use these values to help calculate movement along with the detector images.

Let's now look at the events.

Event line 16 will check if the user has clicked on the left mouse button, if she has clicked in an area that isn't part of the Mask No Walk graphic, and finally if she currently has the mouse cursor set to Walk_Icon. If this is true, then we change Sherlock's animation to "walking" and move the Footprints graphic to the location of the mouse cursor. Event line 17 is an Always event where we set the various detector images around the base of Sherlock's feet. These will be used to determine if Sherlock should continue moving.

Event lines 18, 19, 20, and 21 are all similar except they define the different directions. The events are as follows:

- The Footprints image is visible.

- Every five hundredths of a second.

- Position of Sherlock is not over the Footprints.

- Direction detector is not overlapping the Mask No Walk graphic.

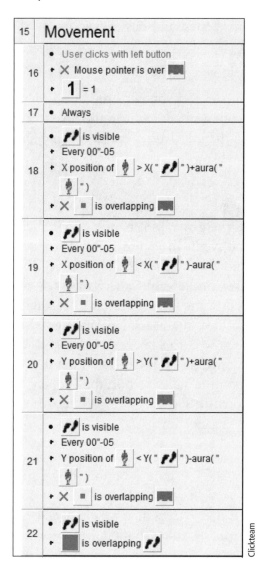

Figure 12.11
The events for Sherlock's movement.

It is important to note the position that Sherlock may need to move in (left, right, up or down) because it will define if the position should be greater or less than the Footprints.

We also have the X or Y position being set less than or greater than the Footprints position minus or plus the aura value. The aura value is set to 5 in the alterable values, which means we move the character a little more than the footprint image. This will move the character more into the middle of the image rather than its edge.

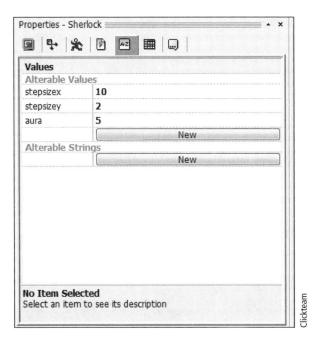

Figure 12.12
The alterable values for Sherlock.

Figure 12.13
A set of actions for one of the movement events.

You can see one of the actions for these events in Figure 12.13. The event will only be true if all is correct. Every five hundredths of a second, we can move our character across the screen by setting the player's new position to be equal to his old position minus the step size. Too big a step size and the character will jump from position to position, so it's important not to set this value to be too large. We also use the Look At action to look in the direction of the Footprints image, which tells MMF2 which direction animation to play, if the character is looking to the left, then it will play the moving left animation.

Note

The X position is from left to right, so 0 is the far left of the screen. If you have Sherlock on the right-hand side of the screen and wish him to walk left, Sherlock's position should be greater than the Footprints value. This means, while his position is greater than Footprints, the character has not yet moved to the left far enough.

Our final event in the Movement group is checking if the Footprints are still visible and if the detector_centre is overlapping the Footprints. If so, we need to tell the skeleton to change its animation to "stopped" rather than "walking," make the Footprints invisible, and move them off the screen. By making the Footprints invisible, the movement code above it will then stop working.

Inventory Reset Group

The Inventory Reset group is quite simple and only contains two Always events. The first sets the InventoryCounter to 0, which will allow the player to make the Inventory_Bar reappear by pressing the "I" key.

The second Always event disables the group so that it can be used again at a later stage when the value has changed again.

Note

It is important to disable groups that are no longer required; otherwise, the code may continue to run and cause undesirable results.

Inventory Fill Group

The Inventory Fill group is used in combination with the Pickup group. When the player picks up an object, we set a value of that selected object into the Inventory_Bar Alterable Value slot. We use the following numbers to identify which object:

- No item = 0
- Apple = 1
- Key = 2
- Newspaper = 3
- Screwdriver = 4

The number in each of the alterable values will determine which animation frame we configure in Inv1, Inv2, Inv3, and Inv4 active pictures.

You can see the code for the first slot in Figure 12.14, using the Event List editor. We check if the alterable value called SLOT1 equals 1 (which would be the apple). If so, then the animation frame of Inv1 active object will be forced to 1 (0 is the default and the blank orange background). If it were set to 1, this means the player has picked up the apple, so we need to make sure the apple is destroyed.

We need to do a comparison for each object's number as the apple may not have been the first object picked up, so we also check if the slot number equals 2, 3, or 4.

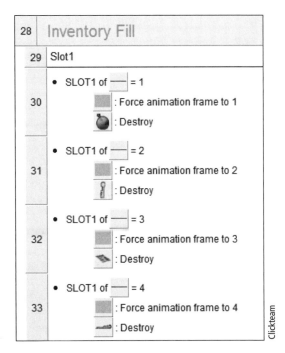

Figure 12.14
Setting a graphic depending on the alterable values in the Inventory_Bar.

Note

This method is fine for a small game with limited objects, but if you are making a larger game this method may become unwieldy. You should consider storing the data in a different manner that can accommodate simpler programming and accessing the data.

Mouse Cursor Group

The Mouse Cursor group is used to check the current value of the MouseCounter and set the correct mouse icon. We have five events that check if the counter equals a value from 5 to 1. Depending on the value, we will make the mouse icons visible or invisible. Only one icon can be visible at a time.

The value 5 means that the player has clicked the right-mouse button after the fourth icon was already set; which means we can reset the counter value back to 1. As the value 5 is above the value 1 in the events, it will change the counter to 5; the action will set the MouseCounter back to 1. MMF2 will continue down the events to line 56, which will now be true and make the correct cursor visible before it disables the group at line 57.

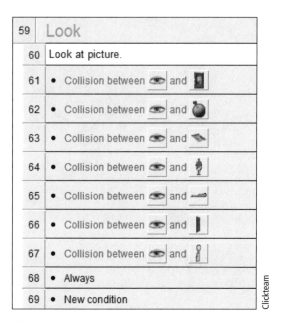

Figure 12.15
Look events.

Look Group

When the player has the Look_Icon selected and then clicks on an object in the scene, a short message appears detailing the object he has just clicked on. This group is quite easy to expand and in combination with Message Timer group can easily be used on many different objects to good effect. You can see the events in Figure 12.15.

The group was activated when the player left-clicked the mouse cursor and the Mouse-Counter equaled the Look_Icon. The events will check for which object is colliding with the Look_Icon and display the correct message. We reset the TimerCounter and then disable the Look group and enable the Message Timer group. This will then start the countdown to how long the message stays on-screen.

Message Timer Group

The Message Timer group has only two events: the first is an "Every 1 Second" condition that adds 1 to the TimerCounter every second. The second event checks when the TimerCounter equals 2, then resets the TimerCounter, resets the String object that displays the messages, and then disables the group.

The biggest issue with using events such as "Every XX Seconds" is that depending on when your group is enabled, it may already be halfway through counting the second(s).

So without resetting the timer first (which we did in event line 11), we could have text staying on-screen for differing amounts of time. By creating this simple group with a counter as the timer, we can be certain that the text will stay on-screen for two seconds, unless another object is clicked on.

Pickup Group

The final group handles picking up the four items. The group is enabled when the Pick_Icon is visible and the user clicks on one of the four objects. You can see the events in Figure 12.16.

If we look at the first event of this group, it has the following conditions:

- User clicks on the left mouse button.

- The Overlapper box is overlapping Pickup_table trigger box, which ensures that the player is close enough to the table to pick up the objects.

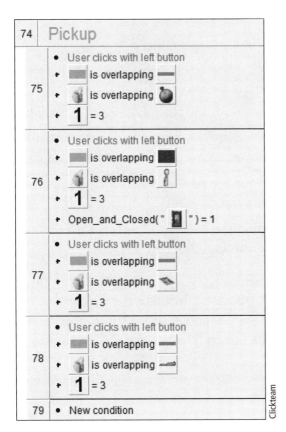

Figure 12.16
The Pickup events.

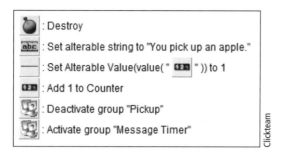

Figure 12.17
The actions needed for picking up an object.

- The Pickup_Icon overlapping the Apple object.
- The MouseCounter equals 3, which is the Pickup_Icon.

If these are all true, run the actions (see Figure 12.17).

The actions cover the following:

- Destroy the apple so that it is no longer visible on the table.
- Set some text so the player knows why the apple is no longer visible, in this case "You pick up an apple."
- Set the Apple value of 1 to the Inventory_Bar alterable value to the correct slot. We know which slot this object is being placed as we have an InventoryItems-Counter keeping track of how many objects we currently have in the inventory.
- We need to increment the InventoryItemsCounter so that when the player picks up the next object, it will appear in the next slot.
- We disable the Pickup group and then enable the Message Timer group so that we can display the "You pick up an apple" message for two seconds.

Event lines 77 and 78 are the same code-wise, but event line 76 is slightly different as we have an object that is hidden behind the picture frame. In this case, we check if an alterable value called Open_and_Closed is set to 1. If so, we pick up the object. We set the value of this alterable value elsewhere in the code when the picture frame is opened.

Final Code

Now that all of the groups have been covered, we have five events left to discuss that can be seen in Figure 12.18. The events do the following:

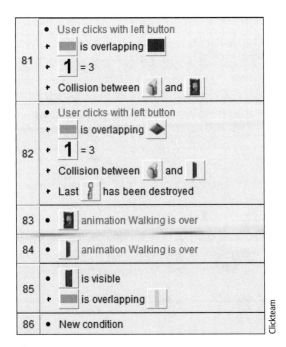

Figure 12.18
The last five events in our first frame.

- **Event line 81:** When the player clicks on the left mouse button and the Overlapper box is overlapping the Frame_Trigger and the user is using the correct mouse icon (in this case, the Pick_Icon), the picture frame opens. We do this by playing the animation for the object called PictureClosed.

- **Event line 82:** This time when the player is overlapping the Door_Check trigger zone, and he has used the Pick_Icon on the door and the key doesn't exist, we can start the door opening animation. If the key has been destroyed, we know that the player has already picked the object up.

- **Event line 83:** This is a simple event that checks to see if the PictureClosed animation has completed. So this works hand in hand with event line 81 and will be true when the picture has finished its opening animation. When the animation is complete, we stop the animation to prevent it looping and set the picture's alterable value to 1 to show that it is now open.

- **Event line 84:** This event checks to see if the Door1 object's animation has completed. If the door is now open, we stop the animation and make the Door_Open_InFront image appear. The big issue with this is that the mouse icons will appear behind this door image, so we also have to bring the mouse icons to the front of the screen in this event.

■ **Event line 85:** If the Door_Open_InFront image is visible and the Overlapper box is overlapping, our DoorTrigger active object then jumps to the next frame. This means the door is open and the player has been moved toward the exit.

To show you what the game would look like without all of the trigger boxes in place, we have created another file with the game in a non-testing state. The testing state is when the game has counters and trigger boxes over the frame to aid in development and is not in a state for release.

You can find the file called Sherlock2Complete.mfa with the downloadable files.

Note

The Door_Open_InFront image is used to create the effect that the player is walking behind the door. Without this, the player would be walking on the wrong side of the door, which would appear graphically incorrect. In this example, we have created a graphic image of the door open and have set this to appear in front of the player's character.

Note

In frame 2, we use the same system as event line 85 to trigger when the player wants to return to Sherlock's living room.

CHAPTER SUMMARY

In this chapter, you created a point-and-click adventure game called *Sherlock Bones Underworld Detective*. The game covered many features that you may want to include in your own games and provided you with a foundation for getting started on your own adventures. Try adding rooms, puzzles, some sound, and music.

If you intend to make larger games, then you will need to re-write some of the code to accommodate the complexity of additional rooms, puzzles, and objects. You should start to consider using arrays and some of the Text Adventure objects for storing object information. Even though some of these objects are used in text adventures, you can easily use many of the features in any other type of adventure game.

In the next chapter, you will learn all about the features of a relatively new adventure game type called hidden object games.

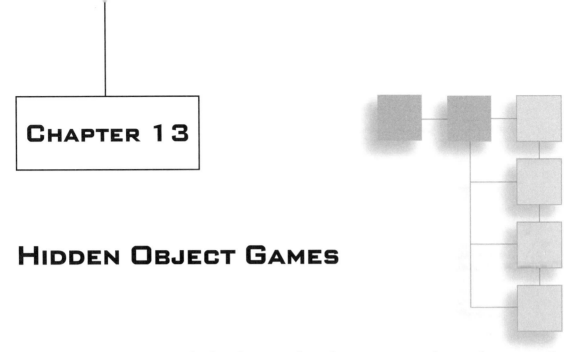

CHAPTER 13

HIDDEN OBJECT GAMES

Hidden object games over the last few years have become extremely popular, especially in the U.S. and U.K. It's quite common to walk into a computer store and see displays full of these types of games.

You may not have ever heard of a hidden object game, so before we get into these games' features, let's explain a little about what they are.

WHAT IS A HIDDEN OBJECT GAME?

The hidden object game is exactly as it sounds; it's like a computer version of the game treasure hunt. There are a number of objects hidden on-screen, and the player's job is to locate the correct object.

Hidden object games are just another type of adventure game. They do not have text entry or use a character in third-person mode that moves on-screen; instead the player navigates through the game using the mouse to point and click.

Note

> Third person is when you can see the character you are controlling, which is different from first person where you are moving around as the character and seeing the situation from his perspective. First-person shooter games, like *Call of Duty*, are a good example of first person, while *Assassins Creed* or point-and-click adventures such as *Future Wars*, *Gabriel Knight*, *Broken Sword*, and *Monkey Island* are examples of third person.

Figure 13.1
Example hidden object game.

Hidden object games can contain many of the features that a great adventure game can, such as an interesting deep story, different characters to meet and, of course, puzzles.

The great thing with the game's design is that even if a concept starts out simple, players will continue to find ways to make it more complex. When hidden object games first appeared, the objective for the players was to find a list of objects, but over the years, these have evolved to include complex storytelling, intricate puzzles, and inventory systems where you have to find an item to unlock a door or chest.

You can see an example of a hidden object game in Figure 13.1.

FEATURES OF A HIDDEN OBJECT GAME

There are quite a few features you can put into a hidden object game, but here are some of the most common ones:

- **Object list:** A text list or graphical icon to represent the objects that you need to find on-screen. As the player finds the objects, they disappear from this list and can be replaced by other objects, depending on the difficulty of the game and the number of objects to be found.

- **Timer/clock:** Many hidden object games use a timer to create a sense of urgency, which puts the player under pressure to find the objects within a set timeframe. Not all games use a timer; the challenge of finding the objects can sometimes be enough. Some games may use a specific amount of time per level, so perhaps five minutes to find all objects on a level. Others use a game total time, which is quite a nice concept but requires lots of testing to get right. The player might have three hours on the clock as he goes into each level. The timer counts down, and if he needs help or presses an incorrect object, then he may lose additional time.

- **Clicking on an incorrect item:** Hidden object games require you to click on objects around the screen, but what happens if you allow the player to just randomly click anywhere on the screen? The player could do this without really trying to find the object. You could consider this a method of cheating the game, and it does remove some of the skill in looking for and finding objects. Some games penalize a user if he does this action multiple times, such as three times in a row. If the level is timed, he then may lose some additional time. You have to be careful implementing such a system as you don't want users to cheat, but you also don't want it to be too frustrating that they cannot click on items they think might be the correct ones. It will also depend on the language you use for an object. For example, a British person may not necessarily understand what an object is by its name, because it might be referred by another name by an American user.

- **Hint button:** These are extremely common in hidden object games and are used to help a player when she is stuck. If a player cannot find an object from the list, she clicks on the Hint button and it will show where one item is currently situated. In some cases, the player will only have a set number of hints, while another game might require a set amount of time to pass before the player can use the hint system again.

- **Maps:** Some games allow the player to navigate to where he wishes to go next; this allows for a less linear route and allows the player the feeling of freedom. It also increases replay value because a player may try a different route the next time he plays. Maps are also very useful to give the player a sense of playing in a "real world" but also a bigger world. If you just present one location to the next, the player won't get that sense of choice and progression. Maps are the easiest way in hidden object games to present this to the player. For example, you can show them a map of the city and the places he can visit.

- **Close-ups:** In some games, when you move the mouse cursor around the game world, the cursor may change to show the player he can get closer to the action; a window will open showing a close-up of the item that was clicked on. For example, if the player clicks on a statue in the distance, the statue will then appear close-up or zoomed in.

- **Mini games:** To broaden the scope of hidden object games, rather than limiting them to just searching for objects, many games have implemented puzzles that you have to navigate to continue with the story. There are many different puzzle-type games such as opening a lock or deciphering a coded message. Some common mini games include spotting the difference, finding matching items, or moving blocks around to put a picture in the correct order.

- **Inventory system:** An inventory system is great for storing objects that have been picked up through the story but also for making the player think about how she might get past a particular point in the game. Perhaps you have a gate that requires four keys to open, but those four keys are hidden around the game world, and without them the player is unable to proceed. This gives the game more depth than if you were just asking the player to find the objects in the list.

Hidden Object Game Designs

When creating a game design for a hidden object game, you will need to consider the following:

- **Story:** In hidden adventure games, the story is the most important part of the game. This will define if you can keep a player interested and continuing to go through different similar levels.

- **Characters:** Characters can be added that appear when required. Having characters appear on-screen will help set the stage for any of the following levels, but it will also give the players a little more information on what these characters look like. If someone is evil, you can show this in the way he dresses or looks.

- **Locations:** The locations that are in your game will depend on the story of your game, but they will also be defined by any time period you are creating. You wouldn't expect to see a car in a driveway in a medieval hidden object game.

- **Puzzles:** Puzzles are used to give players a break from searching for objects. If your game had levels that were just for finding a set of objects, it would become repetitive fast for most players, unless you had a very interesting story. Puzzles allow people to stretch their intellect. If a player is struggling to solve a puzzle, it is a good idea to provide him with helpful hints and clues to ensure he doesn't get frustrated with the game.

- **Objects:** The key components of a hidden object game are the objects that the player finds. The more objects you have, the more variety you can give the player, especially if you provide him with a different list of objects to find every time he plays.

We will now cover some of these items, providing you with more details on what you can implement in your own games.

Story

The story will always play an important part of any hidden object game, as it's the main driving force for the player to continue playing the game.

The great thing about hidden object games is that nearly any story or idea fits well, such as horror, comedy, teen, historical, and so on. So it's generally not too difficult to come up with a story.

There are some themes that seem quite popular with hidden object games:

- **Murder mystery:** In a murder mystery, the player needs to determine who killed a particular character. The "who done it" has been very popular in board games, movies, and in real-life role-playing (the murder mystery weekends). The reason a murder mystery is so interesting is that the keys to this type of game are clues, which can be objects that the player finds through the course of the game.

- **Detective stories:** Similar to the murder mystery games, detective stories can also include serious or less serious stories, such as Grandma gone missing or finding a lost pet. The reason detective stories are interesting is similar to the murder mystery; you need clues and solve puzzles to crack the case.

- **Horror:** These types of hidden object games usually have plot twists with a very strong story element and interesting characters. All of the common character types are to be expected: werewolves, witches, wizards, and vampires. Horror games have always been popular and recently have become even more so due to TV series and movies.

- **Historical:** Many people love historical settings for their games. Being transported back to a time and place that they will never get to experience is one of the big benefits of TV, movies, and computer games. The setting alone may make a person want to play the game, be it in medieval times or in Victorian times. You can find many interesting facts and information about particular time periods that you can then incorporate into your game.

Note

Role-playing is where you act out a story or event as a particular character. In a murder mystery weekend, for example, people go to an event, normally held at a hotel, where a fake murder occurs; the aim of the game for the guests is to figure out who did it.

Story Ideas

Here are a few story ideas to get you thinking about what you can include in your hidden object games:

- **Train mystery:** You have decided to travel on the Orient Express, but not long after the train has set off, there is a murder, and everyone is pointing the blame at you. You have to figure out who the real murderer is and why it took place.

- **Iceberg:** You've just boarded the greatest sea liner of all time, the *Titanic*, on its journey to America. You are a cabin boy whose job it is to look after passengers. The aim of the game is to learn about various people you meet and ultimately rescue them.

- **Wizards:** You are a wizard who has been sent to the open lands to defeat the evil wizards of the north. Can you find the right equipment (spells and potions) to defeat them and bring peace to your lands?

- **Time Traveler:** You are a scientist working on the theory of time and space, but something goes wrong, horribly wrong, and you are transported to a time and place you don't recognize. What's even worse is that every 30 minutes, you are transported to another time and place. Can you figure out what has gone wrong and how to stop traveling through time?

- **Kings and queens:** You are just a peasant who lives in a land that is ruled by a ruthless king. It is said if anyone can find the seven Runes of Albion, he will become king. Can you find the runes and become king?

- **Farm apprentice:** You've always loved the idea of owning your own farm, but every bank you go to refuses to give you a loan. Can you hold garage sales to earn enough money to open your own farm, or can you make even more money to buy equipment so that your farm is successful?

Objects

The core of any hidden object games is the objects that you are asked to find. Some games will have objects that are related to the story and the scene you are currently viewing, while others will just have random objects. For example, your game might have a scene with a Roman temple, but you might find a guitar, a chicken, and a cutlery set in the scene, while other games will have more appropriate objects, such as Roman armor, Roman coins, and other temple equipment.

Some games will have areas that have objects placed around the scene, such as on a table or in a cupboard and floor, while other games will have them scattered randomly.

Having items that are related to the scene will certainly be better for the player, but it may be harder for the player to identify a particular object, especially if you are dealing with a historical-based game, where the player is in a different time period. Of course, this does also add to the challenge of the game.

Here is a list of common items/groups of objects that you will find in a game:

- Animals (dogs, cats, fish, frogs)
- Household goods (such as cups, plates, cutlery, picture frames, light fittings, hat stand)
- Cards
- Spiders and other creepy crawlies
- Fruit and food
- Shapes
- Clothing (boots, hats, gloves)
- Sports items (football, roller skates, bowling ball)
- Weapons
- Stationery items (pen, paper, scrolls)
- Garden gnomes
- Vehicles (planes, trains, and automobiles)

These are just some ideas for objects that you might have in your game. The types of objects you will include will also depend on the locations that the player visits. For example, if you have her visit a shipyard, you might have objects that are associated with the water or sea; if it was a football game, you might have sports equipment.

Note

Some games have very random items within a scene. For example, you might be at a dock, but there will be a dagger, burger, and tank all in the scene. Having random items is certainly easier than coming up with objects that relate directly to the scene, but it is certainly not as good as having the right objects in the scene.

Using Photos

What if you currently don't draw but you want to get your code for your hidden object game up and running? Perhaps you want to just make a game for fun and don't really want to make the art yourself but instead use other sources? Or perhaps you want to complete your code first before getting an artist to help? Well, if either is the case, you could always start with a photo-based hidden object game.

Using photos is a quick and easy way to start building your game. You can take photos of various locations around your town or city, which will serve as the places the player can visit. You can see an example photo of a location in Figure 13.2.

Figure 13.2
An example location.

When taking the photo of a location, remember to take as many photos from different angles and distances as you can so that you can be assured that you will have taken a shot that will work rather than taking one shot and then realizing that it can't be used.

You will also need photos of the objects that you wish to include in your game. You can use photo libraries that allow you to purchase images online, but you may find unfortunately in most cases the cost of these is quite prohibitive. So why not take photos of the objects that you want to include and then cut these out and paste them into your game?

CHAPTER SUMMARY

In this chapter, we talked about what features are available in many hidden object games, as well as about some basic design ideas such as characters, locations, and objects. We also briefly discussed how you might quickly and cheaply get a hidden game up and running.

In the next chapter, we will create our very own hidden object game.

CHAPTER 14

LOST AND FOUND

In this chapter, we will look at making a hidden object game called *Adventures in Endapur*. In the game, you will be cast as an explorer who has to search for a number of objects hidden within a ruined temple. The game consists of a single game screen that will contain all of the code needed to generate a list of objects, pick out those you want the player to find, and then disappear when the player has clicked on them.

The game has the following elements:

- **Objects:** Objects are the key component of any hidden object game. In this example game, there are 16 objects, but you can easily increase this number to accommodate as many objects as you need.

- **Mouse cursor:** A special cursor that replaces the Windows mouse cursor. Replacing the Windows mouse cursor makes the game look much nicer, especially if you have spent a lot of time making pretty graphics for it.

- **Score:** A Score object will keep track of the players' scores. When clicking on a correct object, the score will go up. But to prevent the player from randomly clicking on any object, the score will decrease by a value, which creates a risk–reward situation, whereby the player can click on an area hoping to find an object by chance, but the risk is that they will lose points.

- **Object list:** This is the list of objects the player needs to find. In this example, we will be using some text to let the player know the name of the object, but you can use outlines or clues.

The game works in the following way:

- **Picking objects:** Six objects are picked from a list of sixteen. We use a system of numbers from 1 to 16 to identify every object before picking out at random six objects.

- **Text:** The text is updated within the text boxes in alphabetical order to show the player which objects to find.

- **Object placement:** The 16 objects are randomly dispersed around the screen, so that each time the game is played, the objects are in different locations. To prevent the objects from being placed under the text boxes or the score graphic, we have written the code to place them within an area on the screen.

- **Mouse cursor:** We will replace the mouse cursor with a graphic arrow and then hide the Windows mouse cursor.

- **Mouse cursor tip box:** We place a small graphic box at the tip of the graphic mouse cursor; we will use this to see if the tip of the graphic arrow is over an object.

We will now go through the key parts of the game using a set of examples before we put it all together to create the game.

OBJECTS AND NUMBERS

In our game, we have 16 objects. Our biggest challenge is picking a set of objects from this group and checking when they have been clicked on by the player. We could just code it so that it was the same six objects every time you played the game, but this wouldn't be very exciting, and before long, you would know exactly which objects you were looking for. So we want to be able to select six objects at random and code them so that we know when these particular six objects have been clicked on.

The code for clicking on an object is covered later on in this chapter, but you need to think ahead, otherwise you may create a system that is unusable when creating the next step of the game. When creating this example, I had to think about how the objects were selected and then how I was going to track those six objects through the game. After thinking about various solutions and realizing they wouldn't work, I came up with a solution to give every object a unique number.

There are a number of benefits to using a unique number:

- Numbers are easier to work with than a text string, for example, because you can do calculations with them.

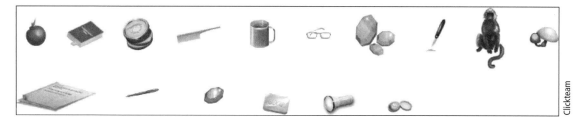

Figure 14.1
Sixteen objects that will each have a unique number.

- We can assign a number to an object and know that this number is unique.

- Numbers scale, which means you can easily add more numbers and program your code to take into account additional objects, whereas using strings or other systems can be much more complicated.

In the following example, we will show how we apply a unique number to a set of objects. We will have a set of objects that will reveal their unique ID number when you click on them.

Load the example file NumberPick.mfa that includes 16 graphical objects, as shown in Figure 14.1.

All active objects have the ability to store values within the object itself. So you can store multiple numbers and strings in each of the 16 objects and retrieve any one value at any time. This is extremely useful when you want to store object-specific data rather than using counters or other objects. In this case, you will know exactly where the data is, instead of searching around for the correct object where you might have stored the data.

Click on any of the graphic objects, such as the apple. In the apple's properties, you will see the Values tab. Click on this tab, and you will now see this object's alterable value, called Alterable Value A, which has the value of 1. This means this apple has a numeric value that can be amended at runtime, but its current value is 1 (as shown in Figure 14.2).

Note

You can rename alterable values and alterable strings to something more intuitive so you can identify them later on; this is particularly useful when using many alterable values.

Note

You can store values in other objects also. To see if you can store and save data within that object, look at the object's properties.

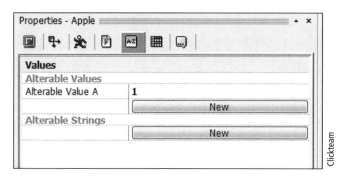

Figure 14.2
The alterable values of the apple object.

On the same frame, you will see a single Counter object; this will display the unique alterable value that we have applied to each of the objects from 1 to 16 when you click on them. This is a simple way of checking that the values are correctly applied, but you can then also use this counter to place the value in your code.

The objects and the values are as shown in Table 14.1.

Table 14.1   List of Objects and Their Unique Numbers

Object	Value
Apple	1
Book	2
Coins	3
Comb	4
Cup	5
Glasses	6
Green jewel	7
Knife	8
Monkey	9
Mushrooms	10
Papers	11
Pen	12
Red jewel	13
Soap	14
Torch	15
Watch	16

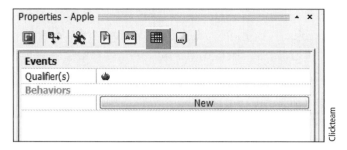

Figure 14.3
The qualifier group.

There is one additional property that has been applied to each of these objects and that is the use of a qualifier group. If you were to write some code to identify the alterable value in each object and place it into a counter, you would have to write 16 events for each mouse click. This would be very inefficient, so to solve this issue we have qualifier groups. By placing all of the 16 objects into a qualifier group, you only have to write a single event since any condition that utilizes a qualifier group can return data on which object has been selected.

If you click on the apple object and see its properties and then click on the Events tab, you will see that it has a small graphic in the Qualifier(s) box as shown in Figure 14.3. All 16 objects have been placed within this qualifier group. You can apply multiple groups or edit a group by clicking on the apple graphic and selecting the Edit button.

Note

A qualifier group allows you to group different objects together and then create conditions and actions that take into account every object in that group.

If you look at the Event editor, you can see the code for this example file (Figure 14.4). The code is only a single event, which is checking for when the user clicks on the left

Figure 14.4
The code to retrieve an alterable value from an object.

mouse button over an object that is within the Good group. The action is to set the counter to the value of the clicked-on object. As mentioned previously, as the event is checking when an object from the Good group is clicked, the action will take the value of the object within the Good group that this has related to.

If you run the example file and then click on one of the objects, the counter will update with the alterable value specified in Table 14.1.

Lists

Lists are great for keeping track of data in real life, such as a shopping or task list. They are also very helpful when making computer games, as you can use lists to store data when running the game as well as using them to sort any data. There will be times where you use lists but don't display the list to the player. In this hidden object game, we won't be showing the lists themselves but using them to sort and display particular data.

We have created an example file called NumberLists.mfa that contains four list boxes. You can see an example of the contents of the example file in Figure 14.5.

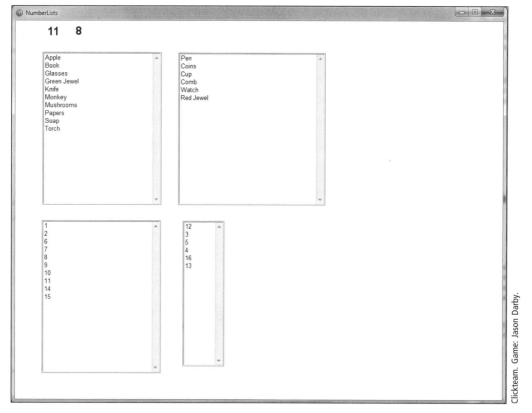

Clickteam. Game: Jason Darby.

Figure 14.5
Four lists containing our objects data.

This example has four lists and two counters and are used in the following way:

- **List:** This will contain the name of all of our objects as the frame starts. We need a text name so we can display it on-screen later when we display the text of the objects that the player needs to find. We will pick six items at random from this list and place them in List2. Once we have done that, we will remove them from the original list so that we don't duplicate the objects.

- **List2:** This will contain the text names of the six objects that we have chosen. In the game, this list is used to display the objects that the player needs to find.

- **NumberList:** This is the alterable values of each of the objects, from 1 to 16.

- **Selected_Numbers:** This will display the alterable values of the six objects that have been selected.

We have used a list for numbers and one for text, because it was easier to duplicate the process than it would have been to come up with a code solution to convert the selected number to a text object or to convert a text name to a number.

When you run the example file, the list of numbers and text in List and NumberList will be the same, which means that in List the top entry will be the word Apple, while in the NumberList will be the number value of 1 (which we've already identified as the first object, that is, the apple). It will randomly pick an item from the List and place it in List2, while at the same time we will use the same random number to do the same with the NumberList and Selected_Numbers.

You can see the values in both List and NumberList in Figures 14.6 and 14.7.

In this example, we have two counters that are very important when selecting the various items within the lists. The first counter is a counter that keeps track of the

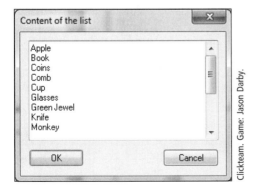

Figure 14.6
The text list of objects in alphabetical order.

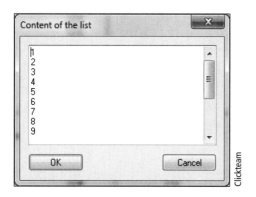

Figure 14.7
The alterable unique ID for each object in numeric order.

number of lines in List and NumberList. We will be picking a line at random, but to use the random expression, you first need to know the range of the items you want to select from. In this case, it's the total number of lines in the list. Because we will need to delete any lines from the lists after using them (so as not to have duplicate objects), we will need to delete the selected line which then changes the number of lines. If we were to continue picking at random from the original number, the list may at times not work correctly because it might select a line that is no longer available.

The second counter is a random number generator. This will generate a number that will select a line in the list. We will then move the item from the left list to the right list. We will also use this counter to remove the old entry from the left lists.

If you look at the code for this example in the Event editor (as shown in Figure 14.8), you will see two events. The Start of Frame event starts a loop called Pick. Since we want to select six items for the player to find, we set the loop to run six times. You can see the actions for this event in Figure 14.9. On event line 2, you can see an event that runs when a Pick loop has been activated (which was done in event line 1). Here we have a number of actions as shown in the Event List editor in Figure 14.10.

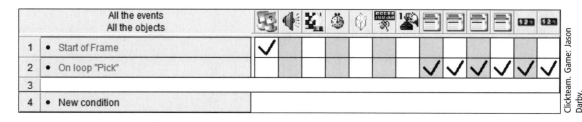

Figure 14.8
Two events to select random items from a list.

Figure 14.9
The loop running six times.

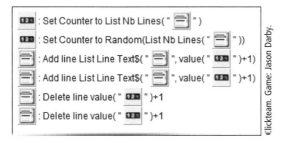

Figure 14.10
The actions for the Loop condition.

The code works in the following way:

- **Action 1:** Sets the Counter_Total_lines counter to the number of lines in the list object.

- **Action 2:** Sets the Counter_RandomPick to one of the lines from the List.

- **Action 3:** Adds a line to List2 from the List using Counter_RandomPick to specify which line to copy.

- **Action 4:** Adds a line to Selected_Numbers from NumbersList using Counter_ RandomPick to specify which line to copy.

- **Action 5:** Deletes the line from List that was copied.

- **Action 6:** Deletes the line from NumberList that was copied.

MOUSE CURSOR

The mouse cursor is an important part of a game, especially in a game where you have spent a lot of time creating especially attractive graphics; the Windows cursor would look particularly boring in comparison. In the following example, we will show you how to use a graphical mouse cursor.

We could use the Cursor object to create a mouse cursor, but there is another way, which is to place a graphic object at the location of the mouse cursor at all times.

You can load the example called Mousecursor.mfa, which contains a simple screen with an arrow cursor, a small red active object, and some graphical objects as shown in Figure 14.11.

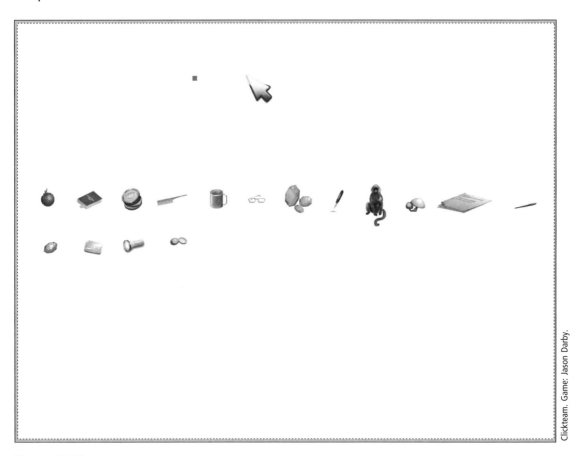

Clickteam. Game: Jason Darby.

Figure 14.11
The frame setup for our mouse cursor example.

We will tell MMF2 to always place the graphic cursor shown in Figure 14.11 to the current coordinates of the Windows mouse cursor. When the player clicks on the left mouse button, we will check if the graphic is overlapping one of the 16 objects and, if so, we will destroy the object, so that it disappears from the screen.

The biggest issue when using a graphic placed at the mouse coordinates occurs if the graphical object is large so that when you click on an object, it may overlap many other objects and produce unexpected results. Hidden object games work on the principle of precision mouse clicking, and as many objects might be over-lapping each other in the game world, you don't want them all to be found at the same time.

In Figure 14.12, you can see the point of the graphical arrow mouse cursor is cur-rently overlapping the cup object.

Figure 14.12
Example of overlapping objects.

Mouse Cursor Example Code

We will now review the code for creating a mouse cursor using a graphic image by always moving it to the Windows cursor position. To do this only requires three events, but there are a small number of other events we use in the game, which will be covered later.

Open the MouseCursor.mfa example file and go to the Event editor. Here you will see the three events, as shown in Figure 14.13.

The first event is an Always condition, which means that this code will always run each time MMF2 reads the events. You can see the actions in Figure 14.14.

The first action places the cursor object at the X position of the X axis of the mouse. This is from left to right. The second action places the cursor at the Y position at the Y axis of the mouse, which will place the cursor at the exact position as the Windows

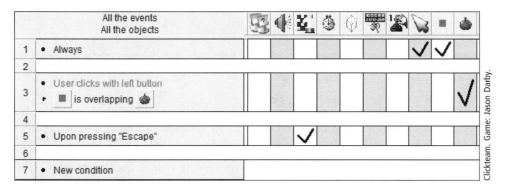

Figure 14.13
The mouse cursor events.

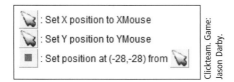

Figure 14.14
The actions for the first event.

mouse cursor. The third action places the red square at the position at the tip of the cursor. Since we are always moving the graphic mouse cursor, this will always be placed over the tip of the image.

The second event will check when the player clicks on the left mouse button and that the red graphic is overlapping an object of the Good group. If this is true, then the action will be to destroy the object. By placing the Destroy condition in the Good action box, it will automatically destroy the correct object.

The final event is a special "Escape" or "Break" key event. Since you will be replacing the Windows mouse cursor with a graphic, you might want to ensure that the player can exit from this cursor, so that when the player presses the Escape key, the application will end.

If you run the application, you will see the graphic mouse cursor, the red box, and the Windows mouse cursor all moving across the screen. If you click on one of the 16 objects, it will be destroyed. In the actual game, we have hidden the red active object and the Windows mouse cursor, but we have left them in this example so that you can see how the code functions.

Note

An Escape or Break key is an old term for exiting an application and commonly used on very old computers where you might need to type a number of commands into a keyboard to initiate some sort of process. If you made a mistake and wanted to stop the process, you would press the Break or Escape key.

Random Placement of Objects

In many hidden object games, the objects are randomly placed over the screen. You could do this manually, but you can also write some code to place them. In the example file RandomPlacement.mfa, we have a frame that has a green set of active boxes around the edge of the window. These green boxes signify our on-screen elements such as a menu bar, score, and text items, and where you would not want any of our 16 objects to appear.

Once you understand the boundaries of your game, you can calculate what part of the screen the objects can be placed in.

To calculate this, you need to know:

- The total screen size/resolution (for this example, it is 1024 × 768)
- The maximum X size of an object

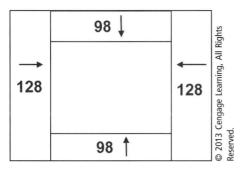

Figure 14.15
Example drawing of the area around the edge of our frame where we don't want to place our objects.

- The maximum Y size of an object
- The starting X point where you can place an object
- The starting Y point where you can place an object

Once you have these values, you can calculate the area where you can place objects safely. We have drawn the area that is not available on our frame in Figure 14.15.

If your screen size was 1024 × 768 pixels, and you don't take into account any object sizes for a moment, the usable area can be calculated as follows:

- X starting area = 128 (the width of the left block)
- X ending area = 896 (the total width of the frame minus 128 for the end block)
- Y starting area = 98 (the height of the top block)
- Y ending area = 670 (the height of the frame minus the height of the Y block of 98 to calculate the area where it should stop on Y)

If you look at the example file, the numbers should represent the white frame area that is not covered by the green blocks, and these numbers represent the four corners of the frame which is where you want to place the objects.

If the maximum X and Y of the largest object is 20 (20 × 20), then you know your usable range is amended to the following:

- X starting area = 148
- X ending area = 876
- Y starting area = 118
- Y ending area = 650

Clickteam. Game: Jason Darby.

Figure 14.16
Our frame layout.

For the start values, we add 20 pixels to move any objects farther to the right or down, while we subtract the value for the end values to bring objects from the right to the center or from the bottom upward. This will prevent objects from moving into the green areas within the example file.

Though our objects are bigger than 20 × 20, this should give you a good idea of what you need to take into account to make sure your objects fit within a particular area of the screen. You can see our frame setup in Figure 14.16.

If you go into the Event editor, you can see the two events needed to randomly place the objects on the screen as shown in Figure 14.17. The first event places the objects within the grid, and the second event sees if any of the objects are overlapping and uses the same calculation to replace the objects on the screen.

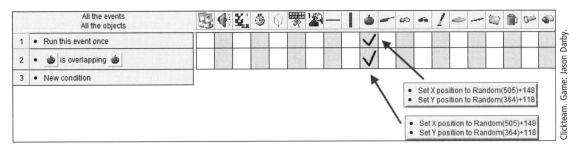

Figure 14.17
The Event editor code to place objects on the frame.

We have used the random expression to place the objects randomly on the screen. We know that the X width is 653, so you might be wondering why we used 505+148. We know that the objects should not be in the first 148 pixels, so by using 505 and then adding 148 ensures no random number is less than 148 pixels on the X axis, and the total width is 653.

If you run the example file, you will notice that every time you run it, the objects are placed randomly around the screen. When you run the example file, you may find that some objects overlap the green area, because their sizes are not precisely 20 × 20. At this point, you can continue to amend the values until you are satisfied that it won't overlap the green area objects, or you can write some additional code to regenerate that object's position so that it's not overlapping.

Note

If there are areas of the screen where you do not want objects placed, but it is not possible to use a simple calculation to place the objects, then you should consider placing hidden active boxes at these locations and then use code to move them if they are currently overlapping one of these hidden boxes.

GAME CODE

Now that you have been introduced to the core parts of making a basic hidden object game, we will look at the final game code for *Adventures in Endapur*. The completed code can be found in the file called HiddenObject.mfa. If you open the file and look at the Frame editor, you will see something along the lines of Figure 14.18.

Note

We have zoomed out to 50% frame width in Figure 14.18 so that you can get an idea of all of the objects used in the frame.

Figure 14.18
The frame for our hidden object game.

You will notice some components of the game that we have discussed previously in this chapter, such as:

■ **Four list boxes:** We have four list boxes that will store the name of the objects and their unique ID numbers, and we will select six objects and place them in the right-hand-side list boxes. These lists won't be shown in the game frame.

■ **Cursor and cursor red box:** We use the cursor to replace the Windows cursor and place the red square at the tip so that we can check when we are clicking over an object.

■ **16 objects:** Each of the 16 objects has a unique alterable value stored in it, and each object is part of the Good qualifier group.

■ **Counters:** We have counters to take into account the number of items in a list and to create a random number. We also have a counter that returns the number of the unique ID of the object clicked on.

Some new items on the frame are:

■ **Score graphic:** A graphic to represent the score.

■ **Six strings:** Six string objects that display the text of the objects to find; this text is retrieved from the list objects.

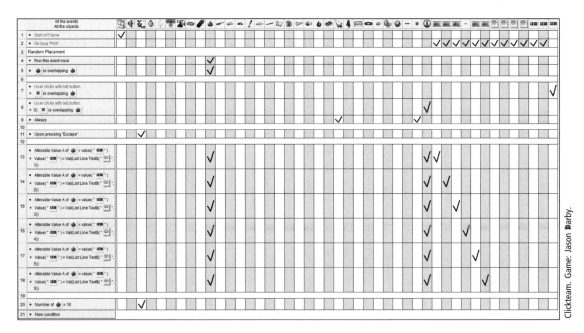

Figure 14.19
The events for creating a hidden object game.

If you click on the Event editor, you will see a few more events than in the example files; in total there are 20 event lines including comment lines. These 20 event lines (as shown in Figure 14.19) provide you with the core game mechanics of a hidden object game and can be used as the basis of your very own game.

Code Run-through

In this section, we will review the events that make up our hidden object game. As we have already discussed how to create a lot of this code, we will concentrate mostly on new features that we have added:

- **Start of Frame:** The Start of Frame event has only a single function and that is to start the "Pick" loop six times. If you wanted to pick more than six objects, you would change the value in this loop.

- **On loop "Pick":** The second event will set up all of the items we want to run in our loop, and this group of actions will run six times. Within this group, we have our object lists—which we have already discussed in the "Lists" section of this chapter. In the loop, we also set the objects' text names into the six text slots at the top of the screen. These will be used by the player to know which objects to find.

■ **Run This Event Once:** This event runs only once and places objects at random places around the screen, as described in the "Random Placement of Objects" section. It uses the qualifier group so only one action is required to apply to all 16 objects.

■ **Good Group Is Overlapping Good Group (event line 5):** This event will continue to move any of the 16 objects around the screen while they are overlapping one another. Be aware that if you have a lot of objects in a small space, then this event may be run many times and may cause your game to slow down if the objects cannot find an area that is free of other objects, so use with care.

■ **User Clicks with Left Button:** If the user clicks and the red square is overlapping an object in the Good group, then it will update a counter with the alterable value stored in the clicked object.

■ **User Does Not Click with Left Button:** If the user does not click on an object from the Good group, then he will lose five points from his score.

■ **Always:** Always set the position of the arrow cursor to the mouse cursor's X and Y screen positions. Also set the red square to the tip of the arrow cursor to ensure that when the player is clicking on objects, the User Clicks code works correctly.

■ **Upon Pressing Escape:** We talked earlier in this chapter about allowing the player to break free of the new mouse cursor using the Escape or Break key. This code currently ends the application in the event you decide to jump to another screen or bring up a menu when pressing a particular key.

■ **Six Events (lines 13 to 18):** This is probably the most complex part of the game code; each event checks the alterable value of the Good group and compares it to the counter that contains the clicked alterable value. It then checks to see if this number exists in the List object, which details the six selected objects. If its alterable value equals the number in one of the six lines in the list, then this means you have clicked on an object that you were expected to find, and the object will be deleted from the screen. The score will have 25 added to it, and the text representing the line item will also be deleted.

■ **Number of Good Group Objects Equals 10:** We have used a Count condition to count the number of objects left on-screen. As we are destroying the objects, this means they no longer exist. As we know, we have 16 objects in total and will be destroying 6. We know that when the number of objects reaches 10, the player has found all objects. In this code, we close the application when the player has found all six objects, but you could easily move the player to another frame, or give him a congratulatory message.

As you can see from the events available, this game is quite simple to make but has all the core components required for a hidden object game. The game will only take you a few minutes to play, so you should consider expanding it with further levels, objects, and puzzles.

HOW TO IMPROVE

Hopefully after looking at the game code and spending some time playing the game, you now have some ideas how to improve the game play experience further.

Here are some ideas to get you started:

- **Messages on-screen:** When a player has found an object, consider displaying an "Item Found" graphic, which creates a little more excitement in the game play experience.

- **Music:** Adding music to a game can be essential to setting the game's scene or mood. For example, what would you think of a scene if it was a horror game with comedy music, or perhaps a serious game theme with circus music? It is important you pick the appropriate music for the right type of game as this will improve your game greatly. There are many websites from which you can purchase royalty-free music, or you can make your own.

- **Sound:** Just like music, game sound is extremely important in helping you raise the quality of your game. Adding a clicking noise when the player clicks on a button or a "magical" sound when he finds an object are just two examples of simple sound effects that can improve the player experience. Adding sound effects will definitely improve your game and can provide essential feedback to the player. For example, imagine clicking on a button and hearing no sound. This might make the user think nothing is happening, especially if there is a slight delay between clicking on a button and the event occurring. Adding sound effects is very important, but you should also take care to play the right sound effects, and where possible, they should not play over one another.

- **Menu:** Create a menu screen where the player can find all of the key links in your game. A menu is a normal location to place all of the top-level options for your game, such as Play, High Scores, and Credits Options. You shouldn't create a game where the game just starts, as the player may not be ready to play at that exact moment.

- **Story:** Consider creating a story as part of the game that tells the player why she is collecting items, as this gives her a reason to play and an emotional attachment to the characters and the game world you have created. You can present the story as text, graphics, a graphical comic, or video.

- **Timer:** Give the player a sense of urgency by adding a timer; this is an easy way to increase the pressure on the player and provides the player with a set time-frame to find all of the objects. You could break this down further and have a time that the player needs to find each object; the quicker he finds it, the more time he has to find the next object.

- **Clicking wrong objects:** In our game, we lowered the player's score if he just randomly clicked around the screen, but you can also lower his score if he clicks on an object that is not available in the object find list. This prevents the player from clicking lots of areas on the screen just to see if one of the expected items is there.

- **Random objects on different screens:** It is important to consider the ability of the player to replay your game. If the objects are always in the same position or the objects that he has to find are always the same, this lessens the chance that you can reuse a particular screen or that a player will want to reload that level and play again. We have already shown you how to randomize the screen locations of the objects, but you can increase the total number of objects, as this will increase the randomness of the objects the player needs to find, or you can create multiple object banks. For example, you have 16 objects in a set of three banks, and you randomly choose from those three banks before choosing the six objects to display for the player to find.

- **Shadows or clues to finding objects:** Rather than using a text name to tell the player which object to find, think of other ways, such as a drawing of the object, or perhaps the outline of the object.

- **Help/Clue button:** Think about the variety of users playing your game, and consider that not all players will be able to find the objects as easily as others. Therefore, consider adding a Help button that will highlight one of the objects the player needs to find. You can restrict the use of this Help button to a set amount of time or number of uses.

- **Difficulty level:** As mentioned in the preceding point, gamers have a wide range of skill levels, so consider adding different selectable difficulty levels or set up your game so that as the player progresses, it gets harder. Always consider a way that a player who gets stuck on a level might be able to play less difficult levels again to "collect" some form of help points that can help him proceed to the next level. You do not necessarily want to block the player from moving to higher levels of difficulty in the game because he may not be as good as another gamer.

CHAPTER SUMMARY

In this chapter, we looked at a hidden object game where you have to find six randomly picked objects from a selection of 16 items. The base code is enough for you to make your own games and expand them to include further features or areas and frames.

You have learned how to create a list and assign it a unique numeric ID, and how to create a list of these objects. You have also learned how to place these objects on the frame, and the issues that might arise with objects overlapping any user interface graphics that might be in place.

In the next chapter, we will look at how to make a graphic adventure game from the first-person perspective using photos taken with a digital camera.

If you are reading the print version of this title, please download Chapters 15, 16, 17, and 18 from the companion website: **www.courseptr.com/downloads** or the author's website: **www.castlesoftware.co.uk**.

INDEX

For those reading the *print* version of this book, page numbers preceded by an "E" (electronic) indicate that they are in Chapters 15, 16, 17, or 18 and can be found on the companion website: www.courseptr.com/downloads.

Index

Index

Index